# Praise for *Manifest Anything You Want*

"In this approachable debut guide to personal transformation, Rajah advocates for moving beyond affirmations, visualizations, and other mainstream methods of manifestation and toward a process of releasing fear and embracing self-acceptance to build a life that reflects what you believe in. Rajah helps readers to identify their core desires and get out of the universe's way so those wishes can come to fruition, a process that is achieved partly by accepting one's circumstances and signaling to the Universe [that] you are ready for the bigger, better, more beautiful reality."
**—PUBLISHERS WEEKLY**

"Shantini is the fresh voice we need, where in today's world, the discussion about manifesting fails to address complexities and inequities, leaving many feeling defeated from the start. In *Manifest Anything You Want*, she brings everyone—from all religions, races, and cultures—into the fold and shows them her simple and accessible approach for a better and more fulfilling life, without the blame and BS."
**—AMY B. SCHER,** bestselling author of *How to Heal Yourself When No One Else Can*

"*Manifest Anything You Want* feels like a breath of fresh air in a world where manifesting is mostly about vision boards and visualizations. Shantini shares unique tools you can apply at any time, including her 1 Healing Breath technique....If you've ever wondered why your most cherished dreams remain out of reach no matter what you do, then this book is a must-read!"
**—DR. NEETA BHUSHAN,** cofounder of the Global Grit Institute and the Dharma Coaching Institute and best-selling author of *That Sucked. Now What?*

"*Manifest Anything You Want* is a refreshing take on how to make your goals and dreams a reality. It is filled with unique and powerful practices that will take you on a journey back to yourself so you can boldly go out into the world and bring your most extraordinary vision to life."
**—AJIT NAWALKHA,** cofounder of Mindvalley Coach, former CEO of Mindvalley, and author of *Live BIG*

T0034804

"Shantini is a bright light in this world…and we can follow that light all the way toward realizing our deepest dreams. *Manifest Anything You Want* is a wise and gentle companion for anyone looking for more magic and wanting to cultivate a manifesting practice that feels powerful and grounded. The book is like a treasure chest of in-depth rituals and in-the-moment tools.…A delightful read, this is the kind of book you'll want to keep close."

—**ANDREA SCHER**, artist, certified life coach, and author of *Wonder Seeker*

"How do you get to a place in life that is so aligned with the truth of who you are that manifesting your desires becomes natural and commonplace? How do you become that person who is referred to as 'lucky' by others because you are a magnet for abundant, powerful, and extraordinary life experiences? You do it by cultivating a healing foundation from deep inside your soul. It is from this place where Shantini Rajah's *Manifest Anything You Want* will guide you to your authentic spirit of wholeness and radiance, where manifesting your dreams happens with ease. It might even feel like a little bit of magic."

—**DONDI DAHLIN**, award-winning author of *The Five Elements*

"Shantini sees people for who they really are and who they're about to become and not just who they are today. She can see their Highest Self— their Highest Being. I told her one time, I want to see me like YOU see me, and she held that space for me to become that person."

—**MANNY GOLDMAN**, founder and CEO of the Sacred Plant

MANIFEST
*Anything*
YOU WANT

# About the Author

Shantini Rajah is a writing and manifesting mentor and energy practitioner. She loves helping conscious entrepreneurs find their true voice and manifest a life and business they love. As a trained physicist and engineer, Shantini brings together a unique alchemy of science and spirituality to everything she does. Her clients are some of the biggest names in personal growth and healing, such as best-selling author and legendary energy medicine teacher Donna Eden and world-renowned leader in transformational education, Mindvalley. Shantini is also a sought-after ghostwriter who has penned best-selling personal growth books for well-known authors. Over the years, her writing has appeared in *Forbes, Inc.*, Hay House books, *ELLE, Harper's Bazaar,* and more. A lifelong lover of books, chocolate, and all things magic, Shantini currently lives in sunny Southeast Asia with her husband and beautiful cats Charley, Charcoal, and Queensie. Visit her at www.shantinirajah.com.

# MANIFEST
## *Anything*
### YOU WANT

## Six Magical Steps to Create an Extraordinary Life

*Shantini Rajah*

Llewellyn Publications
Woodbury, Minnesota

FIRST EDITION
First Printing, 2024

Cover design by Shannon McKuhen
Interior art by the Llewellyn Art Department

Llewellyn Publications is a registered trademark of Llewellyn Worldwide Ltd.

**Library of Congress Cataloging-in-Publication Data**

Names: Rajah, Shantini, author.
Title: Manifest anything you want : six magical steps to create an
    extraordinary life / by Shantini Rajah.
Description: [United States] : [Llewellyn] [2024] | Includes
    bibliographical references. | Summary: "This book shows readers how to
    dissolve emotional pain in a healthy way and provides actionable tools
    and techniques to cultivate a high vibrational state and enhance their
    ability to manifest with ease. It offers readers an effective path to
    bring their biggest, boldest dreams to life from a place of authentic
    desire and true joy"— Provided by publisher.
Identifiers: LCCN 2024000961 (print) | LCCN 2024000962 (ebook) | ISBN
    9780738775043 (paperback) | ISBN 9780738775111 (ebook)
Subjects: LCSH: Magical thinking. | Success—Religious aspects. | Fate and
    fatalism—Religious aspects.
Classification: LCC BF1621 .R34 2024  (print) | LCC BF1621 (ebook) | DDC
    133.4/3—dc23/eng/20240318
LC record available at https://lccn.loc.gov/2024000961
LC ebook record available at https://lccn.loc.gov/2024000962

Llewellyn Worldwide Ltd. does not participate in, endorse, or have any authority or responsibility concerning private business transactions between our authors and the public.

All mail addressed to the author is forwarded but the publisher cannot, unless specifically instructed by the author, give out an address or phone number.

Any internet references contained in this work are current at publication time, but the publisher cannot guarantee that a specific location will continue to be maintained. Please refer to the publisher's website for links to authors' websites and other sources.

Llewellyn Publications
A Division of Llewellyn Worldwide Ltd.
2143 Wooddale Drive
Woodbury, MN 55125-2989
www.llewellyn.com

Printed in the United States of America

*For my handsome, strong, funny, charming, anything-is-possible father who taught me to love and respect the power of words.*

*Papa, you were in my life for just seven years and I miss you every day. You said books would change my life. You were right.*

# Contents

ACKNOWLEDGMENTS...XI

INTRODUCTION...I

## Phase I: Where Our Journey Begins

**One:** Why Traditional Manifesting Doesn't Always Work...13

**Two:** The Missing Piece to Manifesting: Your 1 Healing Breath...25

## Phase II: Build Your Inner Altar

**Three:** Magical Manifesting Ingredient #1: Identify What You Really Want...47

**Four:** Magical Manifesting Ingredient #2: Authentically Elevate Your Vibe...67

## Phase III: Cultivate Un-resistance

**Five:** Magical Manifesting Ingredient #3: Alchemize Fear...97

**Six:** Magical Manifesting Ingredient #4: Tap into Practical Magic...119

## Phase IV: Embody the Magic

**Seven:** Magical Manifesting Ingredient #5: Craft Your Manifesting Avatar...149

**Eight:** Magical Manifesting Ingredient #6: Utilize the Power of Joyful Play...173

## Phase V: Call In Your Destiny

**Nine:** Your Magical Manifesting Recipes...197

**Ten:** The Quiz: Find Your Manifesting Archetype...209

**Eleven:** Breathe Your Way to Anything You Want...223

CONCLUSION...233

RECOMMENDED READING...237

BIBLIOGRAPHY...241

# Acknowledgments

The Universe works through magical beings. There are no words to describe the depth of love and gratitude I feel for every single magical being who helped bring this book to life, but I'm going to give it a shot!

To my mother, Shantha Devi, and my sister, Shamini, who loved me from the beginning and who continue to love me no matter what—I wouldn't be where I am today without you. Thank you from the depths of my soul.

Julian, you've loved and supported me through everything, and I mean *everything*! You made me laugh the first day I met you—it's been over 8,400 days and I'm still laughing. I'm beyond grateful you're in my life. Here's to many more lifetimes of loving each other and laughing together.

Amy B. Scher is a creative force of nature, one of the kindest people I've ever met and one of the greatest writers on the planet. Amy, I can't believe how lucky I am to have had the chance to work with you. You nudged me to meet the edge of my comfort zone so I could transcend it. You gave me wings to fly. I wouldn't be an author if not for you. Thank you, thank you, thank you.

Steven Harris, I hope you know that you're the world's most fabulous literary agent, because you are! Thank you so much for taking a chance on me. There isn't a day that goes by when I don't think about that moment when you said, "Let's do this!" It's a milestone moment and it changed the trajectory of my life.

Angela Wix, we didn't get a chance to work closely together, but I will never, ever forget how you saw the potential in this book (long before it was a book) and you advocated for it. You put your faith and trust in an untested, first-time author, and I'm forever in your debt. Thank you so much!

Amy Glaser, I couldn't have wished for a kinder, more gifted editor than you! You made crafting this book an absolute breeze. I've heard that writing a book can feel like a roller coaster ride, but I don't know anything about that because you made the entire experience feel like a delightfully pleasant boat ride on a bright, sunny day. My heartfelt gratitude goes out to you, Amy, and to Andrea Neff, Donna Burch, Kat Neff, Shannon McKuhen, and the entire team at Llewellyn—you are truly phenomenal at what you do.

Ajit Nawalkha, you are an incredibly gifted coach, a deeply inspiring human, and an unstoppable world-changer. You've transformed countless lives with your love and wisdom, and I feel so blessed that I get to say that mine is one of them. In so many ways you shaped my path, my purpose, and my writing career. I know I can never thank you enough, but I'll never stop trying.

Elysia Hartzell and Kimberlie Carlson, you believed in me years before I believed in myself. Your love for me and your trust in my words are two of the greatest gifts I've ever received. We're soul sisters across lifetimes. This isn't the first time we've met and I know it won't be the last.

Mekala Kannan and Umadevi Ganesan, my oldest and dearest friends, you stood by me, stood up for me, put up with me, and supported my dream of becoming a writer when it was just that—a dream. You are two of the best friends a girl could ever ask for. We've been on many exciting adventures together and I can't wait to go on the next one with you.

I could go on writing these acknowledgments for the rest of time and I know I need to stop, but not before I thank the beautiful souls who see me for who I am, who make it safe for me to be me, and who live in the field of infinite possibilities where love and friendship know no bounds. I'm talking about you, Andrea Scher, Carrie Cento, Cheryl-Lynne Kulasingham, Dondi Dahlin, Jamie Khoo, Johanna Gardner, Lisa Zahran, Manny Goldman, Maricris Dominique Dela Cruz, Marilyn Alauria, Dr. Neeta Bhushan, Randi Buckley, Ruth Poundwhite, Samantha Nolan-Smith, and Stacy Hartmann. Thank you for sharing your light in this world. Thank you for being YOU.

Finally, to my beautiful cats Charley, Charcoal, and Queensie. Your loving energy and gentle purrs transformed my writing space into a sacred, creative sanctuary. Love you forever.

# Introduction

This book is in your hands against all odds, and it's a result of the manifesting approach you're about to discover in these pages. To put it another way, this is a book about a manifesting approach that exists because of the manifesting approach in this book. (Yes, I realize that's super meta and maybe even a little bit unbelievable, but it happens to be 100 percent true!) I didn't expect to beat the astronomical odds of landing a book deal the first time I submitted a proposal, but I did and here we are. Like so many miracles that happen when we choose to dance with the Universe, I'm living my dream of becoming an author in a way that I couldn't have imagined.

Growing up in a little town in the north of Peninsular Malaysia, I'd always dreamed of becoming a writer. But there's no way I could have predicted that I'd have the opportunity to connect with an amazing author I love and look up to who would help me craft a professional book proposal, or that I'd have a wonderfully supportive book agent, who happens to be one of the best in the business and believes in me (plus he totally gets my work— he encouraged me to manifest the book deal the first time we met online!). I couldn't have envisioned that I'd be offered a book deal with the oldest and largest independent publisher for mind, body, spirit books in the entire freakin' world. Even more amazing, my dream became a reality despite the fact that I have almost no presence or following on social media and at a time when a large and engaged audience of fans and followers is often a make-or-break criterion in becoming a published author.

As I write these words, I still can't believe that *I'm writing these words*. I know there's a part of me that will forever remain in a state of awe and delight at the majestic and mysterious workings of the Universe. Sometimes it feels like watching the magic of manifesting unfold is even more rewarding than receiving the results. This book—and the fact that you are reading these words—are just two of the many miracles that have come through when I worked with the six Magical Manifesting Ingredients that I'm about to share with you. In other words, this book is tangible proof that what you're about to learn works, and if you consistently apply these techniques, then manifesting your desires can become a delightful, uncomplicated process that you'll be able to do again and again.

## Becoming a Masterful Manifestor

Let me ask you a quick question: How would your life change if you could have unconditional love, unlimited abundance, joyful energy, or anything else your heart desires *and* you didn't have to strive for it in ways that left you feeling depleted? It's a question that might inspire excitement in your heart or trigger a different sort of emotion—the kind that makes you raise an eyebrow (or two). You might be thinking, "That sounds amazing! Tell me more!" or "Yeah, sure! And the moon is made of Swiss cheese, plus there's a unicorn stomping around my backyard right now!" I'm both a scientist and a writer, so whichever camp you happen to be in, I get you. It's wonderful to wake up every day feeling like the world is full of wonder and wild magic is just around the corner. If this is you and you love following the magic, three cheers to you! There's nothing that cannot be improved with genuine, unbridled enthusiasm and *joie de vivre*.

But maybe that's not you. Maybe you have a mind that questions everything. You see the world through an evidence-based, scientific lens and you have an inexhaustible curiosity that drives you to get to the bottom of things.

If this is the case, I applaud you too. A questioning mind and a heart that tirelessly seeks the truth are priceless treasures, but so often we're chastised or made to feel small because we're not instant believers or endlessly upbeat. The truth is that measured caution is a wonderful thing, and now more than ever, we need people who aren't afraid to ask hard-to-answer questions. Whichever perspective you happen to hold—whether you're magical or measured—you were drawn to this book for a reason.

The world is changing at lightning speed. Most of us feel constantly anxious and stressed trying to keep up, and life has been heartbreakingly hard for so many people. Those of us who've been stoically trudging along and trying to be brave are feeling a level of exhaustion that's beyond just tired or drained; it's the kind of exhaustion that runs deep, right down to the bone. Those of us who are sensitive to energy can feel a strange sense of fearful vigilance unlike anything we've ever sensed before. It's like we're collectively holding our breath waiting for something bad to happen, waiting for the other shoe to drop.

This isn't surprising when you think about it. Global shake-ups brought on by a pandemic that swept the world, the rise of artificial intelligence that seems determined to take our jobs, scary environmental shifts that leave us feeling guilty and powerless, and unexpected revelations and changes in politics, media, finance, and even entertainment have left us feeling frightened, dazed, and confused. Most of what we once believed about our world and our place in it has been uprooted, and it's often impossible to tell the difference between facts and falsehoods.

Everything is changing. As a result, how we work, live, and play is evolving at a rapid pace, and this evolution includes how we manifest. This book is about manifesting all that you desire, but not in the traditional sense (which has become outdated). Yes, we'll be diving into the art of attracting what you want to create a boldly beautiful and magical life. But what you're about to learn has little to do with vision boards and visualizations. It's about discovering who you truly are and what you truly want, and it's about intentionally designing a life that reflects what you believe in and how you want to live. In other words, it's about manifesting a life that feels like *you*. Along the way, you'll learn how to live from a place of wonder and curiosity, self-acceptance, self-kindness, and self-compassion. From that place, you won't just learn to manifest masterfully, you will *become* a masterful manifestor.

We're about to embark on a journey that is strangely fascinating. It's an adventure that promises to surprise and delight you as much as it will stretch and challenge you. But it's worth the effort because you'll emerge feeling so much safer in your body, more tranquil in your mind, more inspired in your heart, and feeling good in your soul. So whether you're an ardent believer in the infinite power of the Universe and the Law of Attraction or not, know that you're in the right place. This book is for you. The manifesting approach you're about to learn is a bit like gravity in that it works whether you believe in it or not. All I ask is that you open your heart and mind to these concepts and ideas and give the activities you'll find peppered throughout the book a heartfelt try.

## What Manifesting Is Really About

If you can legally drink, which is to say that you're over twenty-one in the US, you can probably recall the days when Rhonda Byrne's 2006 book and documentary *The Secret* swept through the world of personal development and spirituality. At that time, just about everyone seemed to be manifesting something or other, with little-known authors and teachers who happened to know even a tiny bit about the Law of Attraction suddenly propelled into public consciousness. But things have changed since then. A lot of people have discovered, much to their disappointment, that visualizing a red Ferrari does not result in a red Ferrari magically appearing in their garage.

Chances are you've tried chanting affirmations and you've practiced positive thinking. Maybe you've put together a vision board or five and you've managed to conjure a few things seemingly out of thin air, such as a couple of parking spots or a free lunch. But you've probably noticed that your ability to manifest is frustratingly inconsistent and often downright disappointing. And no matter what you do or how hard you try, your success rate remains erratic. Okay, so that's the bad news. Now for some fabulous news.

Affirmations, visualizations, and other mainstream manifesting methods work and they work really well, but there's a missing piece of the manifesting puzzle that you need for reliable, consistent results. This piece is something hardly anyone talks about. The truth is that the most carefully constructed vision board in the world holds no magic or power if you're in a place of fear, guilt, uncertainty, or doubt while you're putting it together.

I've written this book so that it's not just another manual about using affirmations, meditations, visualizations, and all the rest of the amazing manifesting tools out there. These are "Google-able" tools, and there are lots of great books and courses that can offer you everything you need to know to make each of them work for you. This book is a little bit different. It's more about the art of becoming a manifestor rather than the craft of manifesting. Attracting all you desire with ease and consistency isn't so much about what you're doing on the outside to manifest true love that lasts a lifetime, a healthy body and mind, a highly profitable business that enables you to donate to your favorite charity without holding back, or any of the other beautiful, illuminating, creative experiences and relationships you might long for. Manifesting is about how you're showing up inside yourself. In other words, becoming a masterful manifestor isn't about *what you are doing* but *who you are being*. That's where the tools and practices in this book can change everything for you.

## The "No Hustle or Hack" Zone

I wrote this book as a companion for your manifesting journey. It's a gentle, fun guide to discover yourself and recognize who you are at your core. It's about identifying what you really want, maybe for the first time in your life, and getting whatever that is just by being yourself.

The first thing to know about the tools and practices in this book is that there's no such thing as doing it wrong. Everything in these pages is intentionally written to rise up and greet you at exactly the right place and the right time. With that in mind, I highly recommend that you read this book all the way through once and then keep it where you can refer to it easily. Any time you need a little boost or guidance, open the book to a random page, or if you have a digital version of this book, close your eyes and scroll through the pages at random until you land on a page. When you do this, I promise you'll read something that is perfect for you at that time.

My intention is for this book to be a loving, reliable friend who knows just what to say to make things better and brighter, rather than an unforgiving coach or teacher whose rules you must follow word for word, step-by-step, or else! This means you can relax and immerse yourself in the experience of becoming a creator of your own life. You don't have to follow any strict rules or, heaven forbid, hack your way to receiving what you desire. No rushing, pushing, or striving required! Think of this space as a "no hustle or hack" zone.

In the following chapters, you'll find a powerful core manifesting recipe that consists of six Magical Manifesting Ingredients. This special recipe creates results with delightful ease and astonishing accuracy, and you can use it to cook up anything you want. You'll also discover how to add flavor, fun, and finesse to your manifesting experience with a breathing practice I developed called 1 Healing Breath. Including 1 Healing Breath in the process is like having the perfect ingredients sizzling and blending together on the stove and then adding that special secret ingredient that transforms a beautiful meal into an unforgettable gastronomic extravaganza.

You'll find that each of the six Magical Manifesting Ingredients as well as the 1 Healing Breath practice can stand alone, and you don't have to do them in sequence, which is great news if you love having freedom and flexibility that lets you fit your manifesting activities into your life and not the other way around. Along the way, you'll learn to cultivate deep inner alignment, enhanced intuition, and embodied safety no matter what else is going on in your life and in the world. You'll learn practical, in-the-moment tools you can use at any time to shift from resistance to un-resistance, release self-judgment and self-rejection, and boost powerful, positive traits such as focus and creativity. You'll also master the art of tuning into your hidden genius through your intuition and falling into a state of relaxed, joyful flow as you take confident, consistent action toward your dream life.

I'll be sharing more about my personal story in chapter 1, and you'll get to know how the 1 Healing Breath practice, which consists of a variety of positive, uplifting, energizing words and images, came to be. (You'll also learn how you can access this special collection of images for free so that you can enter a genuine, high-vibrational state any time you want.) But for now, let me just say that the original practice was given to me in what I like to think of as a Divine Download. I understood exactly what it was the second it dropped into my heart and mind. The rest unfolded from there, like a river flowing to the sea.

Everything you're about to read in this book arose from a confluence of my two obsessions: science and spirituality. Some of the techniques come from deep experimentation and hundreds of hours of reading, writing, and research-ing the guiding principles of neuroscience and psychology, while others are based on spiritual and esoteric ideologies, as well as many of the multiple thou-sand-year-old wisdom traditions from my birthplace of Southeast Asia.

Ultimately, I'd love for you to take the manifesting approach you're about to discover in this book and make it your own. That is the most effective way to maximize the benefits of this deceptively simple yet surprisingly powerful process of creating the life you desire. You'll learn exactly how to fine-tune and tailor the 1 Healing Breath practice so you have a reliable manifesting system that works for you every time.

## How to Use This Book
## (and Supercharge Your Manifesting Skills)

You'll supercharge your manifesting skills if you approach this book like it's an interactive online course that you can't wait to join or an in-person training program that you've been looking forward to rather than just a static reading experience. I encourage you to dive into the practices and activities as you read so you can get your manifesting experience rockin' and rollin' right away!

Get ready for more than a few unexpected surprises about yourself (and maybe even some shocking revelations), like why you secretly don't believe you deserve what you want (even if you think you do) and the real reason why what you want is also what you don't want (and what to do about it). You'll discover that how you feel in your body could be blocking you from achieving all the financial, relationship, health, and other goals you've ever envisioned, along with how you could be unknowingly trying to manifest what I call False Desires, which are based on what other people want for you rather than what you want for yourself.

You'll start to have fun even before you see your manifesting skills take off. (Fun and play are a big part of this experience.) To make things as pleasurable and effortless as possible, I've divided the book into easy-to-follow sections.

### Phase I: Where Our Journey Begins

In this first phase of our journey, I'll share the truth about becoming a masterful manifestor. You'll learn about internal and external blocks that hold you back from being who you are and getting what you want, including common misconceptions about the art of manifesting.

### Phase II: Build Your Inner Altar and
### Phase III: Cultivate Un-resistance

We'll dive deep into the first four of the six Magical Manifesting Ingredients as well as the 1 Healing Breath practice. You'll discover a simple way to nurture gentle, loving awareness of your inner world, so you can follow the voice of your truth and start to release and heal the conscious and unconscious resistance blocking your ability to manifest.

### Phase IV: Embody the Magic

This phase of your manifesting adventure includes the final two of the six Magical Manifesting Ingredients. The Magical Manifesting Ingredient #5 is about creating your Manifesting Avatar, so you can begin living your dream life now. And finally, we'll explore Magical Manifesting Ingredient #6, where you'll learn how to use the power of play and pleasure to amplify your ability to attract anything you want.

### Phase V: Call In Your Destiny

By the time you reach this final phase, you'll be ready to apply everything you've learned. You'll have the option of choosing one or more of the 18

Magical Manifesting Recipes that integrate every single tool and technique in this book, so you can adopt or adapt a manifesting ritual that fits beautifully into your schedule (no matter how busy you are!).

You'll also discover your Manifesting Archetype with a fun quiz! Your quiz results will reveal your personal manifesting rhythm and style, and I'll show you how to use the 1 Healing Breath practice to deepen your manifesting skills and create exciting results with ease and speed.

One more thing to note is that there is a "Manifest Now!" section at the end of many of the chapters, where you'll get to practice what you learned. You'll also find fun, easy-to-do manifesting and healing tools and techniques peppered throughout the book.

## An Opening Declaration

As we prepare to embark on our journey together, I invite you to connect with yourself in a way that ignites a deep sense of safety and security as well as curiosity, inspiration, and creativity. The following is a declaration or prayer called "The Promise," which is adapted from my personal spiritual practice as well as my work with clients. You can read this out loud or to yourself. If you love ritual and ceremony, feel free to light a candle and some incense before you recite these lines. Come back to this if you ever sense the need for renewed commitment or whenever you feel like it.

### The Promise

*With my whole heart, soul, mind, and energy, I am in deepest gratitude.*

*I thank my Highest Self, my angels, my guides, and the divine intelligence of the Universe.*

*Thank you for the light, the love, and the lessons learned.*

*I breathe out all that has come before and all whose time has passed.*

*I know in my soul that I am a part of the light that is the tapestry of All that is Love throughout the Universe and across the time-space continuum.*

*And as such, my power to manifest knows no bounds.*

*I am a masterful manifestor of my life. I design my destiny with conscious, loving awareness and deep joy.*

*I design my destiny with the energies of Earth, Air, Fire, and Water.*

*I design my destiny with the the full power of Shiva and Shakti—the sacred masculine and the divine feminine.*

*And so it is.*

## Phase I

# Where Our Journey Begins

I couldn't be more excited that we're about to begin our manifesting adventure together. In this first section, you'll discover why you might have experienced frustration and disappointment working with so many popular, mainstream manifesting techniques and why feeling safe is one of the most important elements of successful manifesting. You'll also learn how the 1 Healing Breath came to be in a single divine whisper, and how you can use it to supercharge your manifesting skills.

One

# Why Traditional Manifesting Doesn't Always Work

Visualizations and vision boards, affirmations and gratitude journals—when it comes to tips and techniques that help you align with the Universe to attract what you want, you've probably heard it all, or at least most of it. But there's a critical element at the heart of successful manifesting, and it's something a lot of people don't talk about: feeling a profound sense of safety in being who you truly are. Have you ever tried unwinding a tightly wound ball of knotted strings? I've found there's usually that one bit of string that's intertwined with all the others, and when you tug at that one string, the entire ball of knots easily comes undone. Feeling safe to be yourself is that one string that releases the knotted ball of energetic blocks, such as self-doubt, limiting beliefs, and fears, that hold you back from manifesting what you want. When it comes to easy, speedy manifesting, tapping into inner safety is everything.

Learning how to generate safety in the body, mind, and spirit will transform you into an extraordinary manifestor who can confidently and joyfully partner with the Universe to receive everything you desire. We'll return to this truth again and again in our shared adventure throughout the rest of this book, but be patient, because the art of creating inner safety takes time. Most people have no idea what it's like to feel safe, and I was one of them. For most of my childhood and early adulthood, it felt like I was walking a tightrope a hundred feet off the ground without a safety net, and it all started the day I lost my dad.

## The Ravenous Beast

Everyone loved my kind, funny, charming father. He was the friend you called when you were in trouble because you know he'd drop everything to help you any way he could. He was the one who could magically transform a boring dinner party into a lively affair with a funny story that made everyone laugh. I adored my father and I looked up to him. He was handsome, smart, and strong and I thought he was invincible. The day he died suddenly from a heart attack, my world crumbled and my life was never the same again. Those childhood years that most people talk about with wistful nostalgia—the years that are supposed to be full of joyful, carefree abandon—were defined by a strange sense of impending doom for me.

On the surface, everything seemed fine, and even though my dad was no longer around, I knew I was lucky that I had a mother and a big sister who loved me. But despite their best efforts, I hardly ever felt truly happy or calm, and when I did, the positive feelings disappeared as soon as they arrived. The only time I ever felt good was when I had my nose buried in the pages of a book. Books helped me escape the real world, the one without my dad, and I found friends and kindred spirits in the stories that I loved so much.

Despite following Alice down the rabbit hole into Wonderland and taking in the majestic beauty of the mountains with Heidi, I found that the reality of my life without my dad was never far away. To make matters worse, I didn't feel like I was allowed to be anything but happy and grateful because it seemed to me that I had more than I deserved, and certainly more than a lot of people could ever hope to have. I had access to running water, electricity, and an education. I had a roof over my head and food to eat. But even though I knew I had so much to be grateful for, I couldn't shake the awful feeling that something bad was about to happen and it was just around the corner.

In time, I realized that this feeling of impending doom had a name—it was called anxiety—and that revelation was only the beginning.

I battled mightily against debilitating anxiety for years, well into my twenties and thirties. It was like a ravenous beast that threatened to swallow me whole, and so once again, I turned to books for solace and comfort. I first discovered self-help books when I was fifteen, and I've never looked back. My journey to unraveling the fear, anxiety, and unhappiness I felt inside can be mapped across hundreds, maybe even thousands, of self-help books. In the early 2000s, I was enchanted by Rhonda Byrne's *The Secret*, which led me to discover the Abraham-Hicks series, which I treasure and return to every year.

Every single book offered comfort and support, but it would be decades before I discovered the one thing that opened the door to my dream of freeing myself from anxiety and heartache, the one thing that allowed me to co-create my life with the unlimited power of the Universe so that infinite abundance could enter my world. This one thing turned out to be a powerful yet simple thread of wisdom in the form of a question. I happened to chance upon it in a book about finding inner calm, and it transformed my world. The question was this: *Do you feel safe?*

These four simple words haunted me. The question remained in my thoughts and burned brightly in my inner vision: *Do you feel safe? Do you feel safe? Do you feel safe?* I couldn't stop thinking about it, and I couldn't stop turning it over and over in my mind, because the answer shocked me: No, I did not feel safe and I never had. I finally understood why the world felt like a scary place and why nothing I achieved ever felt like it was good enough. Safety was a feeling I did not recognize, and it was something that had eluded me almost all my life.

When you feel safe in your body, mind, and spirit, it's easy to open your heart to the flow of unconditional love from the Universe. A strong sense of inner safety allows you to bounce back after every failure and to get back up again even after the most painful disappointments. In that one moment when I found my answer to that life-changing question, I knew I had to find a way to feel safe even if the world around me was in chaos. What I didn't know at the time was that my path to generating inner safety would arrive in the most unexpected way, in the middle of an otherwise forgettable Wednesday afternoon.

## A Divine Whisper

I was in my kitchen making a cup of coffee and thinking about ideas for an article that I was working on when out of the blue I heard the words "1 Healing Breath." It was a gentle whisper in my right ear, and it was as soothing as the sound of wind chimes ringing in the quiet calm of sunrise. My heart beating fast, I glanced over my shoulder, driven by the irrational thought that someone had whispered those words in my ear, even though I knew the only other people in my house at the time weren't people at all but my two beloved furry feline kids, Charley and Charcoal. I was starting to think I had imagined the whole thing when I heard it again, an imperceptible murmur so quiet it was almost a sigh: "1 Healing Breath." The second time I heard it, I understood. This was an "intuitive hit," or what a lot of my spiritual friends and clients call a Divine Download. It's a knowing that comes from a Higher Power, like the Universe or your guides and angels. What I heard that afternoon was a message, an insight that came from a source that was way beyond my modest understanding of how existence works.

I had been receiving messages, ideas as whispers or spoken messages, since I was a child, so I wasn't startled or afraid. I did what I always do when it happens: I allowed the Universe to guide me through my intuition (we'll explore working with our intuition in chapter 3), and I gave myself permission to follow through with effortless action. As I opened myself to receiving divine guidance from the Universe, 1 Healing Breath became my North Star, my guiding light, my grounding and centering practice, and the vital catalyst in manifesting everything I desired.

## Manifesting from Inner Safety

Most manifesting tools and techniques can add a significant amount of stress and pressure to your energy system, which then works to block your desires from becoming a reality. I discovered this truth by accident.

When I first learned about the Law of Attraction, I loved everything about it. What's not to love? Tap into the unlimited power of the Universe to manifest what you want? Count me in! Create the life you've always longed for? Sign me up! So I dove in with enthusiasm and discovered lots of effective manifesting techniques. But in time, I began to notice something strange: many of the fun and exciting manifesting methods I tried, such as chanting affirmations, trying to think positive, or visualizing my ideal future, left me feeling stressed and anxious rather than brimming with joy and excited anticipation.

As I flipped through magazines looking for images of a dream home to tack on my vision board, I found myself thinking, "What if I never get to live there?" As I faithfully wrote "I'm releasing all resistance to wealth and I'm consistently attracting abundance," I thought, "What if I end up penniless?" As I dutifully chanted "I'm worthy, happy, and at the perfect weight," I found myself thinking, "Nope! You're no big deal, you're not happy, and, *errr*... take a look at those hips and that belly. Yikes! You're at least ten kilograms overweight." This left me feeling disillusioned and disappointed. I was wracked with guilt because I wasn't being positive enough, and I was ashamed of that low-vibrational state of anxiety that seemed to take over without warning every time I tried to do anything remotely related to partnering with the Universe.

This would have likely continued until the end of time if I hadn't tried integrating 1 Healing Breath into my personal manifesting practice. At first I did it just for fun. I let the Universe guide me through my intuition, and when I first received the cosmic nudge to include the 1 Healing Breath practice in my manifesting process, I remember thinking, "Sure, Universe, why not? Thank you." To my surprise and delight, I found that with the 1 Healing Breath, I could begin to release doubts and fears that had been a part of my life for years, and it became much easier to remain in a state of tranquility during any manifesting technique I tried. I started feeling more centered during the day and I fell asleep with more ease and calm in my heart each night. Soon the 1 Healing Breath practice became an integral part of my manifesting experience, and that's when the magic began to unfold. I attracted dream clients, built a wildly successful, fulfilling business that generated more income than I could have possibly hoped for, and more.

As I continued to strengthen my manifesting muscles with the 1 Healing Breath practice, it soon became clear that I'd found an incredibly effective yet simple manifesting tool. I was excited at the thought of helping people who were struggling like I had—people who were constantly disappointed when they tried collaborating with the Universe, people who felt ashamed because they weren't being positive enough or guilty because they'd somehow manifested something negative or unwanted into their experience.

Here's something I want you to know: the Universe is *so* much more than a restaurant from which you can order anything you want, as some manifesting gurus like to say. It's also a source of unconditional love and healing, and it can help to wash away anxiety, pain, and heartache while giving you all that you desire. My consistent positive results with the 1 Healing Breath gave rise to a core manifesting recipe that includes six Magical Manifesting Ingredients. Just like a warm bowl of delicious soup that offers healing and comfort, this manifesting recipe works to *relieve* your anxiety and stress so you can get what you want. And you'll find that's the vital distinction between the approach in this book and that of any other manifesting method you might have come across.

## The Four Failure Factors

Over the next few years, I committed to keeping a promise that I'd made to myself: I'd put together a manifesting process that would give me everything I desired but that would also deliver inner calm, joy, and excited anticipation. During that time, I identified four key factors that trigger anxiety, doubt, and stress, causing many well-known manifesting processes to fail.

### Failure Factor #1: Contracted Manifesting

You might have noticed that lots of gurus and teachers insist that you include specifics in your manifesting process. For instance, if you're looking to attract the love of your life, you need a deadline, such as "I'll meet the love of my life by February 20th of next year." This is like having full access to a magical channel that lets you receive the unlimited creative energy of the Universe and then blocking that channel with a bunch of rocks and boulders.

Dates, times, and any kind of hard data such as numbers and other measurable details belong in the realm of the cognitive, thinking mind, and when you restrict yourself with these measurables, you are in effect significantly contracting and even totally blocking your ability to manifest.

Give the Universe the space and time to bring you what your heart desires or something even better. The Magical Manifesting Ingredients in this book are designed to help you release cognitive control, so you never have to worry about dates, times, numbers, or anything else. Instead, we'll have fun following the energy of potential, so dreams that are bigger than we dare to dream for ourselves can become our reality.

### Failure Factor #2: Proxy Manifesting

I know a bunch of manifesting rock stars who can attract just about anything faster than you can say "I love the Law of Attraction," but only if they're doing it for someone else. A gifted energy practitioner I know envisioned building an abundant business serving clients around the world, and although he was fully committed in his mind and heart, there was a part of him that simply did not believe he was worthy of calling in large sums of money. He believed money and spirituality didn't belong together, which blocked him from receiving the income he desired. Interestingly enough, the abundance he desired flowed freely and quickly into his sister's business when he focused his manifesting skills on helping her attract ideal customers.

You might have experienced something similar. Maybe you helped your best friend land their dream job but couldn't manifest the same for yourself. Maybe you helped a coworker expand their social circle, but you haven't made a new friend in the last twenty years. If you're a serial proxy manifestor, there's a good chance you have no problem believing other people deserve everything they desire but you don't think that's true for you. The six Magical Manifesting Ingredients in this book will help you peel back the layers of false beliefs around what you deserve. You'll connect with the heart and truth of who you are and learn to generate authentic safety in being yourself so you can manifest the life you want with ease and confidence, whether it's for yourself or someone else. And just in case you're wondering, you are a miracle of creation and you deserve everything you desire and more just because you exist.

### Failure Factor #3: Hierarchical Manifesting

Hierarchical manifesting happens when we don't want to shake up the hierarchy we were born into and we hold ourselves back from a life that is vastly bigger and better than the reality we've always known. So many of us feel guilty and afraid of becoming more successful than our family or friends, and it's because we intuitively know that sometimes, being happier, richer, or more at peace than the people around us can stir up a whole lot of trouble. Not fitting in or not being one of the group can come at the cost of cherished friendships and even family relationships. This is a terrifying thought, and it's why we end up playing a much smaller manifesting game. If this is you, it's not your fault. Achieving your biggest dreams might feel like a betrayal of who you are and where you come from, but the opposite is true. When we give ourselves permission to go further and reach higher than anyone we know, we are also giving the people around us permission to do the same. Manifesting at the highest level—the place where you are fully in alignment with the Universe and with high-vibrational emotions such as genuine joy, satisfaction, and wonder—gives your dreams wings. It's how you create all that you want, even if everything in your life seems to show you that what you want is not possible for you. This comes from manifesting through deep, genuine self-love, which we'll explore in chapter 4 and throughout the rest of the book.

### Failure Factor#4: Militant Manifesting

I've run into more than one self-proclaimed manifesting aficionado who has had a hard time holding back from correcting my language or offering an improved way of viewing a difficult situation or challenge. Some of these folks are repelled and sometimes even offended by phrases like "I might" or "I could," which they say signal uncertainty to the Universe, so you end up attracting what you don't want. Unfortunately for the rest of us, these self-appointed guardians of the Law of Attraction think nothing of interrupting and taking over the conversation so they can tell everyone else exactly what they need to say instead. This has happened to me more often than I'd like to admit, like the time I sadly admitted that I was not having a good day and a friend rushed in with a warning. "The Universe hears all, so you need to watch what you say," she said with genuine alarm. When I asked what she'd have me say instead, she piped up cheerfully, "Say you're having a good day when you're having a bad day, and say you're having a *great* day when you're having a good day." She seemed so full of confidence and joy that I didn't have the heart to tell her the Universe wasn't going to be fooled into giving me my desires just because I was careful about switching "bad day" to "good day" and "good day" to "great day."

While there's something to be said about cultivating awareness around the words you use, being overly vigilant and rigorous in controlling your language can trigger strong feelings of shame and guilt when you inevitably say something that's less than positive. Plus, feeling like you have to constantly force yourself to use uplifting language, especially when your emotions don't match your words, is a massive step backward on the path to manifesting what you want, because it creates serious blocks in your ability to connect to and match the authentically loving and joyful energy of the Universe.

## Why Being Yourself Will Give You Everything You Desire

The journey to becoming an empowered co-creator of your life experience with the Universe as your partner is not about what you do but rather who you *are* in this moment—moment by moment by moment. It's about transforming from the inside out and healing emotional pain and limiting thoughts that arise from the environment, inherited belief systems, or what society or your family tells you that you can or should have. This includes preconceived ideas such as "No one in my family runs a business, so there's no way I can be a successful entrepreneur" and "Single women can't be homeowners." I started my business with no network and no friends in high places, and the culture and society I come from can be pretty restrictive, especially if you're a woman, but these obstacles ceased to stand in my way when I started to shift my focus from manifesting as an activity to becoming a manifestor. When it comes to tapping into the right energy to manifest with repeatable success, it's all about who you're being versus what you're doing.

To illustrate my point, I invite you to take a look at a popular manifesting formula that goes something like this:

1. Identify your desires.
2. Activate your manifesting process using tools like journaling, vision boards, affirmations, etc.
3. Align with the energy of your desires by stepping into a positive emotional state.
4. Trust the Universe to work its magic.

Most people breeze through steps 1 through 3 without a care in the world, and then they get to step 4 and think, "How in the world do I do that?!" Step 4 was a major block for me because it's about *not doing anything*. It's about letting the Universe take the wheel, and heaven knows I was terrible at trusting anything and anybody. I simply had to interfere, I had to keep pushing, I had to control everything. I was always striving and hustling hard. It felt like if I didn't, I wouldn't get what I wanted, or worse, something bad would happen. This isn't surprising, especially if you grew up like me not knowing what it feels like to be safe.

This is why most people feel manifesting is an incomprehensible activity. It feels unstructured, unexpected, and most of all, unrepeatable, so they try to do something to make things happen. For so many people, and especially those of us who grew up in a difficult, unsupportive, or traumatic environment, manifesting with any kind of repeatable success can feel like wishing for the moon, the stars and the entire galaxy all at the same time. No matter how hard you try and how many tips and tricks and techniques you use, getting what you want feels like trying to clutch a palmful of water in your hand—it slips through your fingers the second you try to hold onto it by closing your fist. This leads to frustration and disappointment, and at worst it reinforces unhelpful beliefs and thoughts such as "I don't deserve what I desire," "Nothing good happens to me," or "Sooner or later, I lose everything I love."

But here's something I've discovered about successful manifesting, and it works even when it feels like your world is falling apart: what you're doing and feeling right now, at this moment, doesn't matter, because it's all about *who* you're being. The energy of allowing is about receiving and simply being in complete alignment with the Universe, and that's the energy of being who you truly are. My manifesting efforts didn't amount to much until I learned to transition from doing energy to being energy by allowing myself to simply be me. Any manifesting tool or technique in and of itself is nothing more than an empty action or a series of empty actions. But when you tune into the energy of who you are, you'll see that your ability to manifest becomes boundless, and it's because you are naturally attuned to the limitless creative energy of the Universe when you are being yourself. There is a part of you that was never born and will never die, and this is the part of you that is one with the Universe, the part of you that is truly, wholly you. Mainstream manifesting methods create sporadic success because they are made up of tools, techniques, and actions that have very little to do with tuning into a state of being. Most of these processes take you away from presence and from being who you are. But when you manifest from a state of being yourself, when you shift from doing energy to being energy, you are naturally aligned with the Universe, and anything you desire will be drawn to you.

Here's a handy little guide that can help you tell the difference between manifesting by *doing* versus manifesting by *being*.

## Manifesting by doing is about...

- Making things happen with effortful focus and relentless action.
- Struggling with doubt and constantly questioning the Universe.
- Setting ultra-specific, restrictive manifesting goals.

+ Sticking to rules about what it means to be positive and high-vibrational.

+ Holding on to a persona that is not who you truly are.

## *Manifesting by being is about...*

+ Allowing things to happen in service of a higher calling, inspiration, or desire.

+ Trusting the Universe unconditionally.

+ Releasing restrictions and allowing the Universe to deliver without limits.

+ Tuning into your intuition to evaluate and respond to life in the moment.

+ Being who you truly are.

When you are in the energy of doing, you'll find that you must make things happen, but when you are in the energy of being, things happen for you. As you work your way through the rest of this book, you'll find that learning to be a manifestor is one of the most empowering things you will ever do for yourself. A "being manifestor" has the power to shift and transform not just their own circumstances but also their surroundings. This is an extraordinarily empowered place to be in terms of both creating your own life and changing the world around you, and when you manifest from a state of being, you are always allowing, without exception. This means that even when things aren't going your way or don't seem to be going your way, you feel zero anxiety or struggle. You know that beneath the surface, you are allowing the Universe to work its magic (we'll turn up the dial on the art of allowing with a 1 Healing Breath–based method called Conscious Liberation in chapter 6), and you also know that everything is aligning to eventually lead you to where you want to go.

*Two*

# The Missing Piece to Manifesting: Your 1 Healing Breath

Imagine standing in front of a mountain of sparkling jewels. It's a dazzling, multicolored spectacle of diamonds, rubies, sapphires, and emeralds shimmering in the sun. Now imagine that each jewel represents something you long for with all your heart—a heartfelt desire you can't stop dreaming about. This could be a gorgeous home by the beach, a healthy, youthful body, a *New York Times* bestseller, a romantic relationship that fills you with joy, or an abundant, fulfilling business or career that gives you the financial means to donate to your favorite charity with wild abandon. It could be a simple sense of inner peace, equanimity, and love for all. You feel excited and inspired as you gaze at this priceless treasure of desires. You want it all and you're willing to do what it takes to get it. But there's a problem: there's a complicated obstacle course between you and your jewels of desire.

It's a treacherous trip full of steep cliffs, dark forests, hidden pits, invisible walls, and even a fun house of mirrors that can distort your view and take you way off track. These obstacles symbolize objections from your family, other people's expectations of how you should live, beliefs that don't support your path or your purpose, and thoughts and experiences that create conscious and unconscious resistance that becomes embedded in your body, your mind, and your energy system.

Yet, you feel that inner fire of devotion. You don't want to give up, but at the same time you can't ignore the truth: you're exhausted, you're drained, and you're freakin' bone-tired! Even if you've somehow successfully overcome obstacles like other people's expectations and opinions and unspoken cultural, gender-based, or societal rules about what's acceptable and what's not, and you've gathered up the courage to follow the desires of your heart many times before, you're starting to wonder if you can keep it up much longer. Will life ever get easier?

The truth is it's tough to go for what you want when the odds appear to be stacked against you. Dancing to your own beat can feel impossible when just about everyone you know and love keeps telling you the music that stirs your soul is off-key. But there's another way to get to your jewels of desire. It's a safe, joyful path that leads straight to that priceless treasure you've been longing for, and it will have you skipping along, feeling lighter, happier, and stronger with every step.

And best of all, you already found the secret door that opens to this path when you picked up this book. As it turns out, the safest, most joyful way to manifest your heart's deepest desires happens to be the path that leads you back to yourself. And the key that opens the door to this path is something you can feel and experience right now. It's been with you from the day you were born and it's with you in this moment and in every moment—I'm talking about the magical inhale and exhale of your breath.

## Manifesting Unwanted Outcomes

Even though I didn't know it at the time, I've been grappling with anxiety since childhood, and it left me feeling like I was constantly failing, falling behind, or forgetting something important. For years I struggled with the feeling that I was somehow disappointing everyone I knew—my family, my friends, my teachers, and later, the people I worked with. I coped by pushing myself to be perfect and doing everything in my power so I never failed to cross every t and dot every i. Fear of disappointing others turned the dial all the way up on my anxiety, and I found myself saying yes to requests for my time, attention, energy, and money even when I knew I needed to say no. I soon learned that the gnawing inner sensation I felt whenever anxiety had me in its grip would temporarily recede when I received praise or validation for doing a great job or hitting a goal, and I became obsessed with achieving, achieving, and achieving some more. My days blurred into a list of tasks to tick off on a never-ending to-do list as I endlessly attempted to hit bigger, better goals. But that anxious, gnawing pit in my stomach never truly disappeared no matter how much I tried to be perfect or how much I managed to achieve. It was like I was forever racing toward a finish line that drifted farther away every time I approached it, and that background anxiety, fear, and doubt became even more intense, often turning into frustration, impatience, and annoyance that had me lashing out at the world. It never occurred to me to stop and ask myself if I was pushing too hard, or if my goals felt good to me, or if any of those goals were even mine. This was before I understood how to connect with my Authentic Self and my True Desires (we'll learn how to do this in chapter 3), and I know I'm not the only one.

## The Unintentionality Trap

Most people live in response to what's happening in the external world, and it was exactly that way with me. I lived in response to what other people thought or said or believed. I reacted to the environment I was in or the challenge, problem, or obstacle that happened to be in front of me. Every time I became entangled in a sticky web of anxiety, the feeling that I was failing, falling behind, and forgetting would take over. I found myself stuck in what I've come to call the Unintentionality Trap, and it's where we become completely disconnected from our Authentic Self. Most days I was as far away from my Authentic Self as I could possibly be, and I'd manifest unwanted outcomes where I would end up hurting others and myself. Sometimes those outcomes were irreversible, like the time I destroyed a close friendship that I cherished with a dear friend I'll call Rita.

Rita and I first met when we were both hired to work on a major writing project. We loved working together and ended up partnering on a series of creative projects. It was so much fun being friends with Rita. She was fearless, kind, and always up for an adventure. She's the friend you call at 2:00 a.m. when you have a big fight with your boyfriend and you need a shoulder to cry on. She's the first one on the dance floor on a night out and the last one to leave a party because she's helping the host clean up. She always knew exactly what to say to lighten the mood, and the only time I ever saw her at a loss for words was the day when things fell apart between us.

We were working together at our favorite cafe, like we did every Friday. I was expecting a call from an important client and told her to pick up if my cell phone rang while I dashed out for a quick bathroom break. When I returned, I found Rita immersed in her work, staring at the screen, a slight frown on her face. I didn't want to bother her, so I turned back to the article I was writing.

A couple of hours went by before I noticed an email alert pop up on my screen. It was a message from the client I'd been waiting for. He was mad that I hadn't called him back. When I called and told him I didn't know what he was talking about, he became even more upset. "But your friend picked up your phone. She told me she'd let you know that I'd called. Didn't she say anything?" I was livid. I glanced at Rita, who remained blissfully unaware, still immersed in her work. When I told her about my angry client, she was deeply sorry, apologizing profusely again and again, but something in me remained unmoved. I couldn't stop the barrage of angry words that came tumbling out of my mouth. I told her she'd probably cost me an important client (all my clients felt important to me back then, even the ones I didn't want to work with). I told her how disappointed I was, how I had expected more from her, and on and on.

Looking back, I could sense that I was heading straight for the point of no return in our friendship, but I couldn't stop talking. Rita fell silent, listening to my painful accusations, but eventually something must have snapped. Without saying a word, she began packing up her things. When I asked what was going on, she turned to me with sadness in her eyes and said, "I'm sorry, but I can't be around someone who makes me feel bad about myself, and you know what? I wish you'd remembered today's my birthday." I felt like the worst person in the world, and then it was my turn to apologize. We eventually talked it out, but our friendship was never the same again. We saw each other less and less after that, and when I met her for the last time, she told me she was moving to the other side of the world.

I wish I could say I learned an important lesson from my horrible mistake. I wish I could say I never did anything like that ever again, but I can't. There would be many more little and large unhappy incidents that left me feeling like anything but the manifestor or creator of my own life. That is, until I finally discovered the one thing that set me free.

## A Touch of Magic

Most of us go through our entire lives without thinking about our breath or the act of breathing. Our breath is something we largely ignore unless we have trouble breathing, and then it's all we can think about. But the breath is much more than the flow of oxygen into our lungs. Learning how to focus on our breath is one of the most important skills we can develop for greater health and happiness. I learned this important truth in a delightfully unexpected way and from someone I admire but have never met: Jane Fonda.

Not a lot of people know this about me, but I'm a huge Jane Fonda fan. I love that she's a movie star and an activist and I absolutely love her workouts from way back in the day. The festive leg warmers, the happy, upbeat music, the smiling faces—they were an irresistible cocktail of motivation and movement. Jane inspired me to stick to my workout routine, week after week, month after month, and year after year. I loved every one of her video tapes (yes, video was still around back then!), but after all these years it's not her dance moves or the snazzy neon-colored '80s workout outfits I remember best. It's something Jane said as she introduced what was her brand-new yoga workout at the time. In her strong, confident voice, she declared, "The Yogis say that if you can control your breath, you can control your life." The words made me stop in my tracks, and somehow, somewhere deep in my soul, I knew Jane and the Yogis were right. I soon forgot about this powerful piece of wisdom as I tried and promptly failed to do my first downward dog pose. But I guess Jane made an impression after all, because her words came back to me years later, the day I discovered I had trouble breathing.

Just to be clear, I don't have respiratory problems, and as far as I can tell, there's nothing wrong with my lungs. But breathing freely, fearlessly, and naturally didn't come easily to me. Instead, I held my breath multiple times throughout the day, even while I was relaxing in a bubble bath, getting a foot massage, or meditating. When I first became aware of my strange breathing patterns, it dawned on me that I'd been unconsciously holding my breath this way for most of my life.

When the concept of the 1 Healing Breath first entered my heart and mind out of the blue, I instantly knew it was something magical. As I followed that spark of an idea until it grew into a fully developed practice, it became clear to me that a single conscious breath, combined with an intentional word, can lead to peace and healing. It can bring you back to yourself in a second, and it can instantly attune you to the energy of the Universe so you can draw in the magic and the miracles that are waiting to happen.

## Aligning with the Universe

Let's do a quick experiment. Take a second right now and bring your awareness to your breath. Does your breathing feel smooth, natural, and relaxed, or do you find you're taking short, sharp bursts of breath like you're running out of air? You might find that you're holding your breath without even knowing it. I can totally relate, because there were countless times in my life when I was so intensely stressed or upset that I wouldn't let myself breathe.

The breath is the essence of life. It is our soul force. It is a channel through which our awareness flows. Just like all forms of energy, it cannot be seen with our eyes or held in our hands. It leaves no trace, and yet it exists. We know it is real and it is the most important truth of our existence. All living beings are united in this shared experience. Every inhale and exhale is proof that we are alive, because all that breathes lives. It's as simple and as profound as that. I see the breath as a magnificent connector, the translucent thread that links the body, the mind, the heart, and the spirit. It bridges our inner world with the outer world.

At any time (right now if you want to), we can sense the presence of our breath as it travels from our physical self out into the etheric field of the cosmos. I also see the breath as an energetic connector that links the intangible world of energy with the tangible world of our physical reality. In this way, the energy of the breath is the same as the energy of the Universe, which has the power to link the intangible with the tangible and transform thoughts into things, dreams into reality, and intention into action.

The truth is our breath is our closest and most intimate path to attuning with the unlimited creative energy of the Universe, and the best part is that the breath is easily detectable and accessible to anyone. You don't need to be an energy healer or a lightworker. You don't need special skills or the ability to see the unseen. Even if you can't detect auras or angels with your eyes and even if you can't sense when there's an energetic shift in a room, you can always tap into the high-vibrational energies of the Universe using your breath. The 1 Healing Breath practice is an incredibly valuable tool in the manifesting process because it lets you powerfully connect and align with the Universe, and this is a truth I discovered quite by accident.

## Dreaming Audacious Dreams

I first started using my 1 Healing Breath to regulate my emotions so I wouldn't end up hurting the people I loved, like I did with Rita. But over time, I began to see that working with the breath did much more than help me feel better. The practice was so simple and flexible that I found I was enjoying the benefits of meditative mindfulness and intentional living without actually sitting on a cushion in a formal practice. It's why I've come to think of the 1 Healing Breath as a Microaction Meditation and a Microaction Manifesting practice. Bringing intention and attention to my breath through the experience of multiple meditative manifesting moments throughout the day helped me shape my experience and diminish and overcome fear, worry, anxiety, self-doubt, and many other intense feelings that stood in the way of my joy like a big, dark rain cloud blocking out the sun. I could get through hard days with relative ease and with an inner serenity that had eluded me all my life. Among other things, this little Microaction Meditation and Microaction Manifesting practice gave me empowering agency over my own lived experience, and it gifted me a sense of calm and safety like I'd never felt before. It let me cut through the anxious, buzzing, often angry inner voice that filled my thoughts so I could get to know the real me. The practice allowed me to take tentative steps toward accepting myself and being patient and kind to myself even during those times when I thought I was falling short or falling apart. It gave me breathing room to explore the hidden desires and truth of my heart, and it let me reach for goals that felt bold, daring, or even a little crazy. It let me dream wildly audacious dreams and watch them come true.

As I became more relaxed and gentler with myself, as I began to feel safer being me and being with myself without resistance or wanting to change anything, I became more aligned with who I truly am. I found that the more I practiced 1 Healing Breath throughout my day, the more things started going my way and the people, experiences, and opportunities that I longed for began to appear like magic in my life. I attracted synchronicities and opportunities that allowed me to achieve my intentions and desires for the day, the month, or even the year with so little effort and energy that it almost felt like I was cheating!

Everything from an empty parking spot in a packed shopping mall on a Saturday afternoon to creative, lucrative business opportunities that stretched me as a writer and paid more than I ever could have imagined began to fall into my lap with delightful consistency. It often happened without me having to do anything specific or even try to manifest, and that's the most beautiful, enchanting aspect of the 1 Healing Breath as a manifesting tool. When you breathe with intention, when you allow yourself to sink into being the real you, even if it's only for a moment, you are in effect training your body, mind, and energy system to align with the Universe and to vibrate at the energy of creation. In time, this incredibly powerful creative energy began to pour into my life in ways that left me in shock, wonder, and awe.

I became attuned and connected to the part of me that is one with the Universe. The part of me that could manifest friendships with kindred spirits from around the world. The one who attracted abundance in all its forms—such as health, love, and the freedom to do the work I love—seemingly out of thin air. The one who knew in her soul that money and riches can be a force for good and not evil in the world. My personal life began to unfold in ridiculously amazing and magical ways. I wanted to be a successful online entrepreneur writing for international audiences, and that came true. I had envisioned flying first class to the United States for years, and it happened without a hitch just a few months after the 1 Healing Breath technique came into my life. Oh, and I longed to be a published author and ... well, you're reading this book, so you know how that turned out!

Beyond the exciting new reality that began to unfold for me, the 1 Healing Breath practice added layers of richness and meaning to my everyday life. It helped me gently make my way toward authentic self-love and call up genuine courage so I could experiment with expressing myself fearlessly. It let me push the boundaries of my comfort zone and surprise myself with what I could accomplish as a creative, spiritual entrepreneur, and so much more. Despite the heartache of my early years, the 1 Healing Breath began to help me release the past, and I gradually got to know the real me as I let myself come home to myself in a way that didn't feel scary or painful. It allowed me to intentionally shape my experience, moment by moment, so I could become an effective, successful manifestor just by being me.

## Unearthing Buried Treasures of Desire

Most other manifesting methods work in fits and starts because they often lead you away from who you are and what you truly want. For instance, when you flip through magazines or go online to pick an image of a dream vacation for your vision board, you are being subtly influenced by someone else's idea of the holiday of a lifetime and you are looking outside of yourself to figure out what you want. When you chant affirmations crafted by a manifesting coach or teacher, you're unknowingly using someone else's words and energy to create your reality. The 1 Healing Breath method does the opposite. It brings you back to you and only you, so you can unearth buried treasures of desire hidden in your own soul and you'll start to consistently manifest what you want by being yourself.

So why is manifesting as yourself so powerful? We are more than we think we are. We are made of the same creative energy as the stars in the sky, a perfect tender petal of a rose, the golden grains of sand on a sunshiny beach, and everything else that is magical, both seen and unseen. In our natural, aligned state of simply being ourselves, we are in full alignment with the core creative and expansive energies of the Universe, and we are able to channel these energies with ease. The 1 Healing Breath practice brings us back to just being ourselves, and at the same time it magnifies our ability to align with and channel the energies of the Universe to design our reality. It's the reason why every single activity and technique that we are about to explore in the rest of this book begins with either the In-the-Moment Edition or the Extended Edition of the 1 Healing Breath practice, which we'll explore later in this chapter.

When we consistently work with the 1 Healing Breath—when we make it our go-to habit and practice many times throughout the day—we are gently inviting ourselves to return to our natural state of unlimited creativity and expansion again and again and again. With the calming, soothing balm of 1 Healing Breath just a breath away at all times, we are energetically and physically reminded that we are safe in this moment. Little by little, this humble practice can recalibrate our nervous system and our energy system so we remain in the most powerful state we can be in to manifest anything and everything we desire: a state of feeling safe being who we are—which is the only state where we are in full alignment with the core creative energies of the Universe. So how can a practice as simple as 1 Healing Breath do this? Well, it's because there's more to it than you might think. While the act of taking a breath might seem uncomplicated and even elementary, the subtle threads of what's going on beneath the surface are anything but ordinary. This effortless practice contains a surprisingly complex mix of elements from ancient traditions such as spiritual breathwork and the science of neuroplasticity.

There are three main components—self-awareness, presence, and embodied attention—that elevate the 1 Healing Breath from simple breathing to the extraordinary manifesting tool that it is. Let's unpack each of these components one by one. Then we'll look at the step-by-step process of both versions of the 1 Healing Breath practice: the In-the-Moment Edition and the Extended Edition.

## Component #1: Self-Awareness

Picture a little girl playing on the beach. She's scooping sand into her little red bucket one spadeful at a time. Suddenly she drops her bucket and looks up at the sky. She's enthralled by the sight of a seagull swooping down to the water's edge. Her eyes follow the flight of the gull for a second or two before a brightly colored seashell sticking out of the sand grabs her attention. She crawls over to the shell to examine it, overcome by curiosity. Meanwhile, her mother is watching the little girl's every move. Mom's gaze is relaxed but attentive as she observes her child lovingly and without judgment. She is poised and ready for action if she needs to help her little one, but Mom's energy contains no agitation, anxiety, or urgency. Her little girl feels safe and reassured knowing Mom is nearby. You see, the little girl is your mind, darting from one thing to another, curious, distracted, and easily led by what's going on in the environment. Your self-awareness is the loving mother watching her child with calm acceptance and without judgment.

Doubt, worry, uncertainty, fear, and anxiety can easily arise when we lack self-awareness, because we are constantly influenced by an endless loop of random thoughts, emotions, and distractions, like the child playing in the sand. Even worse, when we are unaware of what's going on in our heart and mind, we are also totally disconnected from who we truly are and what we feel. It's like we're walking through life in a daze, stuck in painful habitual thoughts, unhelpful belief patterns, and unwanted behaviors.

You know what this feels like if, like me, you've ever opened a box of chocolate chip cookies meaning to eat just a couple, only to come to your senses a few minutes later to see that you've chomped your way through the entire box without even realizing it. You've experienced this dazed state every time you lost hours scrolling through social media when you meant to check your feed for just a minute. You've been in this dazed state if you've ever felt shredded by guilt because you lost your temper and snapped at the people around you.

This dazed state causes us to go through the motions of our day-to-day life caught in the grip of unwanted habits and patterns, saying and doing things we don't want to do or say. We're angry when we want to be calm. We're impatient when we want to be tolerant and kind. But every time you take 1 Healing Breath, you are cultivating mindful self-awareness and allowing this beautiful energy to grow and flourish from within. You are dissolving the daze a little bit at a time so you can intentionally and courageously be yourself and call all that you desire into your life.

## Component #2: Presence

Some people seem to be born with a natural ability to stay calm and centered even when things are falling apart. I am definitely *not* one of those people! For the longest time, I believed I was forever doomed to live on the razor's edge of hair-trigger, stressful reactivity, jumping at the slightest noise and feeling like I had to be ready to run for my life at a moment's notice. The good news is that anyone can learn to call up inner calm, even in the midst of chaos, and it's because we already have access to deep inner presence at all times. Even if you've had a challenging, stressful life so far, I'm willing to bet you've caught a glimpse of this inner presence. We feel presence when we gaze into the eyes of the love of our life or when we cradle a newborn in our arms. Presence happens when we lose ourselves in the rhythm of a favorite song. We are immersed in presence when we say goodbye to a loved one for the last time. For me, one of the most profound moments of presence happened when I was ten years old.

I had just moved to a new town and started at a new school. No one talked to me those first few weeks, which meant I had to eat alone during recess. The first two days passed without incident, but on the third afternoon, I noticed one of my classmates slowly make her way toward me. I had no idea at the time, but this was the school bully, whose favorite pastime was literally eating other people's lunches. Every day at recess, she showed up, shoved me aside, and grabbed my lunch. This went on for two whole weeks, and it would have gone on indefinitely had something unexpected not happened: I suddenly became tired of being bullied. I was tired of cowering in the corner, tired of feeling scared, so I made a decision. When the bell rang for recess the next day, I watched my classmate stomp over, right on schedule.

"Give it to me!" she said, pointing at my lunchbox. I looked up at her, squinting against the afternoon sun. Time slowed and then stood still, just like in the movies. I could hear the sound of my own breath in the pin-drop silence. I felt fear and courage mix into a pulsating ball of emotion as I spoke up. "No," I said, quietly. "What did you say?" she snarled through gritted teeth, bending low to sneer in my face. "No," I said, a little louder this time.

I can't remember what was in my lunchbox that day. I can't remember if I had blue or white ribbons in my hair (the only two colors allowed at my school). But I can tell you how I felt that day as I stood up to that bully. I was present. I was connected to my body. I was scared, but certain in my conviction. I stared up at my schoolyard nemesis waiting for a response, wondering if she'd slap me hard or maybe pull my hair. Instead, the unbelievable happened. She turned and walked away. She never bothered me again, and we even became fast friends a few years later (but that's a story for my next book!).

Often, we think of presence as a serene or passive energy, but that's not true. Knowing how to drop into presence gives us the capacity to tap into any mindset or emotion, including courage, persistence, compassion, kindness, righteous anger, and more. It allows us to live with intention and access high-vibrational frequencies, and when you take 1 Healing Breath, you can give yourself the gift of presence at any time, anywhere, no matter what else is going on in your life.

## Component #3: Embodied Attention

One of the most wonderful and magical elements of the breath is that while it is invisible and intangible, it allows us to experience the tangible, palpable sensations of our body. Embodied attention with 1 Healing Breath happens as we track the journey of the breath from our nostrils down to our chest and into our belly using not just our mind but also the physical sensory responses that it evokes. It's about tuning into the felt sensations of the breath as it makes its way in and out of the body. We can teach ourselves how to experience embodied attention using the breath by asking ourselves simple questions, such as "Is the breath cool or hot, mild or intense, sharp or smooth? Does my chest feel tight or relaxed as the breath travels through? How about the belly? Can I feel the sensation of the skin expand and contract as my belly rises and falls with the breath?" Tracking the breath in this way may sound simple, but try it and you'll see that it's not as easy as you think. (We'll go deeper into experiencing felt sensations in chapter 5.)

Sensation tracking in the body is a wonderful skill, as it works perfectly with self-awareness and presence to allow the energies of the Universe to flow through to us for powerful manifesting. For some people—especially those who have experienced trauma—long periods of embodied attention can feel scary, because it can unlock hidden, embedded memories of trauma stuck in the body. As Bessel van der Kolk says in his wonderful book *The Body Keeps the Score*, trauma is stored in somatic memory and it expresses as changes in the biological stress response, which explains feelings like fear and anxiety. It's why the 1 Healing Breath method can sometimes work better than long hours of meditation, as it allows embodied attention to happen quickly and without triggering a physical, body-based stress response.

## How to Do the 1 Healing Breath Practice

Now that you understand the three foundational elements of 1 Healing Breath, you're ready to experience the transformational power of taking an intentional breath for yourself. I've developed two versions of the 1 Healing Breath practice: an In-the-Moment Edition and an Extended Edition. You'll find that some of the steps are the same for both versions. You can choose the version that works best for you based on the amount of time, energy, and effort you happen to have at your disposal.

The In-the-Moment Edition of 1 Healing Breath takes just a few seconds to complete, although you might need more time to get the hang of it the first few times you try it. The Extended Edition of 1 Healing Breath takes anywhere from five to fifteen minutes or more if you want to give yourself breathing room to luxuriate in a beautiful, calming experience that feels like a day at the spa. Both versions of this practice include not just the breath but also at least two of your five senses: touch, scent, vision, sound, and taste.

I recommend that you try to do the Extended Edition of 1 Healing Breath as much as possible, especially when you first begin working with this practice, as it can help train your body and mind to quickly drop into relaxation mode for an easier, more enjoyable manifesting experience or simply as a way to give yourself a delightful break whenever you want. A helpful tip to accelerate your progress: 1 Healing Breath is an experiential activity, not a theoretical exercise, so what matters most is that you laser in on experiencing the feeling and the physical sensations that come up for you when you take your conscious breath, rather than simply thinking about it. Sound good? Great! Let's begin.

## 1 Healing Breath: In-the-Moment Edition

Close your eyes and reflect on what you want the breath to bring into your body, heart, mind, and spirit. If this feels overwhelming or you get stuck in the process of trying to identify exactly what you want to experience, you can get unstuck by placing both hands over your heart and simply asking yourself, "What is the feeling or healing I need most right now?" or "What is the emotion I want to immerse myself in right now?" Then go with the first answer that pops into your mind. Trust whatever comes through. Let's give it a try right now. Place your hands over your heart and ask yourself, "What is the feeling or healing I want most right now?" When the answer arises, it's time to take your 1 Healing Breath.

Start by bringing your awareness to the feeling or healing that you identified before. Let's imagine your answer was joy. So you'll start by calling up a memory, experience, thought, image, or sensation that brings up a feeling of joy from within. Reflect on what joy means to you. What does it feel like? Who or what brings you joy in your life? It could be an experience, an image, a memory, a sound, or a combination of all of these elements. It could be a memory of the day you won first place in a singing contest or the day you adopted your puppy. For me, feeling relaxed and joyful has to do with a photograph from my childhood of my very first time at the beach. I was about four years old and I was with my dad. The photograph captures a spectacular sun-drenched moment of the two of us at the water's edge. The waves are pushing against my tiny feet and my handsome dad is laughing in the sunshine as he holds me steady. (I feel joyful just thinking about it now!)

Next, you'll intentionally open up to the energy of joy. You can say to yourself, "I invite the energy of joy." Let the world fall away as you allow joy to rise up and meet you where you are. I like to feel like I'm floating on an ocean of the energy that I desire, and in this case that would be a delightful, enchanting ocean of joy!

If you're having trouble bringing your attention to the emotion, feeling, or healing you want to focus on during this practice, I recommend that you refer to the series of activated, high-vibrational images I've created to help with the process. You'll find powerful positive images to choose from, like love, clarity, serenity, play, and much more. I've found that gazing at a visual representation of the energy of your choosing can help to focus your attention and intention of the breath, so feel free to work with these images. (You can sign up to download a special collection of these images for free at www.shantini rajah.com/manifest.) In the example we're working with, you'll focus on the image for 1 Healing Breath of Joy. Gaze at it for a few seconds and let it guide you toward joy. Allow yourself to feel joy rise up from within.

When you've successfully tuned into joy, you're ready to take your 1 Healing Breath. Place both hands over your heart. Then bring your awareness to a single, conscious breath. Focus on drawing in the breath through your nose. Feel the soothing sensation of life-giving oxygen entering your body. Enjoy the stretch of your chest as you allow 1 Healing Breath of Joy to travel deeper and deeper into your being, all the way down into your belly, into your cells, into your bloodstream, from the top of your head down to the farthest tips of your toes.

Feel the breath fill your lungs and radiate out into all aspects of your being. You can take an inhale and an exhale of seven, five, three, or even just one second. You can even take a series of breaths. Whatever feels good in the moment is perfect. I encourage you to try a shorter inhale and a longer exhale. I like to inhale for three counts and exhale for six to feel an extra dose of calm. The extended exhale flips the switch on the parasympathetic nervous system, which helps to slow the heart rate and de-stress the body. It sends the message to your entire system that it's safe to enter rest-and-relax mode.

When you're done taking your 1 Healing Breath, it's time for a quick self-check. Do you feel calmer and more joyful than you did a minute ago? Don't worry if it doesn't seem to work the first time you try it and you're not feeling particularly joyful just yet. Taking 1 Healing Breath is simple, but it's called a "practice" for a reason! Keep coming back to it at least once or twice a day until you can truly sense the feeling and energy you're looking for in the flow of your breath.

## 1 Healing Breath: Extended Edition

The in-depth version of the 1 Healing Breath practice happens in four phases and involves focusing on each of the three fundamental components we explored earlier: self-awareness, presence, and embodied attention. The Extended Edition of the 1 Healing Breath practice also involves answering a series of questions. If you like journaling, feel free to write down your answers, but you can also keep things simple and answer the questions in your mind. Both methods work well, so it's totally up to you.

### Phase 1: The Initial Invitation

First, you'll set a sacred intention to invite the three components of 1 Healing Breath—self-awareness, presence, and embodied attention—into your practice. Say out loud or in your heart, "I invite the energies of self-awareness, presence, and embodied attention to my 1 Healing Breath practice." If you prefer, use your own words to set the intention. Now you're ready for phase 2, where you'll experientially connect with each of these energies.

### Phase 2: The Experiential Journey

Start by gently focusing on the energy of self-awareness. You'll do this by observing what's happening in your body, mind, emotions, and spirit. What are you thinking in your mind? What are you feeling in your heart? What are you sensing in your body? Are there ideas or visions popping into your consciousness? Rest in the knowledge of your answers for a minute or two. Now you're ready to enter into presence and embodied attention. The body can only be in the here and now, while the mind can travel to the past and future and into fantastical realms that don't exist in our world. So for this segment, you will rely on your body to bring yourself back to presence as many times as you need to. You can sit or lie down for this.

First, bring your self-awareness to your body. Then choose to focus on a part of your body that is connected to the chair or the ground. This might be sensing the feel of the chair under you or feeling your feet on the ground. If you're lying down, you might choose to focus on your lower back on the sofa, bed, or cushion. Let's imagine you've decided to focus on your feet as the point of connection. Bring all your attention and self-awareness to your feet. Now tune into the sensations in your feet. Do your feet feel hot or cold? Prickly, sweaty, or maybe a little numb? If you're barefoot, can you feel the floor? Is it rough or smooth? If you have shoes or socks on, what does that feel like?

Remember, this phase is about bringing your full attention to experiencing the felt sensations in your body. It's not about thinking, "This feels smooth." Instead, allow yourself to experience the smoothness. If you feel your mind wander off, gently bring your attention back to the part of your body that you chose to focus on. Keep doing this again and again. You can do the experiential phase for as long as you wish, knowing you are grounded and in a safe space. Remember, this isn't about doing this activity perfectly; it's about allowing yourself to fully tune into the sensations in your body.

### Phase 3: Choose Your 1 Healing Breath

Now it's time to choose the energy you want to feel or experience with your 1 Healing Breath. Just like you did in the In-the-Moment Edition of 1 Healing Breath, it's good to ask yourself what you want to feel and go with the first answer that pops into your mind. So go ahead and place your hands over your heart and ask yourself, "What is the feeling or healing I want most right now?" When you have the answer, you're ready to move on to the final phase.

## Phase 4: Track the Energetic Pathway

First, bring your awareness to the emotion or healing that you identified before. Let's go with 1 Healing Breath of Joy again. So what you'll do next is call up a memory, experience, thought, image, or sensation that brings up feelings of joy. Tune into a vision, memory, or activity when you experienced joy. As with the In-the-Moment Edition of 1 Healing Breath, if nothing comes to mind, feel free to refer to the series of powerful, activated, high-vibrational, positive images I've created to bring your attention to the emotion, feeling, or healing you want to focus on. (You can sign up to download a special collection of these images for free at www.shantinirajah.com/manifest.) As we did before, we'll work with the image of 1 Healing Breath of Joy. Gaze at the image for a few seconds and let it guide you toward joy. Allow yourself to feel joy rise up from within.

Once you've tuned in, allow the energy of joy to meet you where you are. Feel like you're falling backward into an ocean of joy. Now it's time to take in 1 Healing Breath. If you are lying down, it's time to sit up or, ideally, stand up for this next part. Start by placing both hands over your heart. Then bring your awareness to a single conscious breath. Focus on drawing the breath in through your nose. Fill your chest and belly, and as you breathe in, stretch your arms out to the sides and slightly behind you, then up above your head. With palms facing each other, gently touch your hands together above your head. Now bring your palms down in a straight line, passing in front of your face until you have your hands against your heart in Anjali Mudra (which is also known as prayer position).

As you hold Anjali Mudra, envision 1 Healing Breath of Joy flowing through an energetic pathway that begins at your hands and moves down your arms and shoulders and up to your neck, face, and head before cascading like a waterfall of joy down to the rest of your body, all the way down to your feet. Allow the energy to permeate every cell and radiate into all aspects of your being. Don't forget to do a quick self-check. Do you feel a little—or even a *lot*—more joyful than you did before? If not, no worries. Remember that it takes time to retrain our body, mind, and energetic system to receive beautiful, empowering, uplifting energies, so go ahead and repeat this practice as often as you can. I recommend that you take a few conscious healing breaths of your choosing throughout the day until the 1 Healing Breath practice starts to feel natural, easy, and fun. Keep in mind that you're not confined to taking just *one* breath at a time. You can take a series of breaths around one emotion, or you can take healing breaths focused on different emotions throughout the day. Let yourself have fun with this. This is your breath, this is your manifesting journey, and you get to choose.

Congratulations, you did it! You've learned how to work with 1 Healing Breath to center yourself and bring intentional positive energies into your body, mind, and spirit. We'll be working with the 1 Healing Breath practice throughout the rest of this book to transmit and receive powerful positive energies and emotions in order to connect with the Universe and bring ourselves back to center so we can manifest with delightful ease and accuracy.

# Phase II

## Build Your Inner Altar

In phase II of our journey together, you'll begin to build your Inner Altar from the inside out. You'll discover how to connect with who you truly are and learn wonderfully effective ways to give yourself all that you need to flourish, thrive, and become a master manifestor and intentional creator of your own life. We'll begin with the first of the six Magical Manifesting Ingredients—Identify What You Really Want—where you'll attune to your Authentic Self through the voice of your intuition, so you'll always know you're headed toward your True North when it comes to manifesting what you want. With Magical Manifesting Ingredient #2: Authentically Elevate Your Vibe, you'll learn how to grow your very own Garden of Self-Love, so you can effortlessly align with the highest-vibrational, core energy of the Universe, which is the energy of unlimited, unconditional love.

*Three*

# Magical Manifesting Ingredient #1: Identify What You Really Want

What's the first thing you would need to escape from prison? Yes, I know that's a strange question, but it wouldn't seem strange to you if you happened to be one of George Gurdjieff's students. Gurdjieff was a respected mystic, philosopher, and spiritual teacher who lived in the late 1800s to the early 1900s, and when he posed that question to his students, they were excited and eager to impress their teacher.

One of Gurdjieff's students immediately said that making friends with the prison guards would guarantee a way out. After all, who wouldn't want to help a friend get out of prison? Another student said finding the master key would be the smartest move. That way, escape would be easy. Gurdjieff liked his students' quick thinking but informed them that both answers were incorrect, because the first thing a person needs in order to escape from prison is to recognize they're in prison in the first place. Otherwise, no escape is possible. During his time as an influential spiritual teacher, Gurdjieff was known as a Seeker of Truth, and his answer certainly contains a profound truth.

Too many people spend their lives trapped in an invisible prison. Sometimes it's a romantic relationship that's going nowhere fast or a soul-sucking job that leaves us hating Mondays with a passion. An invisible prison might be a painful, pervasive feeling of unhappiness that defies understanding because on the surface everything seems to be going great. But the most common and most dangerous invisible prison of all is the one that has us unknowingly living by other people's beliefs, values, and expectations to the point that we forget who we truly are or what we truly desire. It's a prison that's built brick by brick over a lifetime of conditioning, and it grows stronger every day, because we consistently set aside what we intuitively know is right for us just so we can do what is asked or expected of us instead. In time, we end up losing ourselves altogether. We fail to remember our inner truth, and we forget how to listen to the inner wisdom of our heart—the part of us that's connected to a Higher Intelligence, knows what's best for us, never lets us down, and always tells us the truth. It's the part that I like to call the Authentic Self, and it's unequivocally, unapologetically who we truly are.

In this chapter, you're going to learn a beautifully simple yet effective method to connect and communicate with your Authentic Self, so you can identify your True Desires: the experiences, things, and relationships that are aligned with who you are and what you want, rather than what others want for you. You'll learn how to identify three to five True Desires using a simple but powerful exercise where you create your True Desires list. But first, let's take a closer look at how to recognize your Authentic Self and discover some essential elements to help you understand this infinitely loving and wise aspect of who you are.

## Recognizing Your Authentic Self

The Authentic Self is known by many different names. It's sometimes called the Higher Self, the True Self, the Divine Aspect, the Soul, the Spirit, or the Universal Mind. It's also known as the Superconscious, Unconscious, or Subconscious. The existence of the Authentic Self is acknowledged in some way in spiritual traditions across the world and is the key to who we truly are in the deepest recesses of our soul. It holds every facet of every thought, emotion, experience, and belief you've ever had. It is the nonphysical part of you that was never born and will never die, and it is forever connected to the Universe with an unbreakable bond that transcends time and space and continues across lifetimes. The Authentic Self contains an incredibly vast grid of wisdom that is accessible to every one of us at every moment, and we can tune into it in less than the time it takes to read these words.

Depending on where you land on the spiritual spectrum, you might be super excited about learning the secrets of communicating with your Authentic Self or you might be thinking, "That sounds like a bunch of mumbo jumbo!" If the latter is you, all I ask is that you give the exercises in this chapter a try. There's no need to believe in the Authentic Self to tune into this magical, mystical aspect of yourself. All you need to do is use the techniques you're about to learn to open the lines of communication so you can start to receive profoundly empowering and aligned messages to manifest effectively and consistently. I believe the ability to communicate quickly, easily, and accurately with your Authentic Self is one of the most important skills you can ever hope to cultivate, because so much of what we think we want to manifest—so much of what we believe we deserve—is shaped and influenced by something or someone outside of ourselves.

For instance, as a result of generational oppression and systemic racism, so many women of color struggle with deeply embedded beliefs of inadequacy and uncertainty. They are led to believe they can't or shouldn't have what they want, and this obstructs their inborn right to dream big and boldly manifest what they truly desire. In some parts of the world, women are constantly pressured to get married and become a mother. Often, the idea of manifesting a fulfilling life as a successful, single, child-free woman is considered abhorrent—even repulsive. And let's not forget about those of us who grew up in a family or in social circles that told us wealth and success are the ultimate goals. The more we achieve, the more validation, praise, and approval we receive. But if we fail to achieve expectations set by our family or community, we are made to feel ashamed. This leaves us believing that the only real way to be worthy of love—the only real way to feel like we belong—is to manifest even more money and more success. In this case, the act of manifesting becomes a painful struggle to feel safe and loved. I don't think I have to tell you that this is not a path to a joyful, fulfilling life!

Staying consistently connected to your Authentic Self is the antidote to these poisonous, often insidious outside influences. It's the path to transcending all else: where you come from, your family, your nationality, your station in life, what you look like—anything and everything that has to do with the external world. The great news is you are never truly disconnected from your Authentic Self. It is an integral part of your being, and chances are you're already receiving messages from this aspect of yourself but you just don't realize it. For instance, you might have had a good feeling about a decision or felt a bad vibe about a location or object. You might have heard a voice direct you toward an action (like the experience I talked about in chapter 1 where I first heard the words "1 Healing Breath" whispered in my ear), or maybe you were shown a vision or had a dream that revealed the perfect solution to a challenging problem. In every one of these instances, your Authentic Self was reaching out to you, offering guidance and answers, and I'm not just making that up! History is filled with stories of the Authentic Self making an unexpected appearance, like it did with August Kekulé.

Kekulé was a brilliant nineteenth-century German scientist who received a game-changing message from what I believe was his Authentic Self. Considered one of the founding fathers of organic chemistry, Kekulé was working on unraveling important foundational structures of carbon-based compounds—specifically the benzene ring, which contains six carbon atoms. He was totally stumped as to how these atoms were connected to each other until the structure was revealed to him in a strange dream. As explained by John H. Lienhard, Professor Emeritus of Mechanical Engineering and History at the University of Houston, in an episode of a radio program called *The Engines of Our Ingenuity*, Kekulé dreamed of twinning serpents seizing each other's tails in the shape of a ring. When he awoke, the answer to the mystery he'd been working on for so long became clear. Kekulé realized that benzene consists of carbon atoms that are linked to each other in the shape of a ring, specifically a hexagonal ring. He was eventually proved to be absolutely correct, thanks to his Authentic Self.

There are countless stories like these—stories of people who received out-of-the-blue insights from their Authentic Self that helped them solve a problem or overcome a challenge. Some people talk about receiving a message that saved their life. They might have heard a voice that whispered, "Stay home" or "Don't get on the plane!" Some people suddenly get an unexplained feeling that inspires them to make a different choice. They might decide to change their schedule or pick a different route only to find out later that they could have been robbed or they might have ended up in an accident if they had followed through with their original plan. This is the infinitely wise, loving Higher Intelligence of the Authentic Self guiding them toward their highest good. An important caveat: sometimes these messages *don't* come from your Authentic Self but are instead just old-fashioned fear and resistance. I'll teach you how to tell the difference between intuition and fear later in this chapter.

## The Essential Elements of the Authentic Self

When you can recognize and communicate with your Authentic Self, you'll know that you're always following your inner North Star even when life feels chaotic. It is the part of you that keeps you safe from harm and lets you connect with the desires, goals, and dreams that are 100 percent aligned with your highest and best good, no matter what else is going on. Your Authentic Self is a powerful accelerating force that can help you become a masterful manifestor sooner than you might think. When you are attuned to receive clear messages from the deepest part of your soul, you'll confidently identify what you truly want, totally independent of other people's expectations, influence, or fears. In this next section, I'll introduce you to the six essential elements of the Authentic Self so you can instantly recognize this powerful, magical aspect of yourself.

### Element #1: You Are Eternal

Your Authentic Self is unceasing. It has no beginning and no end and it never dies. Your Authentic Self will never lead you away from your divine purpose.

The messages, insights, ideas, and inspiration that you receive from your Authentic Self are what's best for you in any given moment.

### Element #2: You Are Never Alone

Your Authentic Self is connected to a Higher Power, Source Energy, God, Divine Perfection, or the Universe at all times. There are no exceptions. This means that even if you are physically by yourself, you are never really alone. This is a powerful truth to hold onto, especially when you're feeling sad, misunderstood, alone, rejected, or abandoned in some way.

### Element #3: You Have Access to Deep Wisdom

Your Authentic Self holds all the lessons you need for your continued evolution. This includes all wisdom, learnings, and truths reaching back to when you were a child and even further back before you were born, from previous lifetimes.

### Element #4: You Are Always Exactly Where You Need to Be

Your Authentic Self operates in divine time, which means you'll receive experiences, information, and knowledge that are perfect for you at the perfect time. Some people completely forget about a trauma or painful incident from their past until the perfect moment when they are able to process and receive the lessons or messages they need to know to continue along their spiritual and life path.

### Element #5: You Are Loved and Supported

Messages from your Authentic Self are never dogmatic, pushy, or forceful. You might feel nudged to step outside your comfort zone or encouraged to be brave and try new ideas and experiences, but your Authentic Self will always communicate with you in gentle, loving, and supportive ways, rather than as an angry or domineering presence that makes you feel guilty or ashamed.

## Element #6: You Are Connected

Your Authentic Self speaks and communicates with you through your intuition, and this could happen through one or more of the four key Clair channels (which we'll explore later in this chapter). This means that every one of your intuitive nudges comes from your Authentic Self, and you always have a choice to follow through with these nudges or not.

I like to think of your Authentic Self as a huge reservoir of learnings, memories, and experiences that are readily available, but most of this vast collection of knowledge remains outside of your conscious awareness. It's a treasure trove of wisdom that isn't easily accessible to your conscious, thinking mind except through your intuition. Your intuition can even allow access to knowledge and wisdom that you never consciously learned or experienced, and all of this happens through thoughts, words, symbols, sensations, feelings, or visions that are part of the language of the Authentic Self. In other words, the voice of the Authentic Self is the voice of intuition. Some spiritual teachers believe that our intuition is pure, unencumbered Universal Intelligence flowing into our human experience, and I absolutely agree.

# Connecting to Your Authentic Self with the 1 Healing Breath

There are two things you need to do so you can consistently and consciously tune into your intuition, receive messages from your Authentic Self, and manifest your True Desires. The first is to set a clear intention, and the second is to enter a calm energetic state. Let's explore why these are essential, and then I'll walk you through the steps.

Setting a clear intention allows you to direct your attention and focus your mind and heart. It gives your entire being a bull's-eye target to aim at, which makes it that much easier to hit your goal—in this case, your goal is to connect with your intuition and the voice of your Authentic Self. Stepping into a calm energetic state is equally important when you want to receive clear messages from your intuition.

In a study published in the journal *Psychological Science*, researchers Annette Bolte, Thomas Goschke, and Julius Kuhl investigated the effects of a group of research participants' emotional states and their ability to make accurate intuitive judgments. In the experiment, the participants were shown three words that were either vaguely connected to a concept (known as coherent triads) or had no common association (incoherent triads). It was discovered that those who were in a calm, positive emotional state could easily associate the words with the right concept, while participants in a negative mood performed much worse.

Your emotions inform your energetic state, which in turn influences the clarity and accuracy of your intuitive connection with your Authentic Self. For instance, if you're trying to decide whether you should accept a job offer when you're feeling terrified that your bank balance is fast approaching a gigantic zero, your fear can—and will—influence your ability to receive an accurate intuitive answer. Thankfully, this does not mean you're doomed to receive inaccurate messages from your Authentic Self every time you feel angry, sad, or upset and you certainly don't have to force yourself to be calm and happy all the time.

## The Stop and Drop Technique
## to Access Your Intuition

Through the ages, highly sensitive people, including intuitives, empaths, and healers, faced the same challenge. They found that when they were overcome by strong emotions such as grief, heartache, anger, or fear, their intuitive powers became diluted and led to less-than-reliable results. So they devised various methods to gently circumvent intense emotions in order to communicate clearly with their intuition and their Authentic Self. We're about to do the same thing using a remarkably effective two-step technique that includes setting a clear intention and safely entering a calm, positive emotional state using the 1 Healing Breath. I use this tool to quickly and confidently connect with my intuition, and I call it the Stop and Drop Technique. Here's how it goes.

### Step #1: Stop and Set a Clear Intention

Setting a clear intention is simple, and it has to do with making a decision and then a declaration. It's about sending out a prayer or invitation to the Universe, God, Source, your angels and guides, or whatever higher wisdom resonates most with you. You can choose to state your intention out loud or quietly to yourself. First take a moment to bring your attention to your heart, then say the words like you mean it. You're making a declaration to the Universe, after all, so you want to make sure your emotion matches your commitment. I usually work with the sentence below, and I like to say it out loud three times, saying it with more volume, power, and conviction each time. Feel free to use this declaration word for word or craft your own. The key is to keep it short and sweet, something you can say in a few seconds.

*I am now open and willing to connect with my intuition*
*to receive wisdom for my highest good and for the highest good of all.*

### Step #2: Drop into a Calm Energetic State

The Drop segment of the Stop and Drop Technique features the 1 Healing Breath practice. I talked about the essentials of 1 Healing Breath in chapter 2, and we'll be working with the In-the-Moment Edition here (page 39). You'll see that this is a simple but powerful technique that involves not just your breath but also at least two of your five senses: touch, scent, vision, sound, and taste. In this case, we'll be working with the 1 Healing Breath of Serenity. We'll drop into a tranquil energetic state as we breathe in a calm sense of serenity.

Maybe for you, feeling calm and serene has to do with the memory of the heavenly scent wafting through your grandmother's kitchen as you helped bake her famous chocolate chip cookies. Maybe stroking the soft fur of your beloved cat brings you a feeling of calm serenity, or maybe you love the serene sound of the wind chime hanging in your balcony as a gentle summer breeze cools the air. If you can't quite come up with something that represents serenity for you, feel free to refer to the image of 1 Healing Breath of Serenity, which can help to invoke the energy of serenity for you. (This is just one of a collection of activated images that you can sign up to download for free. Just go to www.shantinirajah.com/manifest.)

When you have your positive, calming energetic state to focus on, you're ready to experience the 1 Healing Breath of Serenity. You'll be inhaling for three counts and exhaling for six through the nose to activate your parasympathetic nervous system, so your body and energy system can quickly drop into relaxation mode.

Start by closing your eyes and placing both hands over your heart. Inhale slowly for three counts. As you breathe in, gently focus on the memory, experience, location, sound, etc. that you identified earlier, or focus on the corresponding 1 Healing Breath of Serenity included in your free collection of images. This is a no-holds-barred experience, so let yourself become fully immersed in the feeling and sensation of serenity. Allow the feeling to rise up from within and meet you where you are. As you breathe out for a count of six, let the energy and emotion of serenity wash over you. Feel like you're falling backward into a sea of serenity. When you're ready, open your eyes. Now it's time for a quick self-check. Ask yourself if you feel calmer and more serene than you did a minute ago. If your answer is no, go ahead and do the practice a few more times until you start to feel more serene.

## Receiving Intuitive Messages

Now that you know what to do to receive intuitive messages from your Authentic Self using the Stop and Drop Technique, it's time to explore how to connect with your intuition through various intuitive channels. These are essentially the pathways through which you will receive messages from your Authentic Self. The first thing to know is there are no hard-and-fast rules when it comes to tuning into your intuition. Some people get a feeling or an unexplained "knowing," while others hear messages or see a vision, or a combination of those things. It takes time to recognize and understand how your intuitive channels work, so be patient with yourself.

The first thing to know is that there are four main intuitive Clair channels: Clairvoyance, Clairaudience, Claircognizance, and Clairsentience. Your personal intuitive style could be a combination of two or more of the four Clairs. Everyone naturally works with at least two Clairs whether they're aware of it or not, but most people find it really hard to know which ones are theirs. Luckily, that's not going to be you!

In the next section, we'll do a shockingly simple yet effective activity to identify your primary and secondary Clair channels. I developed this exercise for my clients, and most of them get a sense of their primary and secondary Clair channels almost immediately. But I don't want you to worry if that doesn't happen for you. You'll see that I've provided additional guidance and ideas that you can use to home in on your key Clairs after you complete the exercise. I'll also share some signs related to the four Clairs to give you a deeper understanding of each one. Please don't feel like you must have all of the traits listed to consider yourself Clairvoyant, Clairaudient, Claircognizant, or Clairsentient. Having four or five of the traits is a good sign that you're leaning toward a specific Clair channel.

## A Simple Way to Determine Your Intuitive Style

The following exercise shines a light on how you experience the world through your senses. You mostly see, listen, feel, or sense what's going on around you, and knowing how you process information in your day-to-day life is an accessible and accurate way to laser in on your intuitive channels, because messages from your intuition and your Authentic Self are likely to be communicated in the way that is most familiar and comfortable for you.

Before we begin, I'd like you to keep this in mind: Try to focus on the first experience you have, whether that's sight, sound, knowing, or sensation. That's probably your primary intuitive channel, or Clair. The next thing you see, hear, feel, or sense is likely to be your secondary Clair.

Okay, get ready to discover your main intuitive channels. Read the following words carefully, then pause to notice your experience as you focus on them:

*Freshly baked cake*

Did you see, hear, know, or feel messages or information about the cake? Read through the following sections to uncover exactly how you receive your intuitive information. This is going to be a huge help to you, especially when it's time to identify your True Desires later in this chapter.

## Clairvoyance

If you received a strong image or visual of "freshly baked cake," then your Authentic Self is probably connecting with you through "clear seeing," or Clairvoyance. This is one of the most well-known intuitive channels. In movies, TV shows, and books, people who are Clairvoyant are considered to be psychic. Intuition through Clairvoyance happens in a flash of vision or a series of visions that communicate a specific message. The visions are not always literal. As with Kekulé's dream, these visions are often symbolic. Here are more signs that Clairvoyance is one of your key intuitive channels:

+ You like to write or doodle, especially when you're trying to make sense of something.

+ You often use the phrase "I see what you mean" or something similar.

+ You already know you're highly creative, or people around you have recognized your creativity.

+ You can envision or read your thoughts as words in your mind's eye.

+ You can envision images, scenes, and entire storylines in your mind without missing a beat. You're likely to experience visual flashes during the day, and you often have vivid dreams while you're asleep.

+ You sometimes see shapes, symbols, colors, or silhouettes that no one else sees.

+ When you watch a movie, you're drawn to what's going on visually and you might find yourself missing out on the dialogue.

+ You love to daydream and can easily lose yourself in exciting imaginary situations, like fighting off dragons in a fantastical realm or receiving an award on a world stage.

## Clairaudience

If you heard something about the freshly baked cake—maybe you heard "chocolate cake with cream cheese frosting"—then your intuition is likely to be connecting with you through "clear hearing," or Clairaudience. Sometimes this can feel like a voice inside your head and sometimes it might feel like a whisper in your ear. Clairaudience is my primary intuitive channel. When I first received the 1 Healing Breath practice, I literally heard the words "one healing breath" in my right ear, and even though I'd never heard that phrase before, I instantly knew what it meant (this is "clear knowing," or Claircognizance, which is my secondary intuitive channel). Let's look at some signs that tell you Clairaudience could be an important intuitive channel for you:

+ You sometimes speak to yourself out loud when you're alone.
+ You often use the phrase "I hear you" or something to that effect.
+ You learn quickly when you have the option to listen to trainings, recordings, or audio books.
+ You can hear incredibly subtle sounds without even trying.
+ High-decibel noise from traffic, music, or even conversations at your favorite cafe can leave you feeling upset and disoriented.
+ Music moves your soul like nothing else can.
+ You have an uncanny ability to communicate with animals and plants. You somehow know what they're thinking and feeling, and they seem to understand you too.
+ You often know exactly what to say at exactly the right moment. People who know you have told you that your words are loving, comforting, and wise.
+ You sometimes hear unexplained sounds, like buzzing or ringing in one or both ears.

## Claircognizance

If the words "freshly baked cake" triggered a related or unrelated thought, memory, or emotion that nudged you toward doing something, then your

Authentic Self is connecting with you through "clear knowing," or Claircognizance. For instance, you might have felt a sudden urge to bake cupcakes for your bestie, or you might have felt inspired to call your mom or check to make sure you fed your cat. Claircognizance comes through as an undeniable fact to the person receiving the message, even when there's no physical or external evidence to support this knowing. It's one the most prevalent intuitive channels, and it's when you just know something is true or right. These are some of the signs that your intuition probably conveys messages through this channel:

+ You can easily identify if someone's lying or telling you the truth, even if it's a stranger. It's almost like you're a human lie detector!

+ You often use the phrase "I know what you mean" or something similar.

+ You regularly receive unusual ideas or sudden, unexpected insights that make no logical sense at the time but are proven to be perfectly true down the line. For example, you might be introduced to someone at a party and have a sudden flash of insight that they can't be trusted. You're later proven to be absolutely right.

+ You sometimes interrupt people when they're speaking because you already know what they're going to say.

+ You experience déjà vu regularly, where you have the feeling you've talked to someone, experienced something, or been somewhere before although there is no evidence that proves this. For example, you arrive at a foreign destination for the first time in your life but it feels like you've been there before.

+ You've been told that you have an incredibly accurate gut instinct.

+ You've been misunderstood and probably experienced painful rejection and loneliness because you seem to know things but you can't explain how you know them.

+ Creative solutions to complex problems and challenges come easily to you even when everyone else is stuck.

## Clairsentience

When you read the words "freshly baked cake," did you happen to detect a sensation in your body or an emotion like a spark of delight or joy in your heart? If this was your experience, then your Authentic Self is connecting with you through "clear feeling," or Clairsentience. This is the Clair channel that a lot of sensitive people or empaths can relate to. They can feel someone else's pain on a physical level, and they are also prone to experiencing intense emotions across the spectrum, from joy and love to loss and envy. The following are traits that you'll resonate with if you experienced a physical sensation during this exercise:

+ You can easily become distressed and agitated when you're in crowded spaces like at a concert or at the mall on a busy Saturday afternoon.

+ You often experience emotions as sensations in the body. This means you might feel goosebumps when you hear a great idea, feel your entire body go hot when you're embarrassed, or feel shivers run up and down your spine when you're scared.

+ You've been known to go from enthusiastic to hopeless in a matter of minutes (or seconds). It's because you're constantly "receiving" moods and emotions from the environment and the people around you.

+ You often use the phrase "I get the feeling…" or something similar.

+ You've been told you're too sensitive or hypersensitive, which can feel like a bad thing. Don't worry, because it's not. Sensitivity is a superpower, and being able to sense what other people cannot will help you understand yourself and the world deeply.

+ You intuitively know that you absorb information and knowledge quickly and easily when you have the option to learn through a multisensory experience. So if you're learning how to cook something new, you'll want to try it out in the kitchen right away rather than read the instructions in the recipe or watch a video first.

- You can attune to what others are feeling and experiencing just by observing them or having them relate a story about what they've been through.
- You can effortlessly sense the overarching vibe of a building or location. This could be a positive or negative vibe. For example, you might visit an ancient castle on vacation and find yourself feeling extremely uncomfortable or even physically ill when you enter the dungeons where people were imprisoned.

Did you recognize your primary and secondary intuitive channels, or Clairs? I want you to practice and play with activities similar to the "freshly baked cake" exercise so you can home in on your key Clair channels.

For instance, you could take a walk along a beach or some other gorgeous landscape and take note of how you're processing what you see, feel, experience, and sense. Another great way to identify your primary and secondary Clairs is to listen to an audiobook—maybe a novel with lots of descriptions. Make sure you don't know the storyline ahead of time. Pay attention to whether you're seeing the descriptions in your mind's eye, hearing sounds in your ears, and so on. You can also ask friends to help you identify your key Clairs. Ask them to come up with phrases like "cup of coffee," "roller coaster ride," or "red rose" without letting you know in advance. Focus on your inner experience when you hear these phrases and notice what comes up. Recognizing your primary and secondary Clairs is immensely important because it's a whole lot easier to tap into the wisdom of your Authentic Self when you are familiar with the channels through which your intuition communicates with you.

## Recognizing the Difference between Intuition and Just Old-Fashioned Fear

By now you've probably realized that connecting with your Authentic Self and your intuition is an ongoing process and not a one and done deal. The key is to be patient and continue practicing and tuning in. For most people, activating and fully trusting their intuitive messages doesn't come naturally, and one of the biggest bumps in the road to communicating with the Authentic Self is being able to tell if it's a genuine intuitive connection or just old-fashioned fear and resistance.

Let's say you've been offered a great new job, but it involves moving to a new city on the other side of the world. You feel uncomfortable and uninterested in following through, and you think that's your intuition telling you to stay where you are. But is that really true? This is why you need to know how to tell the difference between True Desire and False Desire.

## True Desire versus False Desire

Most people think they know what desire feels like. They see something, they want something, and that's that. For instance, they think they have a deep desire to build a million-dollar business when they see super successful entrepreneurs living the high life on Instagram, but that might not be true. You see, desire has two faces: True Desire and False Desire. True Desire comes through your intuition and your Authentic Self, while False Desire emerges from fear and doubt. When you focus on identifying and manifesting your True Desires, you'll receive far more than you can possibly imagine. (It's why I like to say the Universe always dreams a bigger dream for you than you can possibly dream for yourself!) When you manifest from a False Desire, it can feel like you're not living a life that is true to who you are, which quickly leads to disappointment and heartache.

When you're aligned with your True Desires, you'll feel energized, excited, and enthusiastic about your intentions and dreams. When you're operating from a False Desire, you'll feel unmotivated, disconnected, and disappointed even if you manage to successfully manifest what you think you want. The line between True Desire and False Desire can be razor-thin and almost imperceptible. Luckily, there are easy techniques you can use to quickly tell the difference.

A good way to practice recognizing True Desires versus False Desires is to look for opportunities to use the following techniques in everyday situations. For instance, you could use having dinner at a new restaurant as an opportunity to practice differentiating between the two. First scan through the items on the menu. Then bring your awareness to what's going on in your body, heart, and mind based on the descriptions below. When you read an item on the menu, check in to see if you're experiencing sensations and emotions that point to a True Desire or a False Desire.

In the body, mind, and heart, True Desire feels like this:

+ Open

+ Expansive

+ Light

+ Serene

With True Desire, your thoughts are focused, clear, and uplifting. It's a little bit like opening up a tightly closed fist or the relief that comes when you take a deep breath after being underwater for a little too long.

In the body, mind, and heart, False Desire feels like this:

+ Closed

+ Contracting

+ Heavy

+ Agitating

It's the opposite of True Desire—like squeezing a tightly closed fist even tighter. Your thoughts feel like birds chasing each other around and around in your mind, an endless stream of nervous, anxious rumination.

Knowing how to recognize True Desire can help you make powerful decisions to manifest what you truly want—the experiences, things, relationships that are for your highest and best good—based on the wisdom of your Authentic Self, not what others want or expect.

## Manifest Now! Create Your True Desires List

It's time to identify three to five True Desires that you want to manifest using what you learned in this chapter. This is a powerful and important foundational exercise, so go ahead and grab your journal or digital notebook.

First, freewrite your desires, dreams, and goals. Write down anything and everything that comes to mind without judgment. This includes things you've never talked about before (yes, that means those crazy, big dreams you're too shy to share even with your best friend). Whatever you do, don't give yourself time to reflect. Just open your journal or digital page and start writing or typing. If you're the sort of person who enjoys structure, set a timer for five to ten minutes. Don't check the timer while you write. Allow yourself the freedom to note everything that enters your consciousness without restriction and without thinking about whether or not it makes sense.

## Connect with Your Authentic Self

When you're done freewriting, you should have a fairly substantial list of what you'd like to manifest. Now I want you to work with the Stop and Drop Technique (page 54) to connect with your intuition and your Authentic Self. When you've set your intention and you feel yourself drop into a calm energetic state, it's time to read through the items on the list you just created. Pay special attention to your primary and secondary intuitive channels. For instance, if you discovered that Clairvoyance is your primary intuitive channel and Claircognizance is your secondary channel, be mindful of visuals and imagery that enter your mind's eye and ideas or insights that arise in your consciousness.

As you read through your list, ask yourself if there's anything that needs to be crossed out. Allow your intuition to provide the answers, and get ready to be surprised. A lot of what you thought was important could end up crossed out, while seemingly ordinary experiences or things that don't feel like a big deal to you right now might stay on the list.

Whatever happens, allow yourself to trust what's coming through your intuition from your Authentic Self. Remember that your Authentic Self is the part of you that is connected to the Universe. It keeps you safe from harm and lets you connect with the desires, goals, and dreams that are 100 percent aligned with your highest and best good no matter what. Write down any information, knowledge, or messages that you receive.

## Tune into Your Body, Heart, and Mind

It's time to identify three to five True Desires. Look at your list again. Use the elements of True Desire that I shared earlier to filter your list down to three to five items. As you read each goal, desire, or dream on the list, bring your attention to your body, heart, and mind. Do you feel open, expansive, light, and serene? Are your thoughts focused, clear, and uplifting? These feelings are pointing you toward your True Desires.

When you're done, you'll have a list of True Desires that are fully aligned with who you are, your values, and your beliefs at this time. Your list could include experiences, material objects, emotions, relationships, or even transformations you'd like to see happen in your personal life, at work, or out in the world. This is what you *truly* want, not what others want for you or what you think you should want. Keep your True Desires list safe. You'll come back to it when you're ready to apply the tools and techniques you'll learn later in this book.

*Four*

# Magical Manifesting Ingredient #2: Authentically Elevate Your Vibe

The energy of true self-love is the closest in resonance and frequency to the core energy of the Universe, which is unlimited, unconditional love, and successful manifesting is intricately and inextricably intertwined with our ability to shower ourselves with self-love. When we deny, resist, or push against giving ourselves the love we need and desire, the love that supports our soul, nourishes our spirit, and raises our consciousness, we are inadvertently disconnecting from the Universe and impeding our ability to manifest our True Desires.

One of my favorite songs is "The Greatest Love of All," and I believe it's one of the most inspiring and powerful musical tributes to self-love that's ever been written. The first time I heard the song, the melody and especially the lyrics cast a spell over me. I was instantly mesmerized, but I also noticed that I felt uncomfortable. As I listened, I experienced a strange tightness in my chest that continued to intensify. Eventually I came to understand that this sensation was triggered by the belief that loving myself fully and freely was somehow wrong. All my life I'd been told that nice girls always put others first. This message was reinforced by a nonstop onslaught of advertisements, novels, movies, and television shows. In the culture I was born into and grew up in, good, kind people simply didn't indulge in self-love.

It would be years before I truly understood the simple truth of the song: that the greatest love of all—the gift that attracts all other gifts—is the gift of self-love. If we are to manifest our desires, there is no way around it: we must learn to love ourselves truly, madly, deeply and with unending fervor. Genuine self-love is the most powerful manifesting tool you have access to, and it is the rich soil in which other beautiful qualities and traits can grow. Self-love gives you unbreakable resilience and is the source of an endless flow of self-worth, self-respect, inner strength, and so much more.

In this chapter, you'll discover how to work with Magical Manifesting Ingredient #2, which is about authentically elevating your consciousness so you can manifest with effortless ease using the power of genuine self-love. Along the way, you'll learn how to grow the most exquisite garden in existence, which is the Garden of Self-Love, and we'll plant the seeds of the three Flowers of Self-Love: Self-Acceptance, Self-Compassion, and Self-Kindness.

You'll begin your magical gardening project with the Flower of Self-Acceptance, which is about opening your heart to receive all of who you are, including hidden aspects of yourself called the Secret Shadow. Next, you'll learn to nurture the Flower of Self-Compassion, which lets you cultivate a deep understanding and empathy that will serve as a soothing balm for any kind of pain and heartache. Finally, you'll discover how to cultivate the Flower of Self-Kindness by releasing judgment with a collection of wonderful, easy-to-apply techniques that can free you from a harsh, critical inner voice.

I hope you're excited to begin working on this magical garden where self-love can grow, flow, and flourish. But before we start, we must do what all good gardeners do, and that is to remove unwanted weeds. When it comes to the Garden of Self-Love, I've found that the biggest and most dangerous weed to look out for is something that hides in plain sight: toxic positivity.

# Understanding Toxic Positivity

You might have heard of the Abraham-Hicks Emotional Guidance Scale, which is beautifully described in one of my favorite books on manifesting, *Ask and It Is Given* by Jerry and Esther Hicks. The Scale ranks twenty-two emotions, starting at the top with the highest-vibrational positive emotions, such as joy, appreciation, and love, all the way down to low-vibrational negative emotions, such as fear, despair, and powerlessness. Here's a quick look at the full list of emotions in the Emotional Guidance Scale:

1. Joy/Knowledge/Empowerment/Freedom/Love/Appreciation
2. Passion
3. Enthusiasm
4. Positive Expectation/Belief
5. Optimism
6. Hopefulness
7. Contentment
8. Boredom
9. Pessimism
10. Frustration/Irritation/Impatience
11. Overwhelment
12. Disappointment
13. Doubt
14. Worry
15. Blame
16. Discouragement
17. Anger
18. Revenge
19. Hatred/Rage

20. Jealousy

21. Insecurity/Guilt/Unworthiness

22. Fear/Grief/Depression/Powerlessness/Victim

The Emotional Guidance Scale is a widely known, much loved tool in manifesting and spiritual circles. I love the Scale and use it regularly. It never fails to help me identify the exact emotion I'm experiencing in the moment and to get a sense of where I'm at in terms of my vibrational frequency. For me, the Scale is a reference tool and a guideline, but for a lot of aspiring manifestors, it can feel like a strict measuring device that determines if they're feeling the right emotion or the wrong one, and it leaves a lot of people believing that the emotions at the lower end of the scale are bad and to be avoided at all costs. It's an unrealistic, unhealthy view that, unfortunately, is driven home by loads of spiritual gurus and manifesting coaches who encourage students and clients to rise up the Scale by simply reaching for higher-vibrational, better-feeling emotions to attract what they want. The "how" of doing this is often unclear or left unsaid, leading many aspiring manifestors to unknowingly adopt toxic positivity as a way of life.

In her book *Toxic Positivity: Keeping It Real in a World Obsessed with Positivity*, psychotherapist and author Whitney Goodman explains that toxic positivity denies a negative emotion and forces us to suppress it. In chapter 1, she writes, "When we use toxic positivity, we are telling ourselves and others that this emotion shouldn't exist, it's wrong, and if we try just a little bit harder, we can eliminate it entirely." Toxic positivity is supportive, helpful positivity gone rogue. It's about ignoring difficult emotions such as grief or disappointment and painting over them with false joy and superficial feel-good quotes in an attempt to hit a high-vibrational state no matter what you really feel.

At its core, toxic positivity is about saying and doing just about anything you can to get yourself (and others) to achieve a positive mindset. It asks that we remain upbeat even when our heart is breaking. It expects us to believe that we must express only good vibes even when we have genuine concerns or fear about our wellbeing or the wellbeing of others. Think of times when something unwanted happened. Maybe you lost your job and a coworker or friend came up to you and said things like, "You'll be fine. You'll bounce back. You always do," or "Every cloud has a silver lining. You'll find a better job!" This sounds great, but when you peek beneath the surface, there are unspoken messages that are pretty darn unforgiving. Toxic positivity essentially asks you to instantly snap out of it or simply get over it when you're feeling unhappy, angry, insecure, or any of the emotions at the bottom of the Emotional Guidance Scale.

Just to be clear, *genuine* positivity isn't a bad thing. Having a positive outlook helps us look for the greater good in life and is a wonderful manifesting skill. But toxic positivity is about forcing a cheerful smile when you're feeling anything but cheerful or glossing over real-world problems, like a serious health condition, in the name of staying positive and high-vibe. As Whitney Goodman says, toxic positivity is rooted in denial, and this is one of the biggest reasons why it's a serious, insidious block to genuinely loving and accepting ourselves. It asks that we deny what we're really feeling, and it makes us feel wrong for being, doing, or saying anything that's not positive.

Toxic positivity also rejects the present moment and what we're feeling in that moment, which can send stress levels through the roof. Numerous studies linking stress and emotions show that when research participants were asked to view or watch an emotionally triggering image or video, such as the aftermath of a car accident, physical stress responses such as the heart rate rose to much higher levels in those who were asked to suppress or hide their emotions compared to those who were allowed to freely express how they felt. This shows that toxic positivity does nothing to create genuine positive feelings, and the ensuing stress of holding back what we really feel will inevitably block our ability to manifest what we truly want.

## Recognizing Toxic Positivity

You know you're immersed in toxic positivity when you find yourself dismissing or ignoring difficult emotions or feeling guilty or ashamed when you experience anything less than blazing, in-your-face, brighter-than-the-sun positivity. Here's a fun little guide to help you recognize the difference between negative thinking, positive thinking, and toxic positivity.

### Learning How to Play the Violin

*Negative thinking:* "I'm not musical and I knew I'd suck at this. I'm giving up."

*Positive thinking:* "I'll give it my best shot and keep practicing. Maybe I'll get better."

*Toxic positivity:* "If I can't do this, it's because it's not meant to be."

### Going on a Dream Vacation

*Negative thinking:* "This is too expensive. I can't afford it."

*Positive thinking:* "Maybe I can look into earning a bit of extra cash on weekends and save up."

*Toxic positivity:* "The Universe will provide!"

### Starting Your Own Business

*Negative thinking:* "No one in my family is in business. I can't do this."

*Positive thinking:* "I can learn anything if I try."

*Toxic positivity:* "Life is meant to be easy, and starting a business is tough. I think I'll stick to my day job."

### Feeling Blue after a Romantic Relationship Ends

*Negative thinking:* "I'll never find love again. I'm unlovable."

*Positive thinking:* "This breaks my heart, but I have friends and family who love me. I'll find my way out of this."

*Toxic positivity:* "I didn't really love them anyway. I'm fine!"

### Losing a Loved One

*Negative thinking:* "What have I done to deserve this? I should have done something different. It's my fault."

*Positive thinking:* "I'll never be the same again, but I'll survive."

*Toxic positivity:* "Everything happens for a reason."

# Talking to the Universe

The language of the Universe is the language of emotions, and just as we can't hide what we truly feel from ourselves, we also can't hide what we truly feel from the Universe. The more we tell ourselves that we feel a certain way when we don't, the more we try to force a positive, high-vibrational emotion by practicing toxic positivity, the more we disconnect from our natural manifesting power. In other words, if we are to successfully connect and communicate with the Universe, we must begin to create awareness of how we feel in the moment, so we can begin to think, feel, and vibrate with genuine positivity.

I've discovered that authentic positive energy and all of the good things that it brings, including a heightened ability to manifest, is about learning how to "regulate our emotions," as psychologists call it, which is the ability to accurately identify and then consciously influence our emotional state in a healthy way. When it comes to regulating my emotions for manifesting purposes, my favorite process is the one I'll share next. During this process, you'll give yourself permission to feel what you really feel and then shift into a desired emotion using the three components of the 1 Healing Breath practice: self-awareness, presence, and embodied attention. Doing this will give you the time and breathing room to experience the healing balm of accepting what you feel before inviting an authentic, higher-vibrational emotion. No need for suppression, repression, or toxic positivity!

### *How to Authentically Elevate Your Vibe with 1 Healing Breath*

Begin by taking an In-the-Moment Edition of the 1 Healing Breath of your choice. I like 1 Healing Breath of Clarity, and if you need help invoking this energy, feel free to use the activated image of 1 Healing Breath of Clarity. (You'll find this image in your free gift bundle that you can sign up to download at www.shantinirajah.com/manifest.)

Tune into the first of the three components of 1 Healing Breath, which is self-awareness. You can do this by bringing your attention and awareness to what you're feeling, knowing it is safe to experience what you feel without taking action on it. See if you can name the emotion, whether it's sadness, jealousy, disappointment, or something else. You can do this easily by saying to yourself or out loud, "I'm feeling angry right now," or "I'm feeling frustrated," or some other version.

Next, focus on the second component of 1 Healing Breath, which is presence. Sit with the emotion that you identified for a minute or two while gently maintaining the focus of your awareness on that emotion. Stay in the presence of it until you can start to detect that it is dissipating or decreasing. Often this takes just a few moments, although it can take a minute or more, especially when you first start doing this process. When you notice the uncomfortable emotion begin to decrease in intensity, it's a sign that you're ready to set an intention to call in a higher-vibrational emotion.

Something to keep in mind is that you don't have to actually *feel* this new positive emotion that you're calling in. Simply set an intention with a quick "I'm ready to feel relaxed," or "I'm calling in calm," or "I'm choosing love," or "It is safe to feel better." Be mindful when it comes to the words you use in your intention. Start your sentence with "I'm calling in ...," or "I'm ready to ...," or "I'm choosing to ...," or "It is safe to ...." Don't say "I am feeling..." or "I am ...." This will send you straight into toxic positivity territory, where you're telling yourself that you feel something you don't actually feel. So avoid setting an intention like "I am relaxed" or "I am feeling calm" when that's not what you're actually experiencing.

Once you've set your intention, you can focus on the third and final component of 1 Healing Breath, which is embodied attention. Gently direct your awareness to your breath, and start to track the journey of the breath from your nostrils down to your chest and into your belly, not just with your mind but through physical sensory responses as well. Remember to tune into the felt sensations of the breath as it makes its way in and out of the body by asking yourself, "Is my breath cool or hot, mild or intense, quick or slow?" or "How does my chest and belly feel: tight and knotted or relaxed?" As you allow your body to breathe, gently repeat your intention in your mind: "I want to feel relaxed," or "I'm ready to feel inspired," or "I am choosing to feel better." Continue to do this until you notice an improvement in your emotional state.

# Self-Love: A Strange Concept

We've arrived at the heart of Magical Manifesting Ingredient #2, which is about authentically raising our vibrational frequency with genuine self-love. You might find that this is the hardest part of the book to understand and implement, and I want you to know you're not alone. You might find, like I did the first time I listened to "The Greatest Love of All," that self-love is a strange concept. We might think we know what it means, but so few of us understand what it feels like to fully experience this beautiful, empowering love from within.

I used to believe that genuine self-love was a lofty, unattainable aspiration, something available only to enlightened gurus and masters who spent hours, days, or years in deep meditation, honing their ability to empty their minds so unconditional love could arise unencumbered and radiate out into the world. My quest for true self-love felt hopeless in the beginning, because if there's one thing I know for sure, it's this: I don't have what it takes to meditate for thousands of hours, even if the reward is an endless state of deep love for myself. But I didn't give up on the idea of becoming my own best friend, and my persistence paid off. To my utter delight, the Garden of Self-Love grew and flourished in my heart when I learned how to nurture the three Flowers of Self-Love: Self-Acceptance, Self-Compassion, and Self-Kindness.

The first thing you need to know about the Flowers of Self-Love is that they can't survive without trust. Trust in yourself and the Universe is the soil in which the Flowers of Self-Love can grow strong enough to withstand powerful forces that block our ability to manifest, such as expectations, fears and doubts—our own and other people's. With Self-Acceptance, Self-Compassion, and Self-Kindness seeded in trust, genuine self-love blooms and grows gracefully and naturally.

If you've been around the personal growth and self-help block a couple of times, you've likely come across teachers and coaches who say you need to practice self-love by making time to relax in a lavender-scented bubble bath, or by getting a massage at your favorite spa, or maybe by taking a vacation for a week or two. I have nothing against these suggestions (I'd jump at any excuse to get a massage at my favorite spa!), but massages, bubble baths, and vacations are self-care techniques that are the result of self-love; they do not generate self-love.

Think of it this way: if those well-meaning teachers and coaches were right, we'd experience nothing but self-love after a couple of trips to a luxury spa. We'd find ourselves living true to who we are, asking for what we want, and surrounding ourselves only with that which brings us joy, Marie Kondo–style, after every vacation. So here's the deal: let's keep practicing self-care techniques that bring us joy and lift our vibrational state, but let's also make a commitment to nurture the three Flowers of Self-Love. As you might imagine, this takes a little bit more time and effort than getting your hair and nails done, but I promise it's worth it.

## The Flower of Self-Acceptance

We'll begin growing a healthy, bountiful, beautiful Garden of Self-Love with the first of the three flowers, which is self-acceptance, and we'll be focusing a significant amount of time and effort here. Self-acceptance is the most important, the most rewarding, and also the most challenging aspect of genuine self-love. We'll be growing the Flower of Self-Acceptance primarily through profound, unlimited acceptance of our Secret Shadow, which is the part of us that holds the personality traits we want to hide, even from ourselves (we'll do this with a simple yet powerful exercise called Loving Your Secret Shadow later in this chapter).

The concept of the Secret Shadow is a favorite among novelists, screenwriters, and playwrights, and I'm pretty sure you've come across it in popular TV shows, movies, and stories. One of Stephen King's most celebrated novels, *The Shining*, is about writer Jack Torrance, who starts out a good husband and father but is soon overcome by his Secret Shadow identity. Then there's the classic story of Jekyll and Hyde by Robert Louis Stevenson, which is about the good, upstanding Dr. Henry Jekyll and his Shadow alter ego, Edward Hyde.

These are evil characterizations, and while these stories are incredibly entertaining, they're not exactly accurate. The Secret Shadow is certainly not some sort of dark, scary identity buried deep in your psyche, waiting to take over and destroy your life. In reality, the Secret Shadow is a beautiful opportunity to shine healing light on all aspects of ourselves so we can finally and forever accept all of who we are and shine our light out into the world.

## Exploring the Secret Shadow

For centuries, the concept of the Secret Shadow was shrouded in mystery. Known by practitioners in various esoteric traditions and customs around the world, the Secret Shadow remained largely unexplored outside of spiritual and mystical circles; that is until the celebrated Swiss psychologist Carl Jung put it into clear psychological terms. As explained in an article by Christopher Perry for the Society of Analytical Psychology, Jung was fascinated by the aspect of ourselves that he called the Shadow. He believed that the Shadow holds the dark side of our personality, which are the negative or unwholesome parts of ourselves that we suppress, repress, and hide from the world. It's essentially the part of us that feels unacceptable and unlovable—the things we say, do, and think that we believe are bad or wrong. The Secret Shadow is a fusion of rejected emotions such as conceit, greed, or envy and behaviors we believe are sneaky, stingy, or abhorrent in some way.

Simply acknowledging our Secret Shadow can trigger intense guilt and shame, so we hide it from others and even from ourselves. We deny our unwanted thoughts and feelings because we are deeply afraid of disapproval and of being ostracized, but here's where things get complicated. Like all shadows, our Secret Shadow needs darkness to survive. The more we ignore it, the stronger it becomes, and it doesn't go away just because we reject it. Instead, it remains hidden yet embedded within us, just below the surface, and when something happens to evoke difficult emotions, thoughts, or impulses, such as loss or rejection, the unexamined Secret Shadow rises up and takes center stage in ways that can feel outside of our control. This is partly why you probably know someone who seems friendly, joyful, and calm most of the time, but then you've been shocked to see them gripped by a cushion-throwing, dish-breaking tantrum of epic proportions when something doesn't go their way. And goodness knows we've all read or heard stories of world leaders or authority figures who advocate the virtues of chastity or morality but are later revealed to be practicing the opposite of the principles they preach.

When we dismiss our Secret Shadow or try to pretend it doesn't exist, what we're really doing is practicing self-rejection, which is the opposite of self-acceptance. We start to make choices in our life and work to gain external approval and validation. It takes an enormous amount of energy to hide the Secret Shadow—energy that blocks us from connecting with our Authentic Self and manifesting what we desire. Even worse, the Secret Shadow can and will run your life when it remains hidden and unrecognized, and that's exactly what happened to me.

## The Curse of the Good Girl

I grew up trying not to disappoint anyone or make any kind of mistake. I did what I could to get everything right. I pushed myself to be a good daughter, a good sister, a good friend, and later, a good wife, and I was often overcome by guilt and shame when I thought I fell short. In other words, I was constantly striving to be the quintessential Good Girl. Long before I left high school, I designed the entire trajectory of my life so that things would unfold the way they were "supposed to" for a Good Girl. My plan was pretty straightforward: study hard, go to university, get a degree, get a job at a respectable corporation, get married, and settle down. Through it all, I did my best to be the dependable one, the trustworthy one, the hardworking one; the one who always kept her promises; the one who hit every deadline.

Basically, I moved heaven and earth trying to be the one others could turn to, the one others could rely on no matter what. But by the time I was thirty, it became clear to me that "no matter what" wasn't the end of that sentence. The real end of that sentence was "no matter what the cost," and very often the cost was way too high. The cost was not doing what felt right to me and not taking the path that I wanted to take in my life. The cost was giving up on my dreams, my creativity, my beliefs. It meant giving up on who I truly was in order to be who I believed I was supposed to be, and it fed something dark within me—it fed my Secret Shadow in an unhealthy way.

Wearing the mask of the Good Girl made my Secret Shadow rise up. It made me feel resentful, angry, and misunderstood a lot of the time, and it also made me feel scared. I believed that if I were to live in alignment with my Authentic Self, if I expressed myself, if I said no more often, if I dared to—heaven forbid—set boundaries, if I destroyed the mask of the Good Girl, then people would stop liking me and they would stop loving me. I was terrified. So I continued to do what I was supposed to do, and my Secret Shadow grew bigger, stronger, and meaner. I was short-tempered and irritable with myself and with the people I loved. I developed mysterious aches and pains. I started to lose interest in my work. I didn't like who I was becoming.

Being who we are, expressing ourselves as we are, and connecting to our Authentic Self means embracing our light and our Secret Shadow. Recognizing my Secret Shadow and making friends with the part of me that I was trying to hide—the part of me that felt envious, that played the blame game, the short-tempered, impatient version of myself—led to radically different decisions in my life and my work. I started to speak up for myself and show up as myself, and I found that the more I let go of that which was not me, the more time, love, peace, satisfaction, and, yes, even money started flowing into my life. Now when I help, when I support, when I love, it's with my whole heart and my whole being. No secret resentment. No anger. No shame or blame. Secret Shadow work made way for my Authentic Self to emerge and stand tall. It allowed me to show up wholly and fully and align with the Universe so that all I desired flowed to me with ease. It worked for me and I know it can work for you too.

## Allowing Your Secret Shadow to Step Forward

In this section, you're going to allow your Secret Shadow to step forward. We'll take a gentle approach to this often complicated and challenging task by working with a basic but powerful exercise called Loving Your Secret Shadow. This method does not require an in-depth exploration of your Secret Shadow, but don't be fooled by this seemingly basic approach. This simple exercise can help you connect directly with your Secret Shadow so you can begin to open your heart to this painfully rejected part of yourself and heal through the magical energy of profound self-acceptance. We'll be working with an old-school pen and paper. Before you begin, please read through the entire exercise at least once.

## Loving Your Secret Shadow

Find a quiet corner where you will be undisturbed for at least twenty to thirty minutes. Make sure you have a pen or pencil and a notebook or journal close by. Begin by setting a clear intention. You can use the one below or create your own. Place both hands over your heart and say the following words (or something similar) to yourself or out loud:

> *I wish to recognize and reconcile with my*
> *Secret Shadow with a heart full of love and acceptance.*

Now open your journal to a fresh page, or use a fresh sheet in a notebook. Take 1 Healing Breath of your choice, using either the In-the-Moment Edition or the Extended Edition. (I like to take 1 Healing Breath of Love for this exercise. You can find the image of 1 Healing Breath of Love, along with other 1 Healing Breath images, in your free gift bundle that you can sign up to download at www.shantinirajah.com/manifest.) Next, pick up your pen, close your eyes, and ask this question out loud:

> *My dear Secret Shadow, what would you like me to know?*

Start writing what comes through for you—anything that enters your consciousness. The most important thing to know here is that you must write without giving yourself time to think. This means no thoughtful pauses or reflective moments. Just write and keep writing. You might find that nothing comes to your mind and heart, especially the first few times you do this exercise. If this happens, no worries at all! You can awaken your Secret Shadow with a simple technique.

Go back to the start of this exercise. Say your intention and take your 1 Healing Breath, but this time physically write the following question in your journal or notebook:

*My dear Secret Shadow, what would you like me to know?*

Keep writing the question again and again until you feel answers arise, then continue with the exercise. Remember, write quickly and don't allow yourself time to think. Don't worry about spelling, grammar, and punctuation. You can stop writing when nothing else comes through or when you feel complete. When you're done, sit quietly for a moment with your hands over your heart and declare the following out loud:

## Secret Shadow Mantra

*I love you, [your name].*
*I love you wholly and completely.*
*I love you, my Secret Shadow.*
*I love that which is my Light and I love that which is my Secret Shadow.*

Give yourself a moment to let the words sink in as you allow love to rise up in your heart. Follow your declaration with the following words, which are from the ancient Lovingkindness meditation and mantra:

*May I be happy and free from suffering.*
*May I be safe from harm.*
*May I be healthy, peaceful, and strong.*
*May I live with ease.*

When you're done, take 1 Healing Breath to close this activity. You can go with 1 Healing Breath of Love again or anything else that feels right for you. I like to close this activity with 1 Healing Breath of Ease (which is included in the free gift bundle that you can sign up to download at www.shantinirajah .com/manifest).

*Special note*: Don't be alarmed if you feel anger, fear, or other undesirable emotions rise up as you do this activity. There are hidden aspects of yourself contained within your Secret Shadow that want to come into the light. This writing activity can help you safely accept, heal, and release all that's been suppressed and locked away deep inside.

I highly recommend that you let yourself read through what you wrote during this exercise just once and then perform the Burning Ritual (refer to page 226 in chapter 11 for instructions on how to do this). Knowing beforehand that you will destroy what you write will give you the confidence and courage you need to fully call in your Secret Shadow and write from a place of uncensored and profound self-acceptance and honesty. Burning the page or deleting the words also symbolizes that you are letting go of any negative energies and emotions that came up for you during this exercise.

You can do the Loving Your Secret Shadow exercise more than once, and don't feel like you must stick with the suggested question each time. I encourage you to try a different question if you feel intuitively called to do so. Here are a few questions I like to work with:

*What can I do so you feel loved and accepted?*
*What is your biggest fear?*
*How does your biggest fear influence your choices?*
*What are some ways to tell when you are upset or unhappy?*
*What are some of the times when you felt ignored or unloved?*
*How can I help you heal?*
*What are some of the hidden talents, traits, and gifts that you have?*

Aim to work with just one or two questions every time you do this exercise. You don't want to flood your system with intense emotions or trigger repressed trauma.

Okay, so that's a lot to take in and process, but you did it! I promise the hardest part is over and you're well on your way to growing a beautiful, healthy Flower of Self-Acceptance. Now you're ready to tend to the second Flower of Self-Love, which is the Flower of Self-Compassion.

## The Flower of Self-Compassion

Dr. Kristin Neff is an associate professor at the University of Texas at Austin and one of the world's leading experts on self-compassion. In her book *Self-Compassion: The Proven Power of Being Kind to Yourself,* Dr. Neff explains how "the nurturing quality of self-compassion allows us to flourish, to appreciate the beauty and richness of life, even in hard times. When we soothe our agitated minds with self-compassion, we're better able to notice what's right as well as what's wrong, so that we can orient ourselves to that which gives us joy." While there's no doubt that just about every one of us wants to "orient ourselves to that which gives us joy," as Dr. Neff beautifully puts it, letting in the experience of self-compassion isn't exactly a walk in the park for most of us. We are much more likely to self-punish with harsh criticism than show ourselves compassion when we make a mistake. Thankfully, Dr. Neff comes to our rescue once again with a brilliant breakdown of the three key factors that fuel self-compassion: mindfulness, common humanity, and self-kindness (self-kindness also happens to be our third Flower of Self-Love). Let's look at each of these three factors one at a time.

## Mindfulness

When you are mindful, you have developed the wonderful ability to observe your thoughts and emotions, the sensations in your body, and what's going on around you without becoming lost in the experience (we tapped into mindfulness in chapter 3 when we focused our attention on our thoughts, feelings, and emotions in order to identify our intuitive style in the "freshly baked cake" exercise in chapter 3 (page 57). Mindfulness is fertile soil for the Flower of Self-Compassion to thrive because it allows us to approach difficult emotions and experiences from a place of safety and balance, where we are neither too attached to our own experience nor totally disconnected from it. It's a healthy path to noting our negative experiences so we can allow self-compassion to flow.

I'd like to shed some light on a truth that few others will share about mindfulness. There are a ton of benefits that come from being mindful, such as enhanced concentration and focus, improved clarity, an increased tolerance for discomfort, and of course the ability to experience self-compassion, but there's a problem, and it's a big one: mindfulness is *hard*, folks! Although I'm enormously motivated to live in a constant state of mindfulness, I've never managed to pull it off for more than ten minutes at a time. Luckily, research shows that we can enjoy the benefits of mindfulness without having to practice it every second of every day. All we need to do is to practice being mindful for short moments, many times a day, and the 1 Healing Breath practice—both the In-the-Moment Edition and the Extended Edition—is perfect for this.

Great thinkers, teachers, and masters have analyzed and accurately unpacked the fine art of being mindful, and I encourage you to explore their teachings. You'll find there are entire shelves in libraries and bookstores dedicated to this vital life skill and spiritual practice, not to mention courses, programs, and trainings, so we won't be venturing further into this first factor of self-compassion here. Instead, let's focus on something far more unusual and harder to come by: the concept of common humanity.

## Common Humanity

Dr. Kristin Neff explains that common humanity is about knowing that you're part of a bigger picture—a shared human experience. Cultivating self-compassion through common humanity is about experiencing a sense of belonging, knowing that you're not alone and isolated in your pain and sorrow and that other people face challenges and go through the same or similar struggles as you do. This might feel vague and neither here nor there. After all, how can a sense of belonging contribute to self-compassion? You might be surprised to find that it's actually incredibly effective. Common humanity allows us to gently redirect the compassion we naturally feel for others back to ourselves, and it worked beautifully for a client of mine.

When we first met, Suzanne had been pulling twelve- to fourteen-hour workdays for weeks on end, and she knew something had to change. "It's just nonstop! Between getting the kids ready for school, fixing lunch, doing the laundry, and taking care of my clients, I don't even have time to pee!" she exclaimed during our first coaching session together. She talked about how she couldn't remember the last time she had gone on vacation, and although she was incredibly productive and accomplished, she couldn't seem to shake the feeling that she was letting everyone down. "I feel like I'm falling short on everything," she said. "I love being a mom and I love coaching. My clients are happy and my kids seem fine. The other night my seven-year-old said I'm the best mom in the world, but for some reason it feels like no matter what I do, it's never enough!"

Suzanne came to me looking for help in getting past a particularly vicious case of writer's block. She loved to write for her business, but the muse seemed to have permanently abandoned her. She couldn't seem to string two sentences together and the dry spell had been going on for months. I had a bunch of techniques for Suzanne to use to unlock her creativity and get into the flow of writing, but I knew it would be a temporary solution. I could see that Suzanne's problem wasn't writer's block. She needed a major dose of self-compassion so she could release the pressure and stress that were blocking her natural creative energy. I also knew we were in for an uphill struggle because self-compassion wasn't something Suzanne could call up at will since she had gone on way too long without it. She would have to get to it through a circuitous path: through the experience of common humanity.

In our next few sessions together, I helped Suzanne become habituated to taking regular mini breaks in her day with the In-the-Moment Edition of the 1 Healing Breath practice. Then I showed her how to connect with her Authentic Self so she could listen to her intuition and give herself what she needed to perform at the highest level in ways that were supportive and nurturing to her (including regular bathroom breaks!) rather than harsh and unforgiving. Then we created a list of her True Desires using the process in chapter 3 (page 64), so she could manifest success on her own terms without feeling driven to achieve new and bigger goals based on other people's expectations. At that point, I knew she was ready to tune in and experience self-compassion through common humanity.

We began with a simple question: *Is there anyone in the world going through what you're going through right now?* This question allowed Suzanne to transcend her personal experience and opened her eyes to a comforting truth: she wasn't alone. There were thousands—possibly millions—of single moms just like her all over the world facing the same challenges and obstacles that she was in her quest to be a successful entrepreneur and the best mom she could be. She thought about the women who worried incessantly about paying the bills, just like she did; who wondered if they could provide the best education for their kids; who hoped and prayed they wouldn't let their boss, clients, or coworkers down after being up all night with a sick kid.

As she reflected on the question, Suzanne began to feel deep compassion arise for these women, and as she felt that compassion flow toward them, she began to naturally and easily experience it for herself. She was one of those single moms. She belonged. This realization created a huge emotional shift and release for Suzanne, and the tears began to flow.

"Are you okay, Suzanne?" I asked gently.

"I had no idea just how much I resisted giving myself the compassion that I need and deserve," she replied through tears. Suzanne had broken through the invisible barrier that had kept her compassion flowing out to everyone but herself.

The profound experience of common humanity, and of belonging, allowed Suzanne to shower compassion on those like her and eventually redirect that compassion to herself. I guided her to recognize this feeling of self-compassion in her body so she could call it up when she needed to. From then on, every time she felt like she was on the edge of burning the candle at both ends, she tuned back into the experience of common humanity.

Over the next year, Suzanne began taking vacations and putting up healthy boundaries around her work and her life. Her creativity began to flow again and she started on a bucket list project that was a lifelong dream: writing her first book. Finally feeling good about her work as a coach, Suzanne could enjoy her time with her kids, knowing she was fully present and content just being with them. Suzanne's compassion for millions of single moms around the world and the self-compassion she could now direct toward herself allowed her to experience and express self-love, and her ability to manifest her desires amplified.

The following practice is the exercise that I shared with Suzanne. I recommend that you do this as often as possible until self-compassion starts to feel easy and natural for you.

*Practicing Common Humanity for Self-Compassion*

Begin by taking an In-the-Moment Edition of the 1 Healing Breath of your choice. I like 1 Healing Breath of Tenderness for this practice. (If you'd like to work with the image related to 1 Healing Breath of Tenderness, you can sign up to download it, along with the other 1 Healing Breath images in this book, as part of your free gift bundle at www.shantinirajah.com/manifest.)

Now ask yourself, *Is there anyone else in the world experiencing what I'm going through right now?* Give yourself time to feel into what that's like. Visualize or think about specific situations or scenarios where they're struggling with the same challenges and obstacles as you. Next, it's time to fully feel the compassion that naturally arises, knowing that you belong to this group of people who are just like you. Allow that compassion you feel for them to flow to you, knowing that you belong and that you're one of them.

Feel yourself comforted and held in a blanket of self-compassion, and as you do this, tune into the feeling of self-compassion as it's expressed in your body. What does it feel like? Does your chest feel warm? Maybe you feel a sensation of relaxed strength in your shoulders? Fully tune into this physical sensation. Stay in this space for as long as you wish. The next time you want to quickly connect with self-compassion, simply recall this sensation in your body first so you can ease into feeling compassion for yourself. You can also choose to do the entire exercise again from start to finish.

Now that you've explored mindfulness and common humanity, two of the three components of self-compassion according to Dr. Neff, you're ready to tackle the third component, which also happens to be our third Flower of Self-Love: self-kindness.

# The Flower of Self-Kindness

For most of us, self-judgment is a way of life, and we can barely get through five minutes without it. If you think that's not true for you, I encourage you to take a moment to reflect on a typical day or, better yet, make a commitment to capture every harsh thought, word, or comment you direct toward yourself for just an hour. You may be shocked at just how often you find yourself think-ing and saying things to yourself that you wouldn't dream of saying to any-one else. I'm talking about thoughts like "This is so last-minute! Why didn't I work on this project ages ago? I'm so lazy and stupid," or "Why did I buy those pants? I'm too fat to pull them off!" or "If I was prettier, smarter, taller, thinner, [insert your favorite pet peeve about yourself], I'd be more successful by now."

As you can imagine, facing a hellish firing squad of painful criticism inside your head will take a lot out of you. The Flower of Self-Kindness withers in this unforgiving blaze of heartless judgment, and it becomes nearly impossible to draw in that which you want to manifest. But all is not lost. We can release self-judgment, even if it's deeply embedded in our energy and in our psyche, by learning to recognize when we are immersed in the energy of self-judgment. Here are three critical signs that will tell you that self-judgment is running the show and holding you back from enjoying the soothing, delicious nectar of the Flower of Self-Kindness.

## #1: You Suffer from Comparisonitis

Ever heard of comparisonitis? It's internet-speak for when you find your-self comparing your manifesting skills, or maybe even your whole life, with someone you believe has it all, and you never come out on the positive side of things. In other words, every time you scroll through your social media feed, catch up with old friends for drinks, attend a meeting at work, or simply look around you as you stand in line at the grocery store, you instantly find some-thing that's wrong about yourself compared to everyone else, who seems to be smarter, better-looking, fitter, or more successful than you.

## #2: You Struggle with Coulda-Woulda-Shoulda Syndrome

A thought that begins with "I could have," "I would have," or "I should have" signals that regret is in the house, and here's the thing a lot of people don't know about regret: it cannot exist without self-judgment. Every time you have a thought that begins with "I could have/would have/should have," you're deep in self-judgment and chastising yourself for not doing or saying something different from what you actually said or did. It's a sign that you're not giving yourself room to be who you are, flaws and all, and it's the exact opposite of self-kindness.

### #3: *You Hold Back from Exploring New Opportunities*

Self-judgment works like an insidious poison that drips into your system, eventually rendering you frozen in a deathlike paralysis when it comes to growth and expansion. When you begin to feel hopelessly unmotivated and doubtful of your own skills and abilities and you find yourself avoiding new experiences or holding back from exploring new opportunities, chances are you're in the grip of painful self-judgment.

## Antidotes to Self-Judgment

Self-kindness can arise naturally when we release self-judgment, and it's about learning to see what's going on inside yourself without criticism, blame, or reprimand. You'll probably feel uncomfortable and maybe even kind of weirded out when you first start being kind to yourself. If you've been living with that loud, critical inner sergeant that picks on you and points out every little mistake and flaw, then the gentle touch of self-kindness will probably feel fake and more than a little freaky. But you'll find that once you give yourself the kindness you've been missing out on for years or even decades, it can be delightfully addictive. You'll want more of it, because kindness always feels good and it has the power to heal even the most painful emotional wounds.

I had to intentionally practice being kind to myself every single day, as if I was learning how to play a musical instrument, and I kept at it for a couple of years (yes, years) before it started to feel natural and easy. Now I can't get enough of it. One common pitfall to look out for is that when you realize you've been unfair and overly judgmental of yourself, you'll want to judge yourself for judging yourself in the past! If this is you, it's a wonderful opportunity to practice being kind right away. Begin by taking an In-the-Moment Edition of the 1 Healing Breath of your choice to center yourself and make a commitment to let go of self-judgment. Then choose to do one or more of the following, which are my favorite practices when it comes to growing a beautiful Flower of Self-Kindness that can grow healthier and stronger every day for the rest of your life.

### Be Your Own Best Friend

Any time I feel like I'm stepping into the bad place—the Terrible Land of Self-Judgment—I make a quick U-turn into self-kindness by asking myself, "What would I say to or do if my best friend was in this same situation?" This gives me instant insight and wise guidance on what I need to say or do for myself.

### Soothe Yourself with Loving Touch

Focusing on the sense of touch can be surprisingly soothing and effective in creating space for self-kindness to arise. Research suggests that touch has a de-stressing, calming effect on the nervous system. So the next time you feel that inner mean voice pipe up or when you're feeling particularly mad or annoyed with yourself for any reason, try this: Take an In-the-Moment Edition of the 1 Healing Breath of your choice. Next, close your eyes and touch a nearby object or surface. Immerse yourself in the feel of it in your hands or at your fingertips. Focus on the experiential sensation of the object—the temperature, the texture, the shape and size.

An alternative is to do this exercise on yourself. Close your eyes and touch your cheek with kindness like you would touch the cheek of a beloved child. Feel the texture and temperature of your skin. Sink into this experience and truly let yourself feel the kindness of your loving touch. You can also expand this activity by wrapping your arms around yourself so you can give and receive a hug at the same time. Feel your body under your arms, hands, and fingers and spend a focused moment or two feeling the love and kindness flow. You can also choose to touch, hold, or pick up your pet. Animals are a wonderful source of love, and touching a beloved pet can quickly help you feel kindness begin to flow from your heart.

### Take a Self-Kindness Nap

Have you noticed how you tend to be more critical and self-judgmental when you're exhausted? If this happens to you, a Self-Kindness Nap could be just what you need. Give yourself permission to turn away from the responsibilities and tasks of the day and lie down on a sofa or your bed. You can even take a nap sitting up at your desk. You don't have to fall asleep; all you need to do is shut your eyes. For deeper relaxation, see if you can listen to soothing sounds like waves rushing into shore or the sound of rainfall in the background (you can find lots of free audios of soothing sounds online). Your Self-Kindness Nap can be as long or short as you want. I promise you'll return to your routine feeling refreshed, rejuvenated, and much more inclined to be kinder to yourself.

You've arrived at the end of this chapter armed with techniques and tools to grow your Garden of Self-Love so you can match up with the unconditional, loving energy of the Universe. This is a vibrational match made in manifesting heaven, as it will help you draw in your True Desires with hardly any effort and feel really, *really* good inside at the same time.

These self-kindness practices intertwine beautifully with the practice of mindfulness, along with getting to know our Secret Shadow for self-acceptance and the practice of self-compassion through common humanity. When these accessible and easy-to-do techniques become a part of our lives, we can start to soothe and comfort our psyche, calm our energy, and raise our consciousness at the same time, so we can manifest all that we desire from authentic high-vibrational emotions that arise from genuine self-love.

# Manifest Now!
## Grow Your Garden of Self-Love
## with 30-Second Pockets of Joy

Dr. Rick Hanson is one of my favorite teachers and authors of all time. In his brilliant book *Resilient: How to Grow an Unshakable Core of Calm, Strength, and Happiness*, which he coauthored with his son Forrest Hanson, Dr. Rick talks about how to grow inner strength by encouraging beneficial experiences in your day-to-day life. I've designed the 30-Second Pockets of Joy practice based on his teachings, with a special focus on growing self-love. This practice is essentially about dropping into simple, happy experiences by finding and intentionally focusing on tiny yet delightful moments that happen naturally during an ordinary day, such as the bus arriving on time or receiving an unexpected smile from a busy cashier at the checkout line.

The 30-Second Pockets of Joy practice allows you to rise above painful self-judgment, self-rejection, and self-punishment so you can easily embrace the three Flowers of Self-Love—Self-Acceptance, Self-Compassion, and Self-Kindness—and it also allows you to repeatedly experience short meditative states of focus and intention every day. In this way, you will gain the benefits of a longer-term meditation and spiritual practice without spending hours on a meditation cushion. How cool is that?

You'll begin by looking for what is good and true in your life and focusing on one of those things for 30 seconds or more. The secret to getting the most from this activity is to bring in various aspects of your senses to the experience. This means focusing your thoughts, emotions, sensations, and movements on the experience. For instance, you could be in a cool, comfortable room as you're reading this. Purposefully bring your attention to the sensation of coolness on your skin. Let yourself feel the emotion of comfort as you think about how you are safe in this space and you are reading a book that (I hope!) you intentionally chose to read.

If you're reading a physical book, bring your attention to the feel of the crisp paper, or if you're reading on your phone or tablet, feel the smoothness of the device in your hands. Then do one physical action or movement as you experience all of this. It could be that you flip a page of the book or run your finger along over the surface of your device, or perhaps you shut your eyes and smile, feeling delighted with the comfortable coolness that you're experiencing. Do these things for 30 seconds or more so you can let yourself truly connect with the experience. Teach yourself to consistently and intentionally look for reasons to practice Pockets of Joy throughout your day. It's a fun, easy, and beautifully effective way to authentically raise your vibe and train yourself to experience genuine self-love with ease.

You can also use the 30-Second Pockets of Joy technique to infuse the True Desires list you created in chapter 3 (page 64) with the high-vibrational energy of joy and self-love. The instructions are the same as above. Focus your emotions, actions, sensations, and thoughts for 30 seconds or more as you imagine what it would be like to live out your True Desires. For instance, if one of your True Desires is to manifest your dream home by the sea, use the Pockets of Joy technique to catch the scent of the ocean, and wiggle your toes a little as you picture what it would be like to walk on the warm, sandy beach. Feel excited thinking about how happy you'll be, and maybe even visualize the housewarming party you'll throw when you move in. Do the same with the other True Desires on your list.

# Phase III

## Cultivate Un-resistance

You've arrived at phase III of our journey together, and it's time to apply Magical Manifesting Ingredients #3 and #4 so you can cultivate "un-resistance" and liberate your desires. You'll discover how to use Magical Manifesting Ingredient #3: Alchemize Fear to release Harmful Fear that is blocking your ability to manifest your True Desires. You'll also begin an empowering, life-changing journey where you'll learn to create a soothing, comforting sanctuary inside yourself by generating safety from within using an easy-to-do exercise that layers safety in the mind and body. With Magical Manifesting Ingredient #4: Tap into Practical Magic, you'll connect with the energy of Conscious Liberation so you can create space and time for the magic of the Universe to take effect and allow the manifesting process to unfold in a way that feels empowering and enlightening.

Five

# Magical Manifesting Ingredient #3: Alchemize Fear

If you know even a little bit about the art of manifesting, you know that fear is the biggest block to attracting what you want—and it's because nothing stops creative energy from flowing the way fear can. It doesn't matter whether you're afraid of the rising cost of living, scary environmental changes, or the fact that you noticed an extra couple of lines around your eyes that seem to have appeared overnight. Whatever we happen to be afraid of, that feeling of mild anxiety, worry, or doubt all the way up to the kind of fear that twists our stomach and clutches at our heart can be so distressing that it has the power to send us into a downward spiral that instantly disconnects us from the beautiful, genuine high-vibrational energies and emotions we need to create a life we love with joy and ease. It's a big reason why we fight our fears, and it's why so many of us dream of becoming fearless. But here's the thing: defeating fear has nothing to do with fighting it.

As it turns out, if we want to overcome fear, we must do something that feels incredibly counterintuitive. It's something most people never think of doing, and it might evoke even greater fear in the moment, but this counter-intuitive method is, without a doubt, one of the most powerful antidotes to fear in existence. It's a method that has been passed down through generations of warriors in the East and it's been practiced by legendary spiritual masters throughout history. The good news is you don't have to attain mastery in martial arts or achieve enlightenment to use it effectively, because this all-powerful antidote to fear is available to anyone who is willing to use it—as a humble young basket weaver discovered a long, long time ago.

## The Secret to Becoming Fearless

Once there was a gifted young basket weaver named Divya who lived in a beautiful village by a river high up in the mountains. Divya loved her simple life doing the work she loved surrounded by her family and good friends, but she was often plagued by fear, worry, and doubt that entered her mind and heart uninvited. Fear made her think of everything that could go wrong in her life and all that she stood to lose. What if she fell ill and couldn't weave her baskets anymore? How would she make a living then? What if her friends moved to another village? What if she grew old without ever finding that special someone to spend her life with?

Divya wished with all her heart that she could be free of the gnawing feeling in her stomach that told her fear had come to pay a call. It kept her up at night, made her worry all day, and stole her joy. She decided that her only hope of ever finding peace and happiness was to learn how to beat fear once and for all. But she knew of no one who lived free of fear, so there was no one who could teach her how to become fearless.

One day a stranger arrived in Divya's village, and soon word spread like wildfire. "He's from the Land of the Valiant," the villagers whispered, "where courage flows like sweet honey through the hearts of the people and they know nothing but peace and harmony." Divya couldn't believe her luck. Here was her chance to learn the secret to becoming fearless. She set off to find the stranger, who was resting under a shady tree at the edge of the village. "Kind sir," said Divya shyly, offering the man a cup of clear, refreshing water from the mountain springs. "I hope you don't mind, but I'd love to know the secret of your people—the secret to becoming fearless. How do I beat fear so I'll never have to feel it again?"

The stranger accepted the cup Divya offered with a grateful thank-you and looked at her with a gentle smile. "My dear girl, I'm more than happy to answer your question," he said. "The secret to becoming fearless is simple. Fear gains strength when you are afraid of experiencing change." He paused to take a sip of water before continuing. "But it loses its power over you when you can fully accept the natural, ever-changing ebbs and flows of life without resistance. When you do this, fear cannot hold you back and you will be free to live with peace, love, and happiness in your heart."

Divya thanked the stranger and immediately began to put his wise words into practice. At first, allowing herself to accept the ever-changing nature of life felt overwhelming, but as the weeks turned into months, she realized that the stranger was right: to experience change without resistance was the path to true peace and happiness. Divya went on to live a long and happy life full of unexpected twists and turns. Fear walked beside her for the rest of her days, but it never stole her joy again.

## What Manifesting *Really* Means

What Divya learned from the wise stranger is true: the secret to becoming fearless has to do with living in harmony with the nature of life, which is constantly shifting and changing. Fear cannot survive in our hearts when we learn to live with change, and it's because *all* fear is essentially fear of change. I know this might be hard to believe, but fear of change is an inextricable part of human nature.

Our collective fear of change can be traced all the way back to the days when our ancient ancestors had to survive in incredibly harsh conditions. For thousands of years, everything from a sudden drop in temperature to a rustling of leaves that signaled the presence of a wild animal was potentially a death trap. When something changed—even if it was just the tiniest shift—it usually meant bad things were about to happen. It's why the human brain evolved to see change as a threat. This is where our fear of change comes from, and it's hardwired into the oldest part of the brain, the part that neuroscientists sometimes refer to as the "lizard brain" because of its ancient reptilian "fight, flight, or freeze" response to threats. So right about now, you're probably going, "This is all well and good, but what in the world does any of this have to do with manifesting?" The answer is *everything*.

Manifesting can be defined as the process that brings our desires, dreams, and goals from the intangible realm of energy into the tangible realm of the physical world. Based on this definition, a simple manifesting equation might look something like this:

Manifesting = bringing the intangible into the tangible

But there's a make-or-break element that's missing from that definition, and when we bring it into the equation, here's what the updated definition looks like:

Manifesting = bringing the intangible into the tangible
*through the process of change*

In other words, to manifest is to change, and successful manifesting can happen only if we learn to embrace change. But when you consider how our poor ancient lizard brain lives in mortal fear of change, you'll see why most of us run into big trouble when we try to manifest what we want. Our inborn fear of change gets in the way. It creates serious internal resistance and makes it so what we want is also what we don't want. Whether we realize it or not, the lizard brain is endlessly resisting change even as we consciously go after all that we desire with all our heart.

This fear of change and resistance to change can show up in different ways and in all aspects of life. We might find ourselves procrastinating about completing an important project that could establish our reputation as an expert, even though we long to be recognized for our work. We might push full steam ahead toward a lifelong dream with no regard for our health, so we're drained, depleted, and burned out long before we get to the finish line. We might find ourselves breaking up with a string of partners before we have a chance to fall in love even though we want to find our soulmate. We might chase after a second or third business idea before we've even had the chance to follow through on the first, so we're caught in an endless cycle of chasing after the next shiny object despite our cherished dream of taking our business to new heights. The truth is that fear of change keeps us stuck in place in life, and it keeps us stuck in place when it comes to manifesting our desires.

I'm grateful and happy to say that these days, my fear of change and resistance to change rarely gets the better of me. I've learned to move through life guided by the voice of my intuition, which keeps me focused and moving toward my True North so I can successfully manifest my True Desires. But before I became skilled at tuning into my Authentic Self (using the tools I shared in chapter 3), there was a different inner voice that ran the show. It would wear me out with seemingly helpful, practical advice that consistently threw me off the path leading straight to my dreams, like the time I almost pushed away an amazing flow of abundance in my business.

## How Fear Can Block the Manifesting Process

A few years ago, one of the True Desires on my list went something like this: attract and work with a high-paying dream client on a consistent basis. I patiently applied some of the Magical Manifesting Ingredients in this book, specifically tapping into practical magic (chapter 6) plus working with my Manifesting Avatar (chapter 7), and I was beyond delighted when my persistence paid off a lot sooner than I'd expected. Within a few weeks, I found myself talking to a potential long-term, high-paying client who could help to propel my annual business revenue to exciting new heights. This client was a perfect fit. She was kind, considerate, and an incredibly talented healer who was doing a lot of good in the world. In other words, she was the dream client I had been hoping to attract.

When she sent an email saying she'd absolutely love to work with me, I was over the moon. Here was an opportunity to support a talented client whose work I had admired from afar for years. Plus, I was grateful she hadn't flinched when I mentioned my fees during our call (despite the nervous tremor in my voice). I remember thinking, "I'm on my way to achieving one of my biggest dreams. Pop open the champagne!"

Unfortunately, my celebratory mood didn't last very long, because the annoying but familiar voice inside my head—the one that I would later recognize as the voice of fear—began to do its thing. It was the voice that represented other people's ideas, expectations, and beliefs of what I could and could not do. "Are you sure your fees are okay?" questioned the voice. "You charged way too much. Maybe you should offer her a surprise bonus to make up for it? She's paying you a lot after all! You could throw in extras like free editing services or additional articles and marketing material!" The voice simply would not stop offering advice, and soon it started to turn ugly. "Is your writing any good? You're not ready to work with a client at this level. Are you sure you're not being greedy charging this much? You're not going to be able to deliver what you promised. It could be the end of your business!"

The voice went on and on, and I found myself wondering if I should just go ahead and tell my new client that I wouldn't be able to work with her after all just to get it to be quiet. But when I viewed my situation from a practical perspective, I knew the voice was wrong. I had steadily built a great reputation based on a proven track record of writing high-converting sales and marketing copy for million-dollar online campaigns. I knew I was charging rates that were well within the accepted range in my industry, and I knew I could deliver high-quality work. So why was this annoying voice going on a rampage in my head?

I didn't know the answer at the time, but I do now. I was afraid to earn more than I'd ever imagined I could. Up to that point, feeling anxious, uncertain, worried, and overcome by self-doubt around my work and my business was an uncomfortable but familiar way of being, and anything that was different, anything that felt like a shift in the status quo—even when it was for the better—felt scary and even threatening to me. Somewhere deep inside, my lizard brain was on high alert, screaming, "Stop this madness! Don't change anything! Go back to the way things were!"

I'm glad to say that I didn't end up offering a discount or adding crazy bonuses and extras to the original agreement with my dream client. The first online campaign I wrote went on to become a record-breaker, with over $100,000 in sales in two weeks. My client was so happy that she paid me a bonus, extended my contract, and recommended my services to other successful entrepreneurs in her mastermind group.

Despite all this, every month when her payment appeared in my bank account, I felt a twinge of discomfort and anxiety rather than joy and ease, and like clockwork, the inner voice piped up: "Sure, she's happy with your work now, but you'll screw up next month for sure and she's gonna fire you. It's only a matter of time." It took many months to get to a place where it felt good to charge and receive what felt like ultrahigh fees for my work. Now I'm finally in a place where I can manifest large amounts of money and other positive changes while feeling only gratitude and satisfaction. A big reason for this is because I discovered how to alchemize fear of change, starting with the first step: recognizing the difference between Helpful Fear and Harmful Fear.

## The Difference between Helpful Fear and Harmful Fear

A friendly warning: I'm about to make a bold statement, and you might find it a little hard to believe. Ready? Okay, here we go: All limiting thoughts, blocks, and beliefs, including negative, restrictive belief structures we unconsciously adopt from external sources, such as our family or cultural, racial, or gender-based influences, can be traced back to just one fear, and you can probably guess what it is by now. Yep, I'm talking about the fear of change. But before we label it Manifesting Enemy #1, there's something you need to know: even though a fear of change can hold us back from attracting what we want, it can also be our best friend when we are in serious danger.

Imagine this: It's early in the morning and you're walking down the street on your way to get your daily latte fix around the corner. There's hardly any traffic and you glance left and right before crossing the street. Suddenly and seemingly out of nowhere, you catch sight of a big red bus. It's hurtling toward you at top speed. You don't have time to think, but your legs seem to have a mind of their own. You manage to leap out of the way with seconds to spare, and you have a great story to tell your favorite barista when you get to the coffee shop a few minutes later, flustered but safe. Now imagine if the same thing happened but you had a brain that required time to think for a few minutes before it could get your legs to jump out of the way. That wouldn't be good for you at all. What we want is a brain that detects a shift in the environment on a quiet street—like the sudden appearance of a big red bus—and gets us to safety in an instant.

So it's great when our fear of change keeps us safe, but we also need to know how to consciously release this fear when it blocks the manifesting process. I know that might sound kind of complicated, but it's not. We can manifest what we want without fear of change getting in our way when we can accurately tell the difference between Helpful Fear of Change and Harmful Fear of Change. (For easy reference, I'll go ahead and refer to these as simply Helpful Fear and Harmful Fear from this point on.)

Helpful Fear compels you to take protective or defensive action, like with the big red bus. This means if you're awakened in the middle of the night by the sound of someone smashing a window in the living room, you might reach for the phone to call the police or climb out the bathroom window to get help. If your neighbor's big, angry dog chases you down the street, Helpful Fear gets your body to pump adrenaline so you can successfully outrun the dog, even if you ordinarily have a hard time outrunning a snail (like I do!).

You might have heard stories of a mom getting in an accident and then single-handedly lifting the car to save her trapped child or a son saving his dad's life by lifting a truck after it topples off a jack during a tire change. I used to think these were urban legends, but it turns out there's documented evidence of real people performing these miraculous feats. This is the astonishing power of Helpful Fear in action. It decreases the sensation of pain, triggers focused action, and can even give you superhuman strength. Helpful Fear is the magical fuel that gets you excited and inspired to manifest those big, scary goals and dreams.

Then we have Harmful Fear, which keeps you from getting where you want to go in life. It lives in your mind and yet somehow feels like a serious physical threat, and it gets you to do one of two things: take unfocused, misdirected, meaningless action, like staying up late to binge-watch an entire series instead of preparing for a big presentation you have coming up the next day, or take no action at all. Harmful Fear is what you feel when you think about standing in front of a crowd to deliver a speech. It's the fear you feel when you contemplate asking that special someone out on a date for the first time. Harmful Fear makes us believe that all the things we long to manifest, our deepest desires, goals, and dreams, are somehow unsafe, or that our big, bold visions of a bright, beautiful future might hurt us in some way.

Remember our old friend the lizard brain? Well, it can't tell the difference between Helpful Fear and Harmful Fear. All it knows how to do is detect any kind of change and then sound an alarm that translates to that pit in our stomach or that clutching sensation around our heart—it's that dreadful feeling that says there's a deadly attack heading straight toward us and it's just around the corner. "Danger!!!" screams the lizard brain. "Run for your life! Hide! Don't take that risk. Don't try anything new. Stay in your comfort zone!"

So let's get something straight: When it comes to keeping you safe by keeping you scared, your lizard brain is way ahead of your cognitive, thinking mind (the part of your brain that's reading this sentence). But you can overcome that natural, ingrained impulse to flee at the first sign of change by learning how to accurately identify Helpful Fear, which can motivate laser focus and inspire persistent, powerful action, versus restrictive Harmful Fear, which keeps you from manifesting your True Desires.

Here's a handy guide to help you tell the difference between the two types of fear.

### Helpful Fear versus Harmful Fear: How to Tell the Difference
#### Helpful Fear Is...

+ *Focused:* It motivates you to take focused, direct action.
+ *Silent:* Your mind is quiet and clear.
+ *Emotionally painless:* You don't experience uncomfortable emotions such as anxiety, worry, or doubt.
+ *Present:* Your body, mind, and soul are in the here and now in the face of an identifiable threat to your safety or the safety of others around you. This threat is in your immediate environment or vicinity.

+ *Energizing:* You feel highly energized and physically activated. You're ready for anything.

**Harmful Fear Is ...**

+ *Random:* It motivates you to take unintended, random action or no action at all.

+ *Noisy:* Your mind is noisy and agitated. There's a lot of thinking going on, and you'll consider multiple what-if scenarios.

+ *Emotionally painful:* You feel one or multiple uncomfortable emotions like shame, guilt, frustration, anger, and more.

+ *Future-based:* There is no immediate identifiable threat to your safety or the safety of anyone around you. This perceived threat lives in your mind.

+ *Deflating:* It's a huge energy drain. You feel unmotivated and deflated.

# Hiding in Plain Sight

Developing the ability to differentiate between Harmful Fear and Helpful Fear is the first big step toward alchemizing fear of change to manifest our True Desires. The next step is knowing that Harmful Fear is a master of disguise and hides in plain sight. The truth is that Harmful Fear could be in your heart and mind right now and it could be restricting your ability to create what you want, but it doesn't feel like fear, so it has you fooled.

Next we'll look at emotions, situations, and thoughts that could be Harmful Fear in disguise, trying to keep you stay safe by inhibiting change and your ability to successfully manifest what you want.

### Harmful Fear in Disguise #1: You're Perpetually Bored

You start your manifesting journey in a state of high motivation and enthusiasm, but sooner or later you lose that early excitement and everything starts to feel like a drag. You might catch a glimpse of the vision board you tacked up on your bedroom wall at the start of the year and feel nothing. You stop chanting affirmations because you're yawning too hard. When you think about practicing your manifesting activities, you realize you'd rather be doing almost anything else. It's like you've fallen out of love with your manifesting goals and all that's left is boredom. But there's something else at play.

Harmful Fear loves to hide behind disinterest and boredom, especially when your desires and dreams feel like they're way outside your comfort zone. The Universe requires focused attention and consistency to give you what you want. Boredom keeps you restless, agitated, and disconnected from your Authentic Self. It's an effective way to keep you from fully committing to anything. This way, you get to stay safe from the seemingly dangerous changes that will become your new reality when you successfully manifest your desires.

### Harmful Fear in Disguise #2: You're Trying Too Hard

Picture this: You have a massive manifesting goal and you're doing *all* the things to bring it into your reality. You're reading a ton of books on manifesting (including this one), and you've enrolled in an online course and maybe even hired a manifesting coach. Bringing your True Desires into your reality is all you think about, dream about, and take action on. Your partner and your family and friends can see you're pushing yourself way too hard, and they bring this to your attention. You instantly brush them off, telling yourself, "They just don't understand." Meanwhile, you're bone-tired and you're secretly wondering if you can keep up this pace.

The Universe ignores the energy of pushing or striving. When we're in hustle mode, we're out of alignment with our Authentic Self and we've fallen out of step with the Universe. It seems counterintuitive, but doing all the things to manifest could be a sign that Harmful Fear is standing between you and the beautiful changes you want to invite into your life. So let's remember this simple truth at all times: trying too hard to manifest what we want is the same as not manifesting at all.

### Harmful Fear in Disguise #3: You Seem to Have Endless Patience

They say patience is a virtue, and we do want to practice patience as we allow the Universe to deliver our desires. But patience can quickly turn into procrastination that keeps us from taking inspired action. If you find yourself regularly saying things like "It will happen in Divine Time" or "It will take however long it takes," it's probably because Harmful Fear is trying to stop you from changing your life.

Patience in manifesting is about planting the creative seeds of your desires, receiving clarity around what you want, and following through on the next step that feels aligned and good to you. Procrastination is about avoiding what you need to do to support the manifesting process. It's ignoring the intuitive nudge that tells you to reach out to a potential client you know could change the game in your business or putting off creating your personal profile on an online dating site even though you have "Living My Dream Life with My Soulmate" plastered in large, glittery letters on your vision board. Here's how you can tell the difference between patience and procrastination: Patience is when you've planted the seeds of manifesting and you're waiting on external elements, like the Universe or other people, to help move things forward. Procrastination is when other people or factors are waiting on you to make the next move.

### Harmful Fear in Disguise #4: You're Overcome by Jealousy or Envy

Jealousy arises when we feel that if someone else has what we want—such as a romantic relationship that's straight out of the movies, big money that keeps getting bigger, flawless skin, or a gorgeous home—then somehow we can't have the same. This is the scarcity mindset at play, and where there is scarcity, duality rules. When we see the world through the lens of right or wrong, black or white, or yes or no, it's an all-or-nothing game and there are only winners and losers. But this is simply not true. We have full access to the unlimited creative energy of the Universe, and when we manifest as who we truly are, our desires will become our reality no matter how many other people seem to be living the dream life we desire.

### Harmful Fear in Disguise #5: You Achieve All of Your Manifesting Goals in Record Time

For you, manifesting is easy-breezy lemon squeezy, and you hit every single goal and dream on your vision board or your True Desires list without batting an eyelash. This must mean you're an A-list manifesting maven and the Universe is at your beck and call, so it's time to relax and pat yourself on the back, right? Not just yet! If you find yourself achieving every single thing you desire at top speed and with very little effort or no effort at all, it could be that you're unknowingly short-changing yourself.

Too many well-meaning manifestors set their sights way too low when it comes to their goals and desires. They focus on manifesting an empty parking spot at a crowded mall or a sunny sky on a weekend. I'm certainly not saying these aren't wonderful things to bring into your life, but when all you ever want to manifest is a friendly smile from your friendly neighbor who smiles at you every day anyway, it's a strong sign that Harmful Fear has reared its ugly head. You see, easy-to-achieve dreams and desires let you manifest what you want without rocking the boat. It means Harmful Fear has successfully kept you from experiencing major changes in your life that bring the inevitable risk of temporary roadblocks such as rejection or disappointment.

## Harmful Fear in Disguise #6: You Feel Compelled to Go for Big, Scary Goals

This is the opposite of achieving your manifesting goals in record time. When you feel compelled to go for big, scary goals that leave you feeling frozen and overwhelmed or for a larger-than-life vision that feels so out of reach that it instantly triggers anxiety and stress every time you think about it, you're stirring up inner turmoil that can slow or even totally halt the manifesting process. Once again, this is Harmful Fear keeping you safe by keeping you stuck in place with outrageous dreams that leave you feeling tense and distressed. Yes, it's good to go for bold goals that are a little outside of your comfort zone, but when your desires create major doubt and serious anxiety, it means Harmful Fear is in the house keeping you running in place.

## Harmful Fear in Disguise #7: You're Constantly in a State of Overwhelm

Ah, overwhelm! It's the silent scourge of twenty-first-century living, and it can sneak into your manifesting process without making a sound. If you love going for massive manifesting goals but end up giving up because it feels like you can't get it all done, then beware, my dear ambitious manifestor. This is Harmful Fear holding you in a state of overwhelm so you'll never have to change your life and operate at a higher level when your desires finally appear in your reality. Overwhelm gives you permission to stop doing the work that will get you where you want to go, and it makes you believe that playing small keeps you safe.

### Harmful Fear in Disguise #8: You're Hiding behind Spirituality

Spiritual bypassing happens when a spiritual lifestyle or esoteric practices are used to escape from the reality of our lived experience. Psychologist and psychospiritual guide Robert Augustus Masters, who wrote the classic, celebrated book *Spiritual Bypassing: When Spirituality Disconnects Us from What Really Matters*, defines it this way in the introduction to his book: "Spiritual bypassing is the use of spiritual beliefs to avoid dealing with painful feelings, unresolved wounds, and developmental needs."

Spiritual bypassing is a widely experienced phenomenon, and it offers a justification for those who identify as being highly spiritual but secretly want to sidestep good, old-fashioned hard work or any kind of challenging experience that might help them grow, develop, and become better in favor of what they believe are far more enlightened activities, like meditation. I've often found that spiritual bypassing is really Harmful Fear in disguise, keeping you from experiencing difficult emotions or bravely confronting hard-to-face realities that might signal the need for big changes and transformations in your life.

### Harmful Fear in Disguise #9: You're Suffering from Prince Charming Syndrome

Classic fairy tales like *Cinderella*, *Sleeping Beauty*, and *Snow White* have one thing in common: a handsome Prince Charming who saves the main character from a wicked stepfamily, an evil fairy, and a vicious Queen, in that order. I call this Prince Charming Syndrome, where we wait for someone else or something outside of ourselves to rescue us.

You know you're suffering from Prince Charming Syndrome when you're in a holding mode and your life is on pause while you find yourself constantly torn between blame and shame. Maybe you blame your parents for everything that's not going right in your life. Maybe you're ashamed of where you live, the car you drive, or something else. But despite feeling unhappy with your current circumstances, you don't take action or commit to the manifesting process so you can create the changes you want to see in your life. If this sounds familiar, you can bet Harmful Fear is lurking behind the scenes, holding you back from getting what you want. It keeps you in limbo, waiting for an external problem, challenge, or obstacle to be resolved or someone in your life to be different from who they are before you can move forward.

If you recognize Harmful Fear in your life, don't worry, because we're about to do something about it right now. In the next section, you'll learn to alchemize Harmful Fear with the Bridge of Safety. This is a huge, life-enhancing step toward feeling comfortable, protected, and relaxed so you can be naturally attuned to the high-vibrational energies of the Universe as you take consistent action to joyfully attract your True Desires.

## Layering Safety in the Body and Mind

The Bridge of Safety will help you alchemize fear by generating safety from within. You'll learn to do this by bringing in the awareness and experience of safety on two levels: in the mind and the body. We'll start by creating a strong foundation of safety in the mind using a tool called Fear into Gold, then we'll flow into embodying safety by anchoring effortless presence in the here and now using the Relaxed Protection tool. You can do these exercises every time you feel Harmful Fear come up or any time you like. You'll find that layering safety in both the mind and the body can bring an instant feeling of relaxation and a soothing sense of peace and harmony to your inner world so you can navigate the outer world with ease. You'll also find that you can effortlessly open up to the unlimited creative energies of the Universe when you do this practice regularly. Over time, it will become increasingly easier to slide into an inner state of tranquility, positive expectations, and possibilities, even when life feels chaotic or unsteady.

There are two parts to the Building a Bridge of Safety exercise. The first part, which involves the Fear into Gold tool, is about tuning into your intuition and working with the energy of curiosity. You'll use a simple question to allow the energy of curiosity to flow as you follow through with the wisdom you receive from your intuition. The second part, which is the Relaxed Protection tool, is about giving yourself permission to fully sense what's going on in your body in a way that allows difficult experiences to be fully processed and released.

Each of the two parts of the Building a Bridge of Safety exercise can be done on its own, but for best results and to layer deep safety in your energy system, it's good to do both. Start with the Fear into Gold tool and follow with the Relaxed Protection tool. Read through both parts of the Building a Bridge of Safety exercise so you have a clear idea of what to do ahead of time. If it's a lot to remember (and I think it is), you can find this exercise recorded for you as part of the free gift bundle that you can sign up to download at www.shantinirajah.com/manifest. Alternatively, consider recording the exercise in your own voice. You could easily do this on your smartphone, computer, or tablet.

### Building a Bridge of Safety, Part 1: The Fear into Gold Tool
STEP #1: TUNE INTO ONE
Close your eyes and allow the sounds around you to enter the forefront of your consciousness. You might hear the rustling of leaves outside your window or the sound of passing trucks and cars. Maybe you can hear the gentle whir of a fan. Choose just *one* sound and laser in on it. This will help you start to feel calmer even when you're in the midst of experiencing fear (or any other difficult emotion).

STEP #2: TAKE 1 HEALING BREATH OF WONDERMENT
Be open to inviting the energy of curiosity into your experience. Let yourself feel like a child who sees a gorgeous rainbow stretch across the sky for

the first time. Immerse yourself in a sense of wonder by taking an In-the-Moment Edition of 1 Healing Breath of Wonderment. You can also choose any other energy that helps to bring you to a place of curiosity. (If you'd like a little help with tuning into the energy of wonderment, simply take a moment to gaze at the image of 1 Healing Breath of Wonderment, along with other 1 Healing Breath images, that are part of a collection that you can sign up to download for free at www.shantinirajah.com/manifest.)

## STEP #3: ASK

Now you're ready to ask, "What is my [insert the emotion you're feeling] trying to tell me?" If you're feeling fearful, your question would be "What is my fear trying to tell me?" If you're feeling anxious, your question would be "What is my anxiety trying to tell me?"

## STEP #4: HONOR

Wait for the answer to your question to arise through your intuition. Depending on your primary intuitive channel, you might hear "take a break for a few minutes" or experience a feeling that you need to step outside and take a walk. You might receive a vision that you need to jump up and move or dance. You might receive specific instructions, like "journal what you're thinking" or simply "sit." Honor and follow through on whatever comes up for you. If nothing comes through, that's okay too. Just move on to the next step.

## STEP #5: REST

Take 1 Healing Breath of Wonderment once again and allow yourself to rest quietly. When you're ready, rate your level of calm on a scale of one to ten. How stressed do you feel (with ten as the highest level) and how much personal control do you feel (with ten as total control)? Aim for at least four or five for stress and seven or eight for personal control. If not, please repeat steps 1 through 4 again.

That's it. That's the Fear into Gold tool. As you continue using this tool, you'll find that it takes just a couple of minutes to do, which is great, especially when you'd like to feel calmer and more centered as quickly as possible.

We're halfway through the Building a Bridge of Safety practice. Now that you've tapped into a sense of safety in the mind, you're ready to flow into experiencing it in the body.

### *Building a Bridge of Safety, Part 2: The Relaxed Protection Tool*
STEP #1: FEEL PROTECTED

Choose to sit or lie down in a quiet place, preferably with a wall or something solid behind you.

STEP #2: TAKE 1 HEALING BREATH OF HARMONY

Take an In-the-Moment Edition of 1 Healing Breath of Harmony. You can also choose any energy that helps you to feel comfortable and protected. (If you need help tuning into this energy, feel free to gaze at the image of 1 Healing Breath of Harmony, which is a part of the free gift bundle that you can sign up to download at www.shantinirajah.com/manifest.)

STEP #3: FULLY EXPERIENCE YOUR BODY

Bring your attention to the strongest, most stable part of your body. This could be your seat on the chair, your feet on the ground, or your back against the chair or wall. Next, it's time to sense what's going on in your physical body. Bring your attention to your feet, your back, or your seat, depending on which part of the body you feel is the most stable. What do you sense? What do you experience? Tune into the physical sensation. Maybe your feet feel hot and prickly or your back feels relaxed and strong. Whatever it is, note this feeling. If your mind wanders, gently bring your attention back to the part of the body you were focusing on. You might find that you need to do this again and again as your mind strays every few seconds, but that's totally natural and perfectly okay.

STEP #4: GIVE YOUR BODY PERMISSION

Allow yourself to experience the sensations that come up, knowing you are in a safe, protected space. Sit with this experience until you can feel your body start to relax. You might notice your breath and your heartbeat start to slow a little. You might begin to yawn or experience tremors and shakes. Some people feel their skin start to itch. Let your body do what it needs to. This is absolutely normal, and these are signs that your unconscious lizard brain and nervous system are entering a state of equilibrium. Stay with these physical responses and sensations until they subside and disappear.

*Special note:* If you feel extreme fear, anxiety, or pain rise up, it could be a sign that you have intense emotions and trauma stuck in the body. If this is you, stop the exercise immediately and take 1 Healing Breath of Harmony, Peace, Calm, or Serenity. (You can sign up to download a special collection of these images for free at www.shantinirajah.com/manifest.) Come back to this exercise at another time. If intense emotions continue to be part of your experience, consider consulting a somatic therapist or kinesiologist to help you feel safe while experiencing sensations in your body.

## Easy-to-Do Techniques to Alchemize Fear

The Bridge of Safety is an extraordinarily powerful method to layer safety in the body and mind and alchemize and release Harmful Fear at the same time, but I've found that it's not always convenient to implement this practice. (Can you imagine trying to find a space where you feel comfortable and protected when you're at work or on the subway?) So it's good to have access to other quick, effective techniques you can turn to any time you want to release Harmful Fear. Here are five techniques that work beautifully and that I absolutely love.

### *The Heart on Hand Trace*

The Heart on Hand Trace is an alternative breath technique I developed alongside the 1 Healing Breath practice. Just like 1 Healing Breath, it involves a shorter inhale and a longer exhale, which calms the parasympathetic nervous system, but this technique does not require the inner perception and awareness you need in order to visualize, sense, or feel into a specific energy. This makes the Heart on Hand Trace perfect for those times when you're in a meeting at work or in a noisy restaurant and it's hard to focus.

Start by breathing in as you trace the top left of the universal heart shape on the palm of your hand. Then breathe out as you approach the point at the bottom. Repeat on the other side, starting at the top again. Breathe in as you trace the top right of the heart shape on your palm, and breathe out as you trace all the way down to the point. Repeat until your fear, anxiety, or worry loosens its grip and you start to feel yourself relax. Do this as often as you like.

## Invite Awe and Wonder

Remember what it felt like to catch sight of the ocean for the first time or gaze at a range of mountains that seemed to rise all the way to the top of the world, and that beautiful blend of bliss, astonishment, reverence, and gratitude you experienced? That's awe and wonder, which have the power to neutralize fear in an instant. It's why I'd like you to consciously invite these spectacular emotions into your day as often as you can. It might be something as simple as stepping outside on a bright starlit night, opening your arms wide, and looking up at the vastness of the cosmos, or it might be watching world-class surfers take on a hundred-foot wave (and win) on YouTube. I love turning to a book for inspiration, and one of my favorites is Andrea Scher's delightful *Wonder Seeker: 52 Ways to Wake Up Your Creativity and Find Your Joy*. It's overflowing with fun ideas on how to step out of your everyday routine and experience the magic that's all around.

## Orange You Glad You're Happy?

I learned this little trick from my dad, and it's guaranteed to deliver an instant boost of fear-dissolving delight. Grab an orange, a lime, a grapefruit, or any kind of citrus fruit. Lightly scratch the surface and take a big inhale. The fresh, revitalizing scent will instantly give you a boost of joy. Bonus benefit: doing this can help decrease uneasiness in the stomach and even chase away nausea.

### Give Yourself the Side-Eye

This super simple exercise from Stanley Rosenberg's incredibly in-depth book *Accessing the Healing Power of the Vagus Nerve: Self-Help Exercises for Anxiety, Depression, Trauma, and Autism* can help to dissolve fear and soothe your nervous system. First, lie on the floor, sofa, or bed, and bend your knees so you have your feet flat on the ground. Next, cradle your head in your hands, with your fingers interlaced. Move just your eyes to the right, making sure that your head is still. Hold for ten to thirty seconds. Then do the same on the left side. This exercise might not sound like it will work to reduce fear or anxiety, but try it and you'll be surprised at just how effective it is.

### Energy Medicine

Energy medicine is a noninvasive, incredibly empowering results-driven path to calming and healing yourself on the mental, emotional, and physical levels using your body's energies, and there's no one better at teaching this than Donna Eden, the pioneer of energy medicine and founder of the Eden Method. Whether you're experiencing fear, anxiety, doubt, worry, or something else, there is an energy medicine technique that can take care of it for you. You can discover incredibly simple yet effective energy medicine tools on her YouTube channel (called "Donna Eden Energy Medicine") or in one of her best-selling books (my favorite is *Energy Medicine for Women*).

# Manifest Now:
# Get in the Habit of Performing Fear Checks

Throughout this chapter, we discovered that manifesting is about bringing the intangible into the tangible through the process of change and how layering safety in the body and mind and releasing your inborn fear of change can exponentially boost your ability to manifest what you want. Now that you know how to generate safety within yourself, you're ready to perform regular Fear Checks.

Start with the list of five to seven True Desires you created back in chapter 3 (page 64). Look at the first True Desire on your list (or if you have it written down in a physical notebook, place your finger on the first True

Desire). Now refer to the guide earlier in this chapter to recognize Harmful Fear (page 105). Do this for each of the True Desires on your list, one by one. If you can detect Harmful Fear around any of your True Desires, use the Building a Bridge of Safety exercise or any of the five easy-to-do techniques in the previous section to alchemize fear and release it. Repeat this until you reach the end of each of the True Desires on your list.

I'd also like to invite you to consistently perform Fear Checks on yourself throughout your day. You can do this by setting an alarm so it goes off every hour, or you can leave little sticky notes where you'll see them as reminders. When it's time to do a Fear Check, stop and take 1 Healing Breath of any energy you like. Then place both hands over your heart, bring your attention to your inner world, and check in with yourself. See if you can detect any of the identifying signs of Harmful Fear using the guide on page 105. If your answer is yes, then do the Building a Bridge of Safety exercise, the Heart on Hand Trace, or any of the other techniques you learned. When you're in the habit of constantly releasing Harmful Fear, you will quickly rewire your brain, your nervous system, and your entire energy system to release the grip of Harmful Fear and raise your baseline vibration to higher frequencies such as happiness, abundance, love and freedom for joyful, effortless manifesting.

Six

# Magical Manifesting Ingredient #4: Tap into Practical Magic

One of the first manifesting formulas I ever worked with also happens to be one of the simplest, and it's the one most of us know by heart: ask, allow, receive. When I first discovered this formula, I couldn't believe my luck. I remember thinking, "What? Is that all it takes to manifest what I want? I got this!" But just like every other manifesting method I tried, the formula stopped working when I applied it on some of my bigger manifesting goals, whether that happened to be large piles of cash, a trip around the world, or a stronger animal rights policy in my home country.

Fortunately, I kept meticulous notes at that time, and when I read through my journals, the biggest sticking point—the part that kept me from manifesting some of the bigger things—became crystal clear. I kept getting stuck at the "allow" step, which was shocking to me. Up until that point, I believed allow was the easiest step of all. What could be simpler than letting the Universe bring me my desires? But it turned out to be much more difficult than I could have imagined. Even worse, I soon realized that most manifesting methods had some version of allow inextricably intertwined with the core manifesting process.

Some teachers called it surrendering, and others called it letting go, releasing, trusting the process, or handing over to the Universe. But whatever they called it, the message was the same: step aside, trust in the Universe, and release control. It's a wonderful approach, but I simply couldn't do it, no matter how hard I tried. I was worried I'd never advance to higher levels of magic and manifesting if I had no idea how to tackle one of the most basic and foundational practices of all.

But I wasn't ready to give up on my newfound manifesting adventures just yet, so I did what I always do when I get stuck: I immersed myself in researching the living daylights out of the topic. I read entire books about allowing. I watched YouTube videos. I even enrolled in a couple of online programs that were all about allowing. Although I significantly improved my intellectual grasp of the concept, I still could not master the experience of it. My only consolation was that I knew I wasn't alone. When I talked to clients, friends, and fellow manifestors I connected with online, I found that most of them shared my uncomfortable relationship with "allow."

## Doing the Hustle

Most of us don't realize it, but we're card-carrying members of hustle culture. From the classroom to the boardroom to the Zoom room, we push ourselves to achieve, achieve, and achieve some more. Whether it's getting good grades, sculpting great abs, snagging that promotion, or signing on a fantastic client, we understand what it means to work hard in order to get what we want. We've been told that hustling is the price of success and it's the only reliable way to build a safe, financially secure, respectable life. So we hunker down like we're in for the fight of our lives, and we proceed to do more and try harder until we get to our goals. It's why so many of us are confused and even repelled by the idea of manifesting our desires by not doing more, not trying hard, and releasing control.

When I first began partnering with the Universe to create my dream life, the concept of releasing, surrendering, letting go, and allowing was so alien to me that I had no idea what to make of it. I don't know how long I would have continued struggling with all of it if I hadn't received an intuitive hit that came to me through a half-forgotten memory. I realized that I already knew how to allow because it was just like the time I learned how to float in a pool.

If you know how to swim or if you've taken lessons, you know that every single swim technique has to do with moving your body and breathing a specific way. But the lesson on how to float is totally different. Floating gracefully involves not doing anything. It's about not trying to stay afloat, and in this way the water supports you naturally. Learning to float was a huge challenge for me because my mind did not want to believe the water would hold me up. I was convinced—despite countless assurances from my swim instructor— that I would instantly sink to the bottom of the pool and tragically drown in the middle of my lesson. I had to fight the urge to yell "leave me alone!" at my long-suffering instructor before dramatically getting out of the pool, never to return. It didn't feel safe to release control and let the water support my body weight, but I'm so glad I persevered, because when I finally got there, magic happened. I floated with so much ease that it felt effortless and I felt totally free. It was this memory of floating with effortless ease that led me to stumble on the solution to my problem with the "allow" step in manifesting: I had to find a way to feel good, a way to feel safe, in order to release control so the Universe could work its magic and support me.

In the rest of this chapter, I'll share a comprehensive approach I developed to integrate "allow" into your manifesting journey in a way that feels relaxing, safe, and soothing to your body, mind, and spirit. I call this approach Conscious Liberation, and it's a path that lets us accelerate the manifesting process by opening our hearts to the unlimited magic of the Universe without feeling like we're unsafe and losing control. The Conscious Liberation method does not ask for blind faith or an unshakeable belief in anything that seems unknowable (such as the Universe, a Higher Power, or your own courage). Instead, we'll come home to ourselves and cast an anchor in calm waters using our breath as a loving, comforting guide.

Later, we'll dive into an extended practice called the Light of Empowered Serenity, which invites Conscious Liberation into your energy system so you can become a master manifestor with the power to create the experiences and situations you desire just by being who you are. But first, here's a fun Zen fable that teaches why slowing down is a vital element to speeding up the manifesting process.

## The Tenacious Protégé

There was a young martial arts disciple who was by far the most hardworking and naturally skilled student his teacher had ever seen. Driven by total dedication to his craft and a burning ambition to be the best, the gifted student worked longer and harder than all of the other students combined, often practicing every move again and again, long into the night.

One day the student decided that he was ready to join the advanced class and it was time to leapfrog ahead of everyone else in the beginner group. So he went to his teacher and said earnestly, "Teacher, as you know, I am devoted to studying your martial arts method. How long will it take me to master it?"

The teacher gazed at his tenacious protégé and replied with a hint of nonchalance, "Ten years."

The student was taken aback. He thought for a moment, his face taking on a determined expression. "But I want to master it faster than that. I will work very hard. I will practice every day, ten or more hours a day if I have to. How long will it take then?"

The teacher paused, thought for a moment, and said in all seriousness, "Twenty years."

There are many interpretations of this Zen fable, but the one I love the most is this: rapid advancement is often about slowing down, and if you push too hard, you'll wind up inhibiting your progress. Growth and development need time and space to happen, and manifesting works the same way. The harder we try and the more we strive, the greater the struggle and the longer it takes to receive what we want.

It's why the element of allowing, in order to create space and time for the magic of the Universe to take effect, is a key part of most manifesting processes. It's also why spiritual teachers and gurus from just about every culture and lineage encourage us to surrender or let go, and most of us have an intuitive sense of what that means. Letting go and surrendering are about releasing that which no longer serves you, and this could be limiting thoughts and beliefs, painful memories, or difficult emotions. Unfortunately, most explanations of this practice end there. We may be drawn to the concept and even feel excited about the idea of surrendering to the Universe, but most of us have no clue how to apply it in a way that is practical and doable. That's where Conscious Liberation comes in.

## Experiencing Conscious Liberation

Conscious Liberation is a graceful and actively empowering approach that anyone can adopt when they are ready to open up to the magic of the Universe. This includes those who believe hard work is the only way to achieve anything worthwhile or anyone who thinks surrendering, letting go, and allowing are just fancy spiritual terms for quitting (I used to be one of these people not so long ago!). The truth is the greater your desire, the bigger your goal, and the crazier your dream, the more skilled you must be in letting the energy of Conscious Liberation flow through you. To do this effectively, you need two key elements:

1. **Loving Acceptance:** Giving the Universe permission to create on your behalf in a way that feels safe and comforting
2. **Radical Receiving:** Letting yourself receive so that magical manifestations can come into your life

Let's look at each of these elements one by one, and then I'll share the Empowered Serenity practice. You will learn to use this method to experience Conscious Liberation on every level of your being—body, mind, and spirit—so you can start to feel safe as you naturally release, let go, surrender, and allow the Universe to bring you your True Desire.

## Loving Acceptance

Allowing the Universe to create on your behalf and bring you what you want involves a complex emotion most of us have a lot of trouble tapping into: unconditional trust. The Universe rewards those who can tune into unconditional trust, which is why it's well worth the time and effort it takes to intentionally cultivate and call up this all-important emotion in our hearts. Trusting the Universe without question creates an energetic space for all manner of magic and miracles to come into play, and it's the invisible accelerant that speeds up the manifesting process so you can start to see extraordinary results sooner rather than later.

Unconditional trust in the Universe begins with making peace with what is in order to create space for what wants to be. It's about being okay with what's happening in your life right now, with Loving Acceptance. But most people get caught up in a tangle of inner resistance around accepting where they are in their life or what they're experiencing in the moment, and it's totally understandable. After all, who wants to accept that they're stuck at a job they hate or that they're single and alone when all they want is to live happily ever after with the love of their life? In the world of manifesting, catchphrases like "Energy flows where your attention goes" are misinterpreted to mean that we must turn away from everything we don't want or don't like in our life and in the world or we'll somehow attract all of it into our experience.

While it's certainly not a good idea to focus endlessly on what's going wrong rather than what's going right, steadfastly turning away from what we don't want or like does nothing to make it go away. Instead, ignoring a difficult situation or painful emotion preserves its existence and strengthens its intensity. Pretending everything is okay when it's really not is rooted in the energy of resistance (this is essentially toxic positivity, which we explored in chapter 4). The energy of resistance to reality is disastrous in the journey to creating the life you want because you simply cannot get to where you want to go when you have no idea where you are now. Imagine you want to get to Bangkok in Thailand, but you don't want to see, acknowledge, or accept that you are currently in Hong Kong, which is about 2,000 kilometers (or about 1,200 miles) away and across the South China Sea. Instead, you get in your car and drive down a random road, hoping you'll eventually arrive in Bangkok. Spoiler alert: it's not going to work!

There is an unfortunate misunderstanding about Loving Acceptance where we believe that when we accept what is, we're telling the Universe that we love what's going on or that we want the situation or experience to continue. You are by no means encouraging an unwanted situation or experience by fully accepting it. In fact, the opposite is true. Loving acceptance works like a powerful energetic force that sends a message to the Universe that we clearly see and acknowledge where we are right now and we are ready for sparkling new experiences. When you accept where you are now, you are essentially saying to the Universe that you are ready for the bigger, better, more beautiful reality that you desire.

In Conscious Liberation, the practice of Loving Acceptance is about releasing all that has happened in the past and embracing all that is happening now just as it is. It's about doing what needs to be done without resisting what's real and true for you in the moment. It's the secret elixir that gives the Universe permission to step in and give you something better than you imagined. Let's explore this concept with an example.

Imagine you found your dream home and you're all set to buy it, but the seller has a change of heart at the last minute and decides to keep the house. Does this mean the Universe has left you out in the cold because you're a bad manifestor? Of course not! It's simply an opportunity to transform the situation by practicing the Loving Acceptance of Conscious Liberation so you can let yourself feel what you feel in the moment, whether that's sadness, disappointment, frustration, or something else.

Loving acceptance that the house you had your heart set on has slipped through your fingers will set you free to experience the lightness of relief from resistance. It lets you feel what you truly feel—such as disappointment, rejection, or anger—and safely process your emotions so you can start to entertain the idea that something even more wonderful is just around the corner. It lets you step into the energy of expectant excitement, knowing the Universe is about to bring you something even better, like a home that's far more beautiful than you envisioned, more perfectly suited to your family's needs, and at a price point that leaves you feeling like you struck the deal of a lifetime.

Giving the Universe permission to create with Loving Acceptance means you're giving yourself permission to release painfully stringent expectations of what you want so you can experience the lightness of relief and the breathing room you need to expand into possibility and receive something even better. As I like to say, the Universe always has a much bigger dream for you than you do for yourself, and I've seen this unfold again and again.

When I practiced Loving Acceptance after a failed friendship, I found a kindred spirit who is now one of my dearest friends. When I practiced Loving Acceptance that I did not snag what I believed was a dream job at the time, I attracted work opportunities from around the world and kick-started a wildly successful online business. It's why Loving Acceptance is a big part of our journey here. It lets you make peace with the reality of where you are now while staying inspired and motivated during the hidden manifesting process that leads to an extraordinary new reality, one that might be even better than you can envision.

That's the power of Loving Acceptance in Conscious Liberation. It lets you overcome painful stuck emotions that block your manifesting journey so you can enjoy the freedom of directing your intention and energy in a way that lets you have the life you want. The following practice is a quick, efficient way to enter a state of Loving Acceptance. Turn to this practice whenever you feel disappointed, doubtful, frustrated, or unhappy that it's taking way too long to get what you want or like the Universe has somehow failed to deliver and things aren't going your way.

### The Playful Puppy Practice for Loving Acceptance

Find a quiet space where you can let your emotions move within you and through you. The idea is to sit with your feelings like you would sit and watch a playfully overactive puppy. Know that just like a puppy will run out of energy and eventually curl up and fall asleep, your emotions will do the same. Begin by observing what you feel and naming it to yourself. You might be annoyed, frustrated, or disappointed. Take note of this, and when you've identified how you feel, you're ready to take 1 Healing Breath of Ease, either the In-the-Moment Edition or the Expanded Edition. (If you're having trouble tuning into this energy, gaze at the image of 1 Healing Breath of Ease, which is included in the free gift bundle that you can sign up to download at www.shantinirajah.com/manifest.)

As you take your 1 Healing Breath, say a simple, heartfelt mantra. I like this one: "I know this situation/experience/emotion is here for now, and I accept it with love. I know something wonderful is just around the corner, and I'm ready to invite it in." You'll find that the Playful Puppy Practice is remarkably effective in releasing stressful, painful emotional energy, and it creates spacious breathing room so you can gently shift into Loving Acceptance.

## Radical Receiving

The second element of Conscious Liberation is Radical Receiving. This is an incredibly magnetic energetic force and one that is welcomed and rewarded by the Universe. Letting yourself receive what wants to come to you and helping yourself feel safe to receive is one of the greatest things you can do to amplify your manifesting skills. When you consistently practice Radical Receiving, you will create a synergistic virtuous cycle that continues to grow and expand. To put it another way, the more you receive, the more you'll get to receive.

Unfortunately, in cultures and societies that value independence and self-reliance, receiving can feel uncomfortable and stressful. Those of us who are taught to get things done on our own and without bothering other people feel awkward when it's time to receive help, support, love, kindness, or any kind of gift. This is a huge block in the manifesting process, and it totally makes sense when you think about it. You can't possibly experience your desires—whether it's your soulmate; a flow of ideal clients in your business; youthful, radiant health; a joyful, peaceful, loving family life; or a world that is kinder and more inclusive—if you can't find a way to receive these beautiful creations with open arms and an open heart.

Plus, when we do not practice our inborn right to receive, we can inadvertently interrupt the flow of energies that sustain the delicate balance of our personal energy system. All things in nature exist in this balance. Where there is winter, there is summer; where there is starlight, there is sunlight; and where there is giving, there must be receiving. When we give without receiving, we are disrupting this beautiful, natural balance, which leads to serious energetic blocks that can obstruct the delightful, juicy experiences, situations, people, and things we are looking to draw into our lives.

One of the symptoms that we have an energetic block around receiving is when we're *this* close to manifesting what we want but then something happens at the last minute to keep it from our grasp. For instance, you've been dreaming of meeting your favorite rock band and you manifest a backstage pass in an online contest, but the day arrives and you're down with the worst flu you've ever had in your life (this actually happened to a friend). If you're seeing things like this unfold in your manifesting journey, it's time to double down on practicing the art of Radical Receiving. The good news is there are lots of opportunities to invite this energy into your day-to-day life, and it's as simple as looking for opportunities to practice receiving with grace and gratitude.

Receive compliments and gifts—even big or expensive ones that might make you feel uncomfortable—with a simple thank-you from the heart and 1 Healing Breath of Gratitude, Delight, or any other energy that expresses appreciation and feels aligned for you (you can use the In-the-Moment Edition of 1 Healing Breath, which takes just a few seconds). You'll find that when you receive with 1 Healing Breath, there is little room left for resistance, which often shows up as guilt, discomfort, doubt, and unease. Instead, you'll call in wonderful high-vibrational emotions like joy, gratitude, or delight, and in this way, you are dissolving resistance and essentially telling the Universe, "Yes, please, and I'd love more of this."

When someone offers to help you or gives you a gift, do your best to avoid saying things like, "Oh, that's okay. I can do this on my own," or "You shouldn't have," or "It's too expensive." Not only is this likely to disappoint and frustrate the person who was kind enough to think of you and your needs, but the Universe hears you saying, "No, thanks. I don't want to receive. Don't give me anything." This is definitely not the signal we want to send out to our all-powerful manifesting ally!

Instead, look for reasons, excuses, and opportunities to receive from the heart with 1 Healing Breath and a "Thank you so much!" or an enthusiastic and grateful "Yes! I'd love your help!" Try it and you'll see how this internal shift in your approach and attitude toward receiving can open the floodgates so the desires of your heart become a permanent part of your reality.

The following practice can help you implement Radical Receiving so it feels soothing, calming, and safe. Soon you'll be able to receive gifts, compliments, favors, and offers for help and support from strangers, friends, and family, and from the Universe too, with gratitude, grace, ease, and a big, happy "yes, please!" This is an all-day practice, which means you'll continue doing this throughout the day. If you're feeling particularly ambitious or inspired or you find that you're truly enjoying yourself with Radical Receiving, don't stop after just one day. Go ahead and extend this practice over two or three days or even a week or more.

### The Radical Receiving Practice

It's good to begin this practice first thing in the morning, but you can start at any time during the day. We'll open with an intentional devotion, or, as I like to call it, the Radical Receiving Mantra. Place both hands over your heart, one hand on top of the other, to bring your attention and focus to your heart. Close your eyes and say the mantra to yourself (or out loud):

### Radical Receiving Mantra

*I am ready to receive all that is good and true and aligned for me.*
*It is safe for me to receive all that is good and true and aligned for me.*
*I am ready to receive my desires and my dreams.*
*It is safe for me to receive my desires and dreams.*
*I am ready to receive love and support.*
*It is safe for me to receive love and support.*

When you're done, go about your day knowing this intention is now in your heart. Repeat the Radical Receiving Mantra as many times as you wish, and stay open to receiving compliments, gifts, offers for help, time, attention, and love from those who want to give. When a friend, your partner, or your mom says, "So what do you want for dinner?" receive their kind offer to let you choose and give them an honest answer. Don't say, "Let's have whatever you want!" which is what I used to do all the time.

When you come across a chance to receive, take it with a smile, a thank-you, and an In-the-Moment 1 Healing Breath of your choice that feels aligned or relevant to you, such as 1 Healing Breath of Joy, Pleasure, or Excitement. I personally love to practice Radical Receiving with 1 Healing Breath of Grace. (If you need help tuning into these energies, refer to the corresponding image for each of these energies in the special collection that you can sign up to download for free at www.shantinirajah.com/manifest.) You can also choose any energy that feels good to you or let yourself be drawn to an energy that feels good in the moment.

At the end of the day, write or record an audio about the wonderful Radical Receiving experiences you enjoyed all day, so you can look back at your list and reconnect to the flow of Radical Receiving with a rush of high-vibrational energies. Creating a list is also great for times when you forgot to take your 1 Healing Breath when you received the favor, compliment, or gift or when you were looking to tune into 1 Healing Breath energy using a corresponding image but couldn't for some reason. If this happens, you can take your 1 Healing Breath when you record your Radical Receiving experiences at the end of the day.

Be patient with this practice. Radical Receiving can feel super strange, at least at the start. When you've practiced giving a lot, it can take a while to get to a place where you feel good receiving. But don't give up. As with any muscle, keep using your receiving muscle and you'll build it up to the point where it starts to feel as good as giving, and that's when you'll know receiving is now a part of your natural way of being.

Now that you understand the energy of Conscious Liberation and how it can help you give the Universe permission to create on your behalf through Loving Acceptance and Radical Receiving, you are ready to discover the power of the Light of Empowered Serenity. This is one of the most incredibly high-vibrational energetic methodologies in this book and one of the central practices in our journey together.

## Tuning into the Light of Empowered Serenity

The Light of Empowered Serenity is about intensifying and applying Conscious Liberation in a powerful way, and it involves creating a beautiful, high-vibrational energetic experience on every level of your being. The Light of Empowered Serenity is an inspiring, uplifting methodology that calls in the pure light of our soul through mantras and mudras that have been used for this purpose in Hinduism and in the cultures and traditions of India since ancient times. We'll also be working with guided visualization and meditation to take this practice even deeper.

You'll find that the Light of Empowered Serenity opens you up to making aligned choices as who you truly are and in a way that strengthens your connection and communication with your Authentic Self and with the Universe. When you begin to invite this Light into your life, it becomes possible to allow the Universe to step in and bring you what you want without feeling like you're losing control or losing your right to be the captain of your ship and the master of your destiny. You'll be able to maintain personal, intentional control over your life while gracefully letting the Universe guide you forward in your manifesting journey.

This practice essentially seeds Conscious Liberation so that it can flourish and expand at the soul level and you are continuously immersed in the energies of Loving Acceptance and Radical Receiving.

## What Is the Light of Empowered Serenity?

I like to think of the Light of Empowered Serenity practice as a beckoning of sorts, as an encouraging, loving summons back to who you are, so you can become a masterful manifestor by tuning into the light within. This methodology includes combinations of meditation, mantras, and mudras that can help you guide yourself toward empowering traits such as emotional strength and inner peace, trust, and confidence. In this way, you will learn to release the all-too-common need to control every little detail of the manifesting experience and naturally align with the energy of Conscious Liberation. Ultimately, you will be able to allow the Universe to step in and accelerate the manifesting process as you receive your desires with ease, flow, and grace without feeling like you have to quit, give up control, or otherwise let go or surrender control in ways that don't feel safe to you.

While I'm fairly certain that you're at least familiar with the concept of meditation, and you might also be familiar with mantras and mudras, I'd like to offer my definition of each one so we can begin with a clear understanding of the three elements that make up the Light of Empowered Serenity.

## Meditation

Meditation is the art of focusing our mental energy to light up our inner world. It is about bringing self-awareness to what's going on inside—to the inner experiences, emotions, and constant, never-ending chatter in our minds. Meditation helps us gently focus our attention on ourselves without becoming immersed in our thoughts and feelings. This is so we can arrive at a place of inner tranquility and equanimity and so we can build internal resilience that allows us to remain calm in the midst of external challenges or even chaos.

## Mantra

The word *mantra* is a combination of two words in Sanskrit, which is the ancient language of India. *Manas* means mind and *tra* means tool, so a mantra is a "tool of the mind" that can be used to direct, focus, activate, and calm the mind. I think of mantras as a vibrational meditation of sorts. It's a meditation that integrates the incredible energy of sound. Mantras evoke the infinite transformational power of words spoken with intention, which also happens to be the basis of chanting in tribal rituals and in prayers, affirmations, spells, and other word-based spiritual and magical techniques that have been practiced to great effect for centuries.

## Mudra

A *mudra* is a symbolic hand gesture that channels our body's natural *prana*, or energy. Mudras are used extensively in yoga and in traditional Indian dance and art. Mudras are like energetic invitations that are used to welcome and fulfill specific intentions. There are mudras to elevate your physical energy, boost your confidence, inspire creativity, and just about anything else you can think of.

## The Light of Empowered Serenity Practice

The guided meditation, mantra, and mudra that are the core practices of the Light of Empowered Serenity are designed to stand alone or be threaded together into a cohesive practice that imbues your personal energetic field with the energy of light. This is so Conscious Liberation can become a lived experience and a part of who you are in every moment. Every time you practice, you are training your mind, body, and spirit to embody the two key elements of Conscious Liberation—Loving Acceptance and Radical Receiving—as a natural state of being.

There are two versions of the Light of Empowered Serenity practice that you can work with: the Short and Sweet version and the Deep and Delightful version. I recommend that you do the Short and Sweet version daily and the Deep and Delightful version once a month until you notice that allowing and surrendering through Conscious Liberation, and the energies of Loving Acceptance and Radical Receiving, starts to feel easy, natural, and resistance-free. Let's take a closer look at each of the two versions.

## The Light of Empowered Serenity: Short and Sweet Version

The Short and Sweet version of the Light of Empowered Serenity includes a mantra and a mudra that can be combined and done one after another for a slightly longer practice, or, if you have just a few minutes to spare, choose either the mantra or the mudra. First, let's take a look at the Mantra of Light, which is a quick, powerful invocation in Sanskrit that invites the energy of light, freedom, and Conscious Liberation into your heart and your life. You can say this mantra at any time during the day and as often as you wish. Keep in mind that the more you chant this mantra, the more you will raise your personal frequency, including your mood, emotional and mental vibration, and overall sense of wellbeing. One of my dearest friends in the world, Elysia Hartzell, is also one of the most gifted teachers and healers I know, as well as the founder of the incredible Sacred Soul Alignment healing modality. Elysia has said that chanting mantras throughout the day is a wonderful way to practice letting go of overwhelm, doubt, worry, and fear, and I couldn't agree more! When your mind is alight with sacred words, there is no room left for invasive, troublesome thoughts to rock the boat.

### Short and Sweet Version: The Mantra of Light

The Mantra of Light comes from the Upanishads, the ancient philosophical yogic texts from India that were composed orally in Sanskrit. This mantra translates to "Lead me from the untruth to truth / Lead me from darkness to light / Lead me from death to immortality / Om peace, peace, peace." It is best to say the words out loud, with conscious intention, but if you're out and about or if you can't say the mantra out loud for any reason, say it in your mind and hold the intention for light and freedom to enter your heart. Say the Mantra of Light at least three times each time you practice.

## The Mantra of Light

*Asatao ma sadgamaya*

*Tamaso ma jyotir gamaya*

*Mrityorma amritam gamaya*

*Om shanti shanti shanti*

*Please note:* If you're uncertain about how to pronounce these words, you can listen to a free audio recording of the Mantra of Light. It's a part of the gift bundle that you can sign up to download at www.shantinirajah.com /manifest.

### Short and Sweet Version: Invite the Light Mudra

The Mudra of Light is traditionally known as the Garuda Mudra or Eagle Mudra (see illustration). If you look closely, you will notice that this mudra symbolizes the wings of a bird. The Garuda Mudra elevates your personal energy while inviting the bright, soaring light energies of freedom and independence that allow you to open your heart and trust in yourself and the Universe as you begin embodying the energy of Conscious Liberation.

### The Garuda Mudra (Mudra of Light)

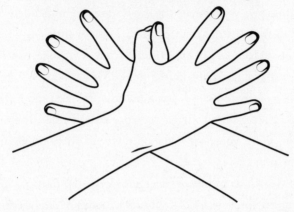

Breathe deeply and hold your hands in the position of the Garuda Mudra for at least one minute. Try to spread your fingers as wide as is comfortable. You can use the Garuda Mudra at any time during your day, and it is especially helpful at times when you're struggling with low energy or feeling blue. Breathe slowly and deeply with the intention of calling in light, freedom, and independence as you hold this mudra.

## The Light of Empowered Serenity: Deep and Delightful Version

The Conscious Liberation approach can greatly speed up the process of manifesting your desires, and it can be hugely and delightfully calming, soothing, and inspiring at the same time. If you're drawn to dive even deeper into the Light of Empowered Serenity practice to intensify the energy of Conscious Liberation in your life, the Deep and Delightful version was made for you!

You'll see that this longer version includes a powerful guided meditation that integrates both the Mantra of Light and the Garuda Mudra from the Short and Sweet version you just learned. You'll also find a calming candle ritual that you can add to your practice. Switch the candle ritual and the meditation around if you want to. In other words, you can start with the guided meditation and end with the candle ritual or do it the other way around. It works beautifully both ways, so it's totally up to you.

## Inviting the Light

Before you immerse yourself in the Invite the Light Guided Meditation, which I will describe shortly, it's good to know a little bit about what to expect. This meditation is a guided visualization, which means it's perfect for you even if you have never meditated before. There is no need to hold still for long periods of time. Instead, you'll find that this is a soothing and pleasant healing journey. Allow yourself to experience it fully. There is no right or wrong here, and if you can't visualize anything, that's totally fine—it still works. Just relax and listen.

There are two kinds of healing energies integrated into this guided meditation. The first is the energy of 1 Healing Breath of Illumination to open up deep self-awareness. (If you feel like you need some help connecting with the energy of illumination during this meditation, I recommend that you take a look at the image of 1 Healing Breath of Illumination, which is part of a special collection of images that you can sign up to download for free at www.shantinirajah.com/manifest.) Gaze at the image just before you begin, so you can easily tune in without interrupting the flow of your meditation experience.

I'm a certified practitioner of the Sacred Soul Alignment energy healing modality, which was brought through by master healer, mentor, teacher, and my dear friend Elysia Hartzell. The Sacred Soul Alignment modality consists of hundreds of healing energy packets or alignments that can quickly link your personal vibration and frequency to universal frequencies to unlock positive energetic states such as abundance, peace, joy, happiness, health, love, compassion, and more. For the Invite the Light guided meditation you're about to experience, I've chosen three Sacred Soul Alignments: Awaken True Happiness, Free at Last, and Diamond Light. Here's a quick snapshot of what each alignment means and what it can do for you.

### Sacred Soul Alignment #1: Awaken True Happiness

True happiness feels like freedom. We are free to be ourselves and to love and be with who we want. We are free from the need or desire to blame others. True happiness is independent of other people's beliefs and desires, and this releases us from having our personal happiness influenced or restricted in any way by others. When we are happy, we are able to make decisions from the heart and to live from the heart.

The Awaken True Happiness Sacred Soul Alignment will activate the emotions of joy, satisfaction, and fulfillment, as it eliminates the beliefs, thoughtforms, oaths, vows, and contracts that stand in the way of true and lasting happiness. This alignment also releases blame and the need or desire to have someone or something to blame.

### Sacred Soul Alignment #2: Free at Last

We can be held in an invisible prison that is made up of many things: the past; our own beliefs and emotions such as anger, guilt, and shame; outdated oaths, vows, and contracts; and hooks and cords to people or places that are not serving us. Being in this energetic prison causes us to stay stuck where we are, even if we have big dreams and desires that we want to bring forth into reality.

The Free at Last Sacred Soul Alignment will free you from what is holding you prisoner. It will give you the Creator's understanding of true freedom on every level, and it will help you to live in this energy of freedom so you can move forward and create the reality that you desire.

### Sacred Soul Alignment #3: Diamond Light

Diamonds symbolize luxury, beauty, and strength. They are considered to be the hardest substance in the world and also one of the most beautiful. This is a rare and amazing combination that represents an important truth: we can exude strength and beauty in all its forms, including kindness, love, gentleness, understanding, and compassion.

The Diamond Light Sacred Soul Alignment will bring in the incredibly high-energy vibration of the pure diamond, including the knowledge that you are precious and deserve the best of everything that life has to offer. This alignment also activates your cells and DNA with the full power of Diamond Light vibration.

In addition to the 1 Healing Breath of Illumination and the three Sacred Soul Alignments, the Invite the Light Guided Meditation integrates both the Mantra of Light and the Mudra of Light from the Short and Sweet version of the Light of Empowered Serenity practice. Before you begin this guided journey, I recommend that you try to sit with your spine straight to allow the prana, or energy, to easily move up and down your system. If it feels comfortable, you can assume the lotus position, or Padmasana, which is the traditional cross-legged meditation and yoga pose. Sit on the floor, a yoga mat, or a meditation cushion. If this feels awkward or if there is discomfort of any kind, feel free to sit on a chair with your feet flat on the ground. You can also lie completely flat on a couch or bed (minus a pillow). A guided recording of this meditation is available for free as part of a gift bundle that you can sign up to download at www.shantinirajah.com/manifest. Alternatively, you can record yourself saying the words and then listen and follow along.

### Invite the Light Guided Meditation

Begin by holding your hands in the position of the Garuda Mudra (page 135). Now say the following words out loud or to yourself.

*I invite freedom and serenity into my heart and into my life.*

Hold the mudra as you breathe in for a count of 6 and breathe out for a count of 6. Breathe in, 2, 3, 4, 5, 6, and breathe out, 2, 3, 4, 5, 6. Relax your hands and let them lie naturally in your lap or at your side. Bring your attention to your heart chakra, in the center of your chest.

Take 1 Healing Breath of Illumination. Intentionally open up to the energy of illumination and say to yourself, "I invite the energy of illumination." Let the world fall away as you allow illumination to rise up and meet you where you are. Feel like you're floating on an ocean of illumination. Inhale the energy of illumination and exhale the energy of illumination.

Next, bring your attention to the space between your brows, and relax that space. Now bring your attention to the corners of your eyes, and relax them. Next, bring your attention to the corners of your mouth and your jaw-line. Relax the muscles in your face. Move down to your neck and shoulders. Allow the muscles in your neck to relax and then let your shoulders relax. Let them feel heavy and drop downward.

Now bring your attention to your arms, and relax your upper arms and your lower arms. Next, focus on your wrists, your hands, and your fingers. Then bring your attention to your torso and your hips. Allow yourself to relax in these areas. Now your thigh muscles and legs, your knees, calves, ankles, and your feet and your toes. Relax your legs. Feel the ground beneath your feet, and if you're sitting in a lotus position or lying flat, feel the support of the cushion, yoga mat, bed, or couch beneath you. Feel yourself connected, stable, and strong as your energy anchors into the earth.

It is time to call in the healing energies of the three Sacred Soul Align-ments: Awaken True Happiness, Free at Last, and Diamond Light. Set the intention to receive these energies as you say quietly to yourself, "I'm ready to Awaken True Happiness, be Free at Last, and embody Diamond Light." Sit quietly for a moment as you allow these energies to work their magic.

Now you're ready to enter the Light of Empowered Serenity. In your inner vision, slowly look up above your head and see clouds floating by against a bril-liant blue sky. Then look straight ahead and see a stretch of golden sand spar-kling in the sun. Look down and see fine golden sand under your feet. It feels warm and you feel the delicate, tiny grains. In your mind's eye, you look up and look beyond the stretch of sand and catch sight of the ocean, and you realize that it's a vast, luminous, translucent ocean that's made of pure Light.

The Ocean of Light is magical, and it stretches out as far as you can see. You are mesmerized by this gentle Ocean of Light, and you watch as the waves ebb and flow and ebb and flow. You watch as wave upon wave of pure light rolls continuously onto shore. You notice sparkles of gold and aquamarine blue on the surface of the Ocean of Light, and you feel your heart fill with grace and gratitude. As you continue to gaze at the Ocean of Light, you feel yourself becoming lighter and lighter and lighter as you start to rise up above the ground.

Soon, you're lighter than air and you're floating gently up among the clouds. You feel expansive and elevated. You feel loved and protected, safe and free to be you. As you float among the clouds, you look around and see the Light of Unconditional Love, the Light of Source Energy, the Light of Your Authentic Self, and the Light of the Universe, and you can see what that looks like. You catch a beautiful scent, and you know it's the scent of this Light. You reach out your hand and touch the Light, and you feel its texture. Now you can feel the Light moving gently throughout your entire being. You are filled with this Light. Immerse yourself in this magnificent Light and feel it light up every aspect of your being. This is the Light of Your Authentic Self. It is the Light of Healing, Truth, Wisdom, Unconditional Love, Awareness, the Light of Infinite Abundance, the Light of Source Energy, the Light of I AM Energy. It is the Light of Empowered Serenity.

Breathe in this Light. You are an infinite being who can do, be, and have anything and everything you desire. Feel the energy of this Light flow through your entire body as you release all that has come before. Letting go, letting go, letting go. You are embracing who you are and you are loving who you are fully and freely. Now it's time to say the Mantra of Light (from page 134). You can say it quietly to yourself or out loud:

## The Mantra of Light

*Asatao ma sadgamaya*
*Tamaso ma jyotir gamaya*
*Mrityorma amritam gamaya*
*Om shanti shanti shanti*

(Remember, if you're uncertain about how to pronounce these words, you can listen to a free audio recording of the Mantra of Light. It's a part of the gift bundle that you can sign up to download at www.shantinirajah.com /manifest.)

You feel quiet in your heart, mind, and soul—quieter and more silent than ever before. You feel peace, tranquility, serenity. You feel empowered. You begin to feel yourself floating back down to the earth—back to the ground, back to your body—and you can feel the ground beneath your feet or feel the couch, chair, or bed supporting you. Feel yourself anchored back in your heart and in your body. You feel strong, serene, at peace. Now open your eyes.

Know that this meditation is here to guide you to reclaim your Light and to recognize Light within yourself so you can open up to Conscious Liberation, gently release the need to control every single thing, and allow the Universe to work on your behalf. You can do this visualization any time you wish. I recommend doing it at least once a week for at least four weeks and then once a month.

## Creating Light

You can strengthen and intensify your heart-opening experience of the Invite the Light Guided Meditation in the previous section with the Invoking the Light Candle Ritual. This is a simple, potent ritual that involves lighting a ceremonial candle and reciting a devotional declaration to call in the Light that gives you the calm and serenity you need to fully embody the energy of Conscious Liberation.

It's important that you work in a quiet space where you will not be disturbed for a few minutes. If you're inspired to go deeper into relaxation mode and bring in high-vibrational, sacred ceremonial energies, arrange some of your favorite crystals around the candle and light some incense or use an aroma diffuser with a single relaxing pure essential oil, such as lavender, sandalwood, bergamot, or rose. You can perform this ritual before or after your Invite the Light Guided Meditation experience.

The act of lighting a match is a traditional symbolic gesture of creating light, so try to use an old-school match—not a modern lighter—for this ritual, and choose a large, unscented candle. Please be careful when lighting the candle and make sure there are no flammable items around. You can work with a candle in a color that is associated with a specific intention.

Here's a list of the meanings behind some of the more popular candle colors.

+ *White:* Purity, peace
+ *Black:* Protection, banishing negative energy
+ *Red:* Strength, passion, good luck
+ *Pink:* Romantic love, friendship, healing
+ *Green:* Abundance, fertility, growth
+ *Yellow:* Clarity, confidence, action
+ *Orange:* Joy, energy, vitality
+ *Purple:* Wisdom, sacred knowledge, influence
+ *Blue:* Calm, creativity, communication
+ *Gold:* Abundance, wealth, spiritual evolution
+ *Silver:* Goddess energy, psychic development

You can go to www.shantinirajah.com/manifest to sign up to download an audio recording of the Invoking the Light Candle Ritual as part of your free gift bundle, and then listen to the recording as you do the ritual. If you prefer, you can simply say the words out loud as you light your candle.

### Invoking the Light Candle Ritual
Place your candle in front of you on a heatproof surface. You can be standing or sitting down. Light the candle and say the Invocation to the Light Devotional Declaration out loud:

## Invocation to the Light Devotional Declaration
*As I light this candle, I call in*
*The Light…*
*The Light of Healing*
*The Light of Truth*

*The Light of Wisdom*
*The Light of Unconditional Love*
*The Light of Awareness*
*The Light of My Soul*
*The Light of Infinite Abundance*
*The Light of I Am*
*The Light of Empowered Serenity*
*This is the Collective of Light Energies that is my Sacred Inner Light.*
*Allow me to trust this Light within.*
*The Light that holds me close and never lets me go.*
*The Light that lifts me up and shows me the way.*
*This is the Light that illuminates my path and my purpose.*
*The Light to which I devote my heart focus and mind focus.*
*May this Light flow through me and bless my entire being.*
*May I recognize this Light in myself and may I see it in all beings.*
*May this Light show me who I truly am and allow me to know in*
    *every fiber of my being that I am Empowered Serenity, I am Healing,*
    *I am Truth, I am Wisdom, I am Love,*
*I am Awareness, I am Soul, I am Infinite Abundance, I Am that I Am…*
*Light loves and protects me at all times.*
*I come from Light and I will return to Light.*
*I am eternal and I am Light itself,*
*And that which is the Divine Light in me sees the Divine Light in All.*
*It is so. It is so. It is so.*

You now have everything you need to connect with the beautiful, freeing energy of Conscious Liberation. When you practice these rituals consistently, you'll find that you will begin to dissolve resistance and blocks to allowing and receiving and you will gently recalibrate your entire energy system to safely open up and surrender to unlimited cosmic support and magic from the Universe. In time, you no longer will simply perform the act of manifesting but instead will become a masterful manifestor just by being who you are.

## Manifest Now! Let the Universe Talk to You

Embodying Conscious Liberation with the Light of Empowered Serenity can accelerate the manifesting process, and sometimes you'll see the results of doing this almost immediately. Often, you'll notice that what you want to attract will come to you months or even years before you expected. For instance, manifesting this book and creating a successful and abundant online business happened for me years before I imagined it would. Another simple, powerful way to speed up the manifesting process is to look for signs that your desires are about to enter your reality. Your natural excitement and inspiration, which are high-vibrational energies, will propel the process forward.

If you've been practicing various manifesting techniques for some time, you might already know how to recognize signs from the Universe, such as seeing repetitive numbers or angel numbers like 111 or 22. It's good to ask for signs that your desire is on its way. A client asked to see a butterfly as a sign that her desire to become a mom was close at hand, and soon after she saw not just one butterfly but hundreds of them everywhere—she was suddenly surrounded by butterflies! She saw butterflies in the middle of the city and in her mom's garden. She saw butterfly logos and designs on mugs and T-shirts, on a friend's new living room wallpaper, and on someone's shoulder as body art. She had a beautiful baby boy the next year, and she's loving every minute of being a mom.

Feeling a deep sense of peace and clarity is also a good sign that what you want is just around the corner. Another interesting sign is when you notice *others* receiving what you've been asking for. This means your desire is beginning to enter your energetic space. It's important to support their wins with gratitude and love, as this signals to the Universe that you are ready to receive the same.

You can also connect to the energy of the Universe by choosing a sensory experience of your manifestation and then allowing your body to tell you if you're about to receive your desires. For instance, maybe you want a new car. Tune into that fabulous new car smell. See the car you desire in your mind's eye if you wish. Feel the touch of brand-new, sparkling paint. What does the experience of driving a new car feel like in your body and in your emotions? Are you filled with excited anticipation? Alternatively, do your body and your breath start to feel tight and restricted? Maybe a new idea pops into your head, like "do research on car prices." This is the Universe talking to you through your intuition and your Authentic Self, letting you know the next steps and that you are on the right track in attracting what you want.

I encourage you to apply this exercise to your list of True Desires from chapter 3 (page 64). Choose each of the three to five True Desires you listed and use any one of these methods to discover if what you want is around the corner. You can ask for a sign, notice if you're seeing angel numbers, identify if you feel peaceful and clear when you think about your True Desire, or connect with the Universe by experiencing your True Desire through your body as you stay open to receiving messages and intuitive nudges. If you find yourself feeling stressed, resistant, fearful, anxious, or worried when you think about your True Desire, it means there is still work to do around alchemizing Harmful Fear. In that case, it's good to do the Building a Bridge of Safety exercise (page 112) or one of the five easy-to-do techniques to alchemize fear (page 115) that we explored in chapter 5.

# Phase IV
# Embody the Magic

In this fourth phase of our manifesting journey, you'll learn how to embody the unlimited magic and creative power of the Universe using Magical Manifesting Ingredient #5: Craft Your Manifesting Avatar. Your Manifesting Avatar will accelerate the energetic process of change so you can quickly start seeing the results you're looking for from your manifesting practices. You'll also discover how to use Magical Manifesting Ingredient #6: Utilize the Power of Joyful Play to immerse yourself in the energy of play, so you can heighten your manifesting skills and fully enjoy every moment of your journey as you speed toward the bright, beautiful future you've been dreaming of!

*Seven*

# Magical Manifesting Ingredient #5: Craft Your Manifesting Avatar

One of my favorite spiritual teachers and authors, Louise Hay, says in her classic book *You Can Heal Your Life*, "The point of power is always in the present moment." Louise is absolutely right, and when I'm filled with doubt and worry about the future, her wise words rise up to greet me like a warm sliver of sunshine on a cold, windy day. Being in the now, which we experience as a deep sense of presence, is a crucial element in our journey to manifest anything we want.

So far we've learned that we need presence when we want to connect with our Authentic Self and the voice of our intuition (Magical Manifesting Ingredient #1), we need it when we're growing the Garden of Self-Love to elevate our vibe (Magical Manifesting Ingredient #2), it's a vital factor in building a Bridge of Safety to alchemize fear (Magical Manifesting Ingredient #3), and it allows us to tap into practical magic with the power of Conscious Liberation to supercharge the manifesting process (Magical Manifesting Ingredient #4). But as we move to Magical Manifesting Ingredient #5: Craft Your Manifesting Avatar in this chapter, the notion of presence takes an interesting twist. You see, the act of manifesting happens in the now, created by the current version of who you are, but what you manifest, the result, is received by a future version of you.

As we discovered in chapter 3, your Authentic Self is eternal, because it is the essence and energy of you that has no beginning and will never die. But every other part or aspect of who you are is in a continuous transitional state of transformation based on your intentions, choices, and level of consciousness. Our emotions are always changing and we change our minds, sometimes from moment to moment. The body is also governed by an endless flow of natural change. Blood cells are being created and discarded even as you read this sentence. Our hair and nails never stop growing, and we shed about 30,000 to 40,000 skin cells per minute (yes, we are literally shedding our skin every sixty seconds!).

The current version of you, or the Present Self, will become your Future Self no matter what, so why not take charge of this inevitable transformation? There are a ton of brilliant benefits to doing this. For one thing, the Universe is an unending field of Infinite Possibilities, which means there's the potential for infinite versions of ourselves to come into being. When you take charge of the process of who you are becoming, you get to pick and choose character and personality traits and—believe it or not—even skills and gifts that you don't yet have but would like to possess in the future.

This is because your desire for any trait, gift, or skill is an undeniable sign that it already exists in your energy field, in one of the many infinite possible versions of you in one of the many infinite possible futures that are constantly unfolding and evolving. You will have zero desire for that which is absolutely not for you. For instance, I've never wanted to be the world's fastest runner, and I'm definitely not (but I suspect I just might be the world's slowest runner!). Meanwhile, I've dreamed of becoming an author and writing my book for as long as I can remember, and here I am. It's why discovering your True Desires (which we learned to do back in chapter 3) is crucial, because your success rate in manifesting can and will drop like a stone to the bottom of a lake if you try to manifest anything that is not your True Desire and not within your energy field.

One of the biggest benefits of tapping into the energy of your brilliant Future Self is that it activates and then accelerates the manifesting process of your True Desires. Connecting with your Future Self lets you call in the energies of your delightful, delicious future even before the fruits of your manifesting efforts arrive in your reality, and it is hugely helpful in sustaining high-vibrational emotions in your day-to-day life. It's like you're saying to the Universe, "I'm the version of me that has already received what I want to manifest, so I'm ready to experience the results of my manifesting efforts in the here and now." Lots of authors, teachers, and coaches offer guided meditations to tune into the energy of the Future Self to amplify this message to the Universe. While this is a valid approach, there's a drawback: the Future Self can feel far away and out of reach for most of us, which can add unwanted, often unconscious stress and anxiety to our manifesting journey. It's a big reason why we'll be doing something different and far more accessible.

In this chapter, you'll discover how to intentionally cultivate something I like to call the Manifesting Avatar, which speeds up the energetic process of change so you can start to see your efforts pay off sooner rather than later. Intentionally creating and activating your Manifesting Avatar allows you to shift and change your current energy so you can embody the creative power of the Universe as you align with the energy of your Future Self, who already has everything you want. It's one of the boldest moves we'll be making in this book, and it's also one of the most exciting. But first, let me share a story on how focusing solely on your Future Self can potentially slow down rather than speed up the manifesting process.

## Lila's Rich Life

Lila was a client of mine who wanted to manifest a rich life in every sense of the word. She was excited about creating overflowing abundance in her relationships, her energy, her time, her finances, and her health. She was looking forward to attracting an ever-increasing flow of revenue in her online business so she could dedicate more time and energy to the things she truly loved, including traveling to exotic new locations each year and helping to build animal sanctuaries around the world.

As a life coach and avid practitioner of self-help methodologies, Lila knew she needed to drop outdated stories about who she was allowed to be or what she was allowed to manifest in order to see results. She had successfully identified a major obstacle that stood in her way: deep down, she didn't believe she deserved to live her dreams. She knew she needed to let go of thoughts and beliefs that she was not good enough for the rich life she longed to have.

Not one to shy away from hard work, Lila immediately set about doing everything she could to make this happen. She chanted affirmations all day, and she created multiple digital and physical vision boards and set them up on her devices and all around her house (she even had a mini vision board in her car, tucked away in the glove compartment). She meditated, performed a gratitude practice every morning, and diligently recorded positive intentions and experiences in a manifesting journal. But her favorite tool, by far, was the Future Self technique. Lila had spent an entire year working with Future Self visualizations, and while she could clearly picture her Future Self in her mind, she couldn't quite embody the version of herself that already had everything she desired. This left her feeling frustrated and stressed, which only blocked her ability to manifest with any kind of lasting success.

When I introduced Lila to the Manifesting Avatar approach, she immediately fell in love with the concept of aligning with the energy of her Future Self in the now, and she was excited to try it right away. Within a couple of weeks, Lila began to feel a shift within herself that she'd never experienced before. She began to display some of the traits, skills, and gifts she had visualized in her Future Self, like the courage to speak up and ask for what she wanted and to feel genuinely confident and deeply worthy and deserving of all that she desired. In just a few months, one of her True Desires came to life: Lila hit the highest monthly revenue in her business, which was just over $10,000. And when we talked again a few months after that, things were really starting to take off for her. She was in the midst of making plans to go on safari in Kenya, and she had started to donate a portion of her business revenue to a favorite animal sanctuary in her hometown. This is the most wonderful thing about cultivating a Manifesting Avatar: it's a clear, safe, and accessible path to call in and embody your Future Self in the now and without spending months or even years waiting to see your True Desires enter your reality.

## Collapsing Time and Space

The word *avatar* is used in various contexts today, but when it is roughly translated from the original Sanskrit, it simply means downward or descent. An avatar was believed to be a divine being who descended into our physical, earthly realm to raise the consciousness of humanity and to protect and restore cosmic order. In some spiritual circles, Jesus, Muhammad, the Buddha, and Krishna are believed to be avatars who made the journey down to Earth to teach, support, and uplift humanity.

For our purposes here, the Manifesting Avatar symbolizes the journey of bringing the energy and essence of your Future Self into the physical realm of your Present Self and into your present reality. Cultivating and consistently calling in your Manifesting Avatar lets you collapse time and space so your Future Self can immediately start to assimilate with your Present Self. In this way, you'll begin to experience your day-to-day life as your Future Self. Soon you'll be able to fully live as your Future Self in the now, just like Lila learned to do.

I like to think of the Manifesting Avatar as a safe passageway that allows the Future Self and the Present Self to meet and merge in the middle. It's an extraordinarily effective way to speed up the energetic process of change (I'll talk about this more in the next section) and accelerate the process of transforming into your Future Self. Crafting your Manifesting Avatar will also allow you to uncover incredible traits, gifts, and skills that you never even knew you had, and when you get in the habit of regularly activating your Avatar, you'll find that you can respond to life with intention and with far more grace, flow, and ease.

So how does it all work? Let's imagine that you dream of becoming a world-class motivational speaker and you're looking at ways to share your wisdom with more people. Your business coach feels it would be good to start a podcast to grow your audience. You think this is a wonderful idea, but every time you think about recording your voice, you're overtaken by an overwhelming sense of terror. What if no one listens to your podcast? Or even if they do, what if they think you're boring beyond belief? This leaves you stuck in freeze mode, so you do nothing. Six months go by and then a year. You don't record a single podcast episode and you're nowhere close to becoming a motivational speaker.

This is where crafting a Manifesting Avatar can change the game. When you can connect with your Avatar at a moment's notice, you'll have the power to bring your far-off Future Self—the version of you that is unafraid of being heard by thousands or even millions of people—into your now. And that's not even the best part. By simply designing your Avatar, you are preparing your energy system to receive what you want—even those desires that seem out of reach—in a way that feels relaxing and enjoyable.

Developing your Manifesting Avatar is an exhilarating and exciting approach to creating a life you love. But before we begin, I'd like to shine the light of clarity on exactly what a Manifesting Avatar is and what it most definitely is not. Here's a helpful little guide you can use to quickly understand the difference.

### Your Manifesting Avatar Is Not...

+ Rooted in the energy of fantasy: It's not about dreaming up a persona or creating a false identity. You know you've gone too far when your Manifesting Avatar shoots laser beams out of her eyes, has gigantic purple wings, and fights crime. (I know that's exciting, but that's not what we're doing here!)

+ Confined to a specific time: Your Manifesting Avatar does not recognize the passage of clock time and will not respond to sequential timelines.

+ A version of you that feels inconceivable or fake

+ In opposition to the natural inner essence or energy of your Authentic Self

+ An escape route: Your Manifesting Avatar is not about ignoring the truth of your reality by getting away from the real world.

+ Ethereal or something that exists in the realm of dreams, without the physical sensations of the body

+ Devoid of emotion: Your Manifesting Avatar experiences the entire spectrum of emotions, and it's not just a bundle of happy thoughts and feelings.

+ An amalgamation of skills or gifts you wish you had or believe you need in order to gain praise or validation from others

## Your Manifesting Avatar Is...

+ An aspect of you that can do the things that you never thought would be possible, within the boundaries of the physical world: For instance, you might believe you'll never have the courage to speak onstage to large audiences, but your Manifesting Avatar has what it takes and then some.

+ Fluid and freely able to emerge in the moment when you call upon it

+ A version of you that feels genuine, conceivable to you, and real

+ Always in full alignment with your Authentic Self: Your Manifesting Avatar will never do or say things that are disconnected from your Authentic Self.

+ You, but better! Another way of looking at it is that your Manifesting Avatar is an elevated, enhanced version of who you are.

+ Something that exists in the realm of physical reality, where we can easily connect with our physical senses: Your Manifesting Avatar can touch, taste, see, feel, and smell.

+ Able to feel all that you feel and able to process these emotions and doubts to take action in ways that your current Present Self finds challenging

+ A persona based on traits, skills, or gifts that you already have inside but are unaware of: Some of these amazing attributes may be available to your conscious mind and some may be hidden in your unconscious mind.

Now that you have a clear picture of what a Manifesting Avatar is, it's time to discover how this enhanced version of you can help to speed up your manifesting journey because it includes all aspects of the energetic process of change. Knowing how this process works can help you fully accept and embody your Avatar, which is the ultimate agent of profound and powerful energetic change.

## The Energetic Journey of Change

In chapter 5, we explored our innate fear of change and how our physical brain detects and processes it. Here we'll be looking at change through a different lens. On the energetic level, change happens through the flow of transformation. It begins as an invisible process and unfolds in the visible world: it starts in our invisible inner world of thoughts, feelings, and consciousness before becoming visible in the outer world through our actions and behaviors.

In the world of energy, change involves more than just our tangible physicality; it also includes our energy bodies, or subtle bodies. Most spiritual teachers and texts talk about five to seven subtle bodies or even more. But when it comes to designing and developing the Manifesting Avatar, there are just four subtle bodies we need to get into: the Mental, Spiritual, Emotional, and Physical Bodies. Let's look at each of these one by one.

### Change in the Spiritual Body

The Spiritual Body is essentially the energy of higher consciousness, wisdom, and knowing. It holds the egoless identity of the I AM, where the Authentic Self is united with the Universe. The Spiritual Body brings through ideas, insights, aspirations, and inspirations and is where the desires that align with our soul purpose and mission are born. We can cultivate change at this level through contemplative practices such as meditation. But it's important to know that although change at this level is astonishingly powerful, as it creates soul-level transformations and shifts our entire consciousness, it's also incredibly hard to achieve. When you hear of yogis, masters, gurus, and teachers who experience instantaneous enlightenment, you know they have successfully created deep-lasting change in the Spiritual Body.

### Change in the Mental Body

The Mental Body is the energy of the mind and holds our conscious thoughts. This body is where our belief systems reside and is where we can tap into the powers of imagination and memory. The energy of the Mental Body is incredibly powerful and immersive, which is why we can find ourselves lost in daydreams and fantasies.

We can effect intentional change in the Mental Body a little more easily than in the Spiritual Body, but this is by no means a simple task. The Mental Body contains habitual patterns of thinking, and it is extraordinarily challenging to purposefully create change at this level—if you've ever tried not to think of a pink elephant, you know exactly what I mean! Change in the Mental Body can be identified through a transformation in understanding of concepts and ideologies or a shift in position, opinion, or worldview.

### Change in the Emotional Body

The Emotional Body is the energetic home to the entire spectrum of our feelings and emotions. Our reactions to stimuli from the outside world often begin at this level. Our emotions can change in an instant, which is why for most people, the Emotional Body is wildly active and even a little bit erratic. The Emotional Body is closely tied to the Mental and Physical Bodies, and change at this level is influenced by both, as well as what's going on in the environment around us.

For instance, the Emotional Body is influenced by the Physical Body when we are hugged or held close by a loved one and we feel safe and comforted. When we feel wonder and awe as we watch a glorious sunset, the influence is the environment, and when we feel annoyed thinking back on a time when someone cut us off in traffic, the Mental Body has cast its influence. The Emotional Body shifts easily in response to stimuli but can be incredibly challenging to change through intention. It's why most people feel like emotional mastery is hard to achieve, and we can sometimes feel overcome by our emotions. Change at the level of the Emotional Body can be recognized through a shift in attitude, temperament, or personality.

### Change in the Physical Body

The Physical Body is the energy of our physicality and holds the energies of the body. As you know, the Physical Body is greatly affected by the physical world, and just about everything that happens to the Physical Body is a direct consequence of what's going on around us. The energies of the Physical Body are far slower and denser than those of the Spiritual Body, and creating change at this level can feel a lot easier than at any other level. The downside is that changes made here are usually temporary. The transformations that happen solely in the Physical Body rarely reach the level of the egoless identity of the Spiritual Body, which is why these changes can be transient and fleeting.

## The Incredible Power of the Manifesting Avatar

Lots of personal development and spiritual courses, workshops, and seminars don't work because most of the tools, techniques, and teachings are focused on creating transformation in just one of the four subtle bodies. If you've ever tried meditating for hours every day hoping to experience deep calm and lasting inner peace, but you still feel like you could bite someone's head off if they're rude to you, you know that focusing on just the Spiritual Body doesn't guarantee change. The same is true for the Physical Body. Ever tried sticking to a healthy eating habit for a few weeks, let alone for the rest of your life? Then you know that changing just your actions and behaviors, like working out sixty minutes a day, drinking green juices each morning, and avoiding desserts at all costs, barely makes a dent in your quest to reach the top of the Healthy Eating mountain. It's the same with doing just mindset work on the Mental Body or transforming your emotional landscape with tools and techniques designed to heal the Emotional Body. This is where the Manifesting Avatar is different. This is where it shines.

The Spiritual, Mental, Emotional, and Physical Bodies overlay to create an energy field around us that is sometimes referred to as the auric field or biofield, and your Manifesting Avatar allows you to speed up the ultra-long, arduous process of energetic change by triggering comprehensive transformation on the level of your biofield, where the four subtle bodies mix and mingle. When you work with your Manifesting Avatar, you are in fact creating change through all four subtle bodies at the same time, which is the secret sauce that allows your Future Self to merge with your current Present Self. The magic begins in the design and development stage, which involves integrating your Manifesting Avatar into the energies of the four subtle bodies.

Aside from that, your Manifesting Avatar lets you tune into the future where you already have what you desire. Your desire is a sign that what you want already exists in one of the many infinite possible futures that are constantly unfolding and evolving, and you will have no desire for that which is not for you. This means that if you long to be stronger, braver, calmer, and more confident but you don't feel like you can access any of that, your Manifesting Avatar allows you to connect to the possible future where you are already strong, already brave, already calm and confident (even if you currently believe that you have never felt these things before). Your Avatar can also bring forward gifts and skills that are hidden within you and that you didn't know were there. It is the best version of you, and you can connect with it when you need it the most. This skill is essential in your path to moving beyond the act of manifesting so you can become a masterful manifestor.

Developing your Manifesting Avatar is a profoundly eye-opening experience, and it can be deeply loving, supportive, and healing at the same time. You'll channel and direct the energies of the subtle bodies to step into the most powerful version of you. I promise this is going to be so much fun, because you get to be your best and live from that place no matter who you are, where you come from, or what your story happens to be. All I ask is that you open your heart and mind to fully commit to designing your Manifesting Avatar. Doing this will help you see yourself in a wonderful, uplifting new light as you receive the energies you need to think, act, and make choices in a way that will bring your already manifested future reality into your current everyday life.

## Designing Your Manifesting Avatar

Designing your Manifesting Avatar consists of three stages: Stage #1: The Genesis, Stage #2: The Merge, and Stage #3: Instant Activation. In Stage #1: The Genesis, we'll identify and then assemble powerful, high-vibrational traits, attributes, and energies you want to call in before we move into the ritual aspect of this process in Stage #2: The Merge, which involves an empowering inner journey. In Stage #3: Instant Activation, we'll learn how to bring forward our Manifesting Avatar anywhere and at any time. Through it all, we'll be tuning into the energies of all four subtle bodies—the Spiritual, Mental, Emotional, and Physical Bodies—to invite and encourage lasting change.

Your Manifesting Avatar marks the start of a whole new beginning and is the birth of the version of you that can effortlessly channel the energies of the Universe and carry you forward to your dream future. With this in mind, I highly recommend that you approach this process like it's a luxury mini retreat for the soul, because it is! Set aside a whole half day on a weekend. Light some candles, bring in fresh flowers, and surround your space with images or photos of places, people, and pets that you love. I did all of these things when I designed my Manifesting Avatar, and it felt safe, comfortable, inspiring, and calming to breathe in the scent of traditional Indian incense and be surrounded by a vase of wildflowers and photos of my darling cat Charley and my dad, plus images of the Buddha and Saraswathi (the goddess of music, art, education, and culture in the Hindu pantheon).

I invite you to do the same. Take your time with this so you can experience each stage with a sense of calm and ease. This is a gentle process, but if you find yourself feeling scared or anxious at any time, turn to the Fear into Gold tool in chapter 5 (page 112) to gently release these emotions.

## Stage #1: The Genesis

We'll be using Sacred Promises, which is the fundamental practice in the Genesis stage, to identify ideal qualities for your Manifesting Avatar that you can use to live as your Future Self in the now. The Sacred Promises are essentially qualities you are naturally drawn to. Your attraction to these qualities and desire for them means that you recognize them within yourself, whether you realize it or not. These traits, gifts, or skills are in your energy field and are easily accessible to you via your Manifesting Avatar even if you're not currently aware of them. Throughout the Genesis stage, we'll be working with the thinking mind and the Mental Body as well as the Spiritual Body and the energy of higher consciousness.

### STEP #1: ASSEMBLE

In this step, we'll assemble a collection of words that are character attributes, traits, virtues, and skills you'd like to integrate into your Manifesting Avatar. I like to use an online dictionary and thesaurus for this exercise. Choose as many words as you wish. These can be nouns, verbs, or adjectives, and you can also combine two to three words to create a short phrase. Have fun— there are no rules! Below is a list of my personal favorite words and phrases, which you can use for inspiration as you create your own.

Before you begin assembling your Manifesting Avatar's skills and traits, connect with your Authentic Self and your intuition using the Stop and Drop Technique from chapter 3 on page 54 (we definitely want the wisdom of our Authentic Self guiding us here). Then record your chosen words in a journal or on a digital device, and make sure it's within reach so you're ready for the next part of this exercise. Keep in mind that one of the biggest pitfalls with this process is that we can overthink it. We start to wonder, "Is *loving* a good word, or maybe I want to go with *compassionate?*" This can go on and on! It's why I recommend that you work through this step in fifteen minutes or less. Otherwise you might get stuck in mental chatter for hours, days, or even weeks.

**My List of Favorite Words and Phrases**
Brave
Curious
Dazzling
Empowered serenity
Free
Holy pleasure
Intuitive
Magical
Rich
Serendipity

### STEP #2: REMEMBER

Whether you realize it or not, there have been moments in your life when your Manifesting Avatar took center stage. These have been times when you felt uplifted, inspired, motivated, happy, empowered, brave, or anything that made you feel wonderful about yourself, about life, and about the world. What we're going to do now is bring these moments forward.

Think about events, experiences, or milestones in your life when you felt grounded, connected, and real and when you felt like everything was exactly as it should be. You can note these moments or experiences in your journal. This is a beautiful part of this process, so take your time with it. Use all five senses and focus on what made you feel good. What time of day was it? What was the weather like? What were the scents you could detect in the air? Could you feel a gentle breeze on your skin? Allow yourself to become fully immersed in your recollection of the greatest moments and experiences of your life, and note it all down.

### STEP #3: CHOOSE

Now that you've tuned into the incredible, uplifting energy that represents the highlights of your life, it's time to look at your list of words again. Let yourself be drawn to five to seven words that reflect this beautiful energy for you. You'll be using your intuition to guide you to the words that are aligned for you, so go ahead and work with the Stop and Drop Technique again from chapter 3 (page 54). When you're feeling calm and connected with your intuition and your Authentic Self, refer to the Tune into Your Body, Heart, and Mind activity that I shared at the end of chapter 3 (page 66) and choose five to seven words from your list. As you read each word on your list, bring your attention to what's going on inside yourself. Which words make you feel open and light? Which ones make you feel closed, contracted, heavy, or agitated? Filter your list down to five to seven words that make you feel open, expansive, light, and serene.

I invite you to go old-school with this exercise and physically write the words with pen and paper. If you're having a hard time choosing just five to seven words, don't forget that you can combine words so you have phrases or terms that are unique and meaningful to you. (One of my phrases is *empowered serenity*, which I developed into the Light of Empowered Serenity practice in the previous chapter.)

When you're done, you have the traits, attributes, and gifts that will be a part of your Manifesting Avatar! You can come back to this exercise any time you want, but I recommend that you choose no more than seven words at a time so your energy remains stable and you don't feel fragmented or stretched in too many different directions. For that same reason, I invite you to stick to one set of five to seven words for at least a month before you consider adding more qualities to your Manifesting Avatar.

*Fun twist:* If you'd like to invite the Universe to be your partner in this activity, write each individual word you chose in step 1 on its own piece of paper. Then fold the papers (so you can't see the words) and ask the Universe to guide you as you pick your words from the pile of folded papers.

## Stage #2: The Merge

Now that you've successfully identified the five to seven traits and attributes of your Manifesting Avatar, it's time to officially meet and merge with this powerful aspect of yourself. The Merge is an inner journey that integrates all four subtle bodies—the Physical (body and movement), Mental (thoughts and mind), Emotional (feelings), and Spiritual (consciousness) Bodies—to speed up the process of energetic change so you can start to live today as your ideal Future Self. We'll be doing this with a simple yet richly sensory inner journey that involves connecting with your Manifesting Avatar with three eye-opening questions. It's best to immerse yourself in this process, so I suggest that you read and record the entire journey in your own voice. A simple audio recording on your smartphone or any other device will work nicely. (Alternatively, you can find this inner journey recorded for you as part of a free gift bundle that you can sign up to download at www.shantinirajah.com /manifest.) In this journey, you will open up your heart, mind, and energy to connect to, attune to, and embody your Manifesting Avatar through all four subtle bodies.

## BEFORE YOU BEGIN THE MERGE

Go back to your list of words from step 3 in Stage #1: The Genesis and breathe in each of your five to seven words with an In-the-Moment Edition of 1 Healing Breath. You can do this by choosing a corresponding energy for each word. So if you have five words—such as joy, gratitude, love, beauty, and transcendence—take 1 Healing Breath of Joy, 1 Healing Breath of Gratitude, 1 Healing Breath of Love, 1 Healing Breath of Beauty, and 1 Healing Breath of Transcendence. (Again, if you feel like you need some support or inspiration in connecting with these energies, feel free to refer to the collection of 1 Healing Breath images and energies that you have access to for free. Just go to www.shantinirajah.com/manifest to sign up to download them.)

## INNER JOURNEY TO MERGE WITH YOUR MANIFESTING AVATAR

Sit on a chair with your feet on the floor or in a comfortable, cross-legged position on your bed, yoga mat, or cushion. Relax and gently keep your spine straight. Close your eyes. This time is for you. Allow yourself this beautiful gift of space and time to nurture yourself as you begin to intensify and strengthen your connection to your Manifesting Avatar through the four subtle bodies: the Physical, Mental, Emotional, and Spiritual Bodies.

In your mind's eye or inner vision, beautiful glittering pink light appears all around you. This is the light of unconditional love from the Universe. This pink glittering light is showering down on you, silently and gently. As you watch this pretty sparkling pink light, you feel deeply loved and held, and you feel safe and free to be who you truly are. As you continue to gaze at the pink light of unconditional love, you begin to see the silhouette of your Manifesting Avatar walking toward you. As your Avatar enters your view, you see that they look just like you but there is something a little different. You can sense that they have all of the traits and skills you desire and that you chose earlier, and it feels so good to recognize these attributes in them. Take a moment to fully enjoy this feeling.

As your Manifesting Avatar moves closer, you see a loving smile just for you, and you feel gentle and powerful yet serene energy radiating from your Avatar. You see that your Avatar is inviting you to step into a breathtakingly beautiful open space surrounded by tall trees. The sun is shining and there's a gentle breeze blowing; you can hear it whispering through the leaves. The air is perfumed with the delicate scent of wildflowers. Your Manifesting Avatar turns to you, and the two of you sit on the grass, facing each other. You ask the following question in your heart, and you know your Manifesting Avatar can hear and understand you:

*What do I need most right now to connect deeply and completely with you?*

Let your Manifesting Avatar answer, and listen quietly. When your Avatar is done, ask your next question:

*What can I do to strengthen and nurture my connection with you?*

As before, let your Manifesting Avatar answer, and when your Avatar is done, ask your final question:

*What would you like me to know right now? What is your message for me?*

When you receive the answer, you are ready to connect with your Manifesting Avatar in the Merge. Both your Avatar and you stand up in unison. You take a step forward toward your Avatar, and you see that your Avatar is doing the same. You reach out your hands, palms facing up, and you see your Avatar placing their hands, palms facing down, on yours. Take one more step forward and feel yourself merge with your Manifesting Avatar. Give yourself a moment to take this in. You might feel lighter—or heavier. You might feel a glorious sense of wonder, bliss, ecstasy, or joy. Allow yourself to experience this for a few moments, knowing you are safe.

You are now ready to return from your inner journey, and you are ready to make your way back. Feel yourself coming back to yourself in the room. Feel your body touching the surface of the chair, yoga mat, or cushion. You are grounded, strong, and centered in your body, connected to the earth. Gently wiggle your fingers and toes. Slowly open your eyes, and know that you and your Manifesting Avatar are one and that you can now call on your Avatar any time you want to.

This Inner Journey is the first phase of connecting with your Manifesting Avatar, and you might not feel different or changed in any way for a while. But know that through this process, you have activated your energy so it is continuously shifting and adapting to include the energy of your Manifesting Avatar. The Merge process will continue to unfold over the next few days. In the meantime, take good care of yourself. Drink lots of water and get as much rest as you can.

If you'd like to strengthen your relationship with your Manifesting Avatar, revisit the Merge process every two to three weeks until it feels like the traits and qualities of your Avatar are now a natural part of who you are. For instance, if you chose *confident* and *sociable* as desired traits for your Avatar, you'll find that in a few weeks or months, some of the things that used to feel hard to do, like meeting new people, will now feel easier and eventually it will become effortless. Isn't that cool? Now that you've successfully completed stage 2 and you're connected with your Manifesting Avatar, there is one final stage to complete.

## Stage #3: Instant Activation

The Instant Activation is a simple activity that allows you to do two important things: instantly tune into your Manifesting Avatar and consistently strengthen your bond with your Avatar every time you do it. Instant Activation involves something I like to call the Symbolic Gesture, which is a symbol that you can use to connect with your Avatar at any time (kind of like using the Bat-Signal to connect with Batman!). The Symbolic Gesture works like a magnifier, and what we're actually doing is repatterning our energy to flow into and fuel our Manifesting Avatar in order to bring it into existence in moments. But first let me explain what a Symbolic Gesture is and why it's important.

A Symbolic Gesture is any physical action you choose that sends a signal to your subtle bodies and the Universe that you're ready to move forward with your intention. In this case, your intention is to connect with your Manifesting Avatar, but it also works for any intention. The Garuda Mudra (page 135) from the Light of Empowered Serenity practice in the previous chapter is a Symbolic Gesture, and so is Anjali Mudra, which is part of the Extended Edition of the 1 Healing Breath.

Your personal Symbolic Gesture that you use to call in your Manifesting Avatar could be a movement, a logo, or a sacred geometric shape that you sketch on a piece of paper in a couple of seconds or trace on your open palm. Every time you use your Symbolic Gesture, you are inviting your Manifesting Avatar into your energetic field. It's good to use your Symbolic Gesture multiple times throughout your day so you can consistently embody your Manifesting Avatar.

The fun thing about this practice is that you get to create your own Symbolic Gesture, and you can do this in a number of different ways. You can ask the Universe to show you a sign. You can choose a favorite symbol that makes you feel happy and protected, or you could simply use the Stop and Drop Technique from chapter 3 (page 54) and let your Symbolic Gesture come to you through your intuition. Another great way to receive your Symbolic Gesture is to ask your Manifesting Avatar to show you what it is, which is the method I used when I received mine. The following is a quick visualization in which you will meet with your Manifesting Avatar again to receive your Symbolic Gesture.

Just like you did with the Inner Journey to Merge with Your Manifesting Avatar in the previous stage, you'll be immersing yourself fully in this experience. So go ahead and record this visualization in your own voice on your smartphone or any other device so you can follow along without referring to this page. (You can also sign up to download and listen to the free recording of this journey at www.shantinirajah.com/manifest.) Don't forget to take note of your Symbolic Gesture as soon as you're done with this visualization. You'll be surprised at how easy it is to forget what you received from your Manifesting Avatar if you don't do this immediately! Describe your Symbolic Gesture in words, or better yet, draw it in your journal or on a piece of paper, and keep it in a safe place.

### ASKING FOR YOUR SYMBOLIC GESTURE VISUALIZATION

Sit on a chair, with your feet on the floor, or in a comfortable, cross-legged position on your bed, yoga mat, or cushion. Relax and gently keep your spine straight. Close your eyes.

In your mind's eye or inner vision, beautiful glittering pink light appears all around you. This is the light of unconditional love from the Universe. This glittering pink light is showering down on you, silently and gently. As you watch this pretty sparkling pink light, you feel deeply loved and held, and you feel safe and free to be who you truly are. As you continue to gaze at the pink light of unconditional love, you begin to see the silhouette of your Manifesting Avatar walking toward you.

As your Manifesting Avatar enters your view, you see them holding a gift just for you. It's wrapped beautifully. This gift is the key that activates your instant connection to your Manifesting Avatar. Go ahead and open your gift. You see it's a symbol, insignia, logo, sign, or gesture. Take a moment to take it in.

You are now ready to step out of your inner journey and make your way back. Feel yourself coming back to yourself and back to the room. Feel your body touching the surface of the chair, yoga mat, or cushion. You are grounded, strong, and centered in your body, connected to the earth. Gently wiggle your fingers and toes. Slowly open your eyes.

## Consistently Working with Your Manifesting Avatar

You did it! You have successfully created your incredibly powerful Manifesting Avatar to link your Present Self to your ideal Future Self. You now have the ability to speed up the process of energetic change through the subtle bodies and accelerate the manifesting process. Go ahead and call on your Avatar regularly so you can consistently attune to the high-vibrational energy of your ideal Future Self in the now.

Here's a list of situations and experiences where it's good to activate your Manifesting Avatar using your Symbolic Gesture. You'll be delightfully surprised when you find yourself responding as your best self and in exciting new ways that feel totally out of reach for your Present Self.

## When You Need to Channel a Specific Trait in Your Manifesting Avatar

Your Manifesting Avatar contains qualities that are in your energy field but feel out of reach to your Present Self. For instance, maybe you wish you were more adventurous. You've included this trait in your Avatar, but you spend your weekends on the couch in front of the TV, flipping through one streaming service after another. To switch things up on a Saturday morning—and finally get up off that couch—you could call on your Manifesting Avatar using your Symbolic Gesture to bring in the energy of adventure and let yourself be guided by this energy.

## When You're Feeling Topsy-Turvy or Off Track

Call on your Manifesting Avatar when you're feeling stressed or upset or when you're going through a challenging time in your life. This will allow you to make high-vibrational choices and decisions and take aligned action that will quickly get you past obstacles that stand in the way of your ideal future.

## When You Need to Do or Say Something That Feels Difficult

Your Manifesting Avatar can be there for you when you know you have a difficult conversation ahead of you, for instance, if you're planning to break up with a longtime love or ask for a promotion at work. Your Manifesting Avatar can help you speak your truth in a way that is fully aligned with the best version of you that is your ideal Future Self so that you can receive the outcome in the highest service of your soul purpose and mission.

### During Manifesting Activities

Whether you're chanting affirmations, creating a vision board, or doing a daily gratitude practice, begin by activating your Manifesting Avatar. Doing your manifesting activities as your Manifesting Avatar will add remarkable power, confidence, and speed to your ability to create what you want.

### When You Need a Quick Vibrational Boost

Your Manifesting Avatar vibrates at a high level of consciousness, and allowing this part of you to come forward can create a beautiful, fresh surge of high-vibrational energy any time you need a positive energetic boost.

### When You're Writing or Doing Creative Work

Your Manifesting Avatar is the part of you that feels all the emotions but can easily practice healthy detachment. Allowing your Avatar to come forward when you need to write, paint, sing, or do anything else that requires creativity and ingenuity can help you release self-doubt so that you can get into the flow state and create with ease and speed. Your Avatar has the power to open up your energy system to magical experiences of flow where you feel like your book or artwork is creating itself!

The more you work with your Manifesting Avatar, the more you're likely to see quick results with your manifesting efforts. Your Avatar will also help you to start living as your ideal Future Self. Doing this can lead to beautiful choices and decisions that allow an ongoing flow of joy, abundance, incredible opportunities, and synchronicities to come through into your present reality with ease. So don't be surprised if you start to see major positive transformations start to happen like magic in key areas of your life.

## Manifest Now!
## Stay on Track with Your Manifesting Avatar

You can connect with your Manifesting Avatar to track your progress in bringing your True Desires into your reality and to receive guidance that can help you accelerate your manifesting journey. Remember, your Manifesting

Avatar is connected to the energy of your ideal Future Self, and it contains the vision, mission, and wisdom of that future version of you that is already living the life of your dreams.

Receiving answers from your Manifesting Avatar involves taking the Inner Journey to Merge with Your Manifesting Avatar that we explored in the Merge stage earlier in this chapter (page 163). All you need to do is follow the same instructions but switch out the questions that you asked earlier (*What do I need most right now to connect deeply and completely with you? What can I do to strengthen and nurture my connection with you? What would you like me to know right now? What is your message for me?*) and insert whatever burning questions you have about your True Desires or your overall manifesting experience. As a rule of thumb, keep your questions short, clear, and to the point, and stick to three questions or less each time you do this practice.

It's also important to avoid asking questions related to the past. Your Manifesting Avatar is a powerful force for energetic change, which is why it's good to focus your attention and energy on transforming your life in your future without looking back at the past. A question like "How could I have avoided losing all that money in the stock market last year?" not only is meaningless but could end up drawing you into lower-vibrational energies and emotions that will slow your ability to manifest.

It's good to ask questions that begin with "What" or "How," such as "What do I need to know to improve my manifesting skills?" or "What's blocking me from receiving my True Desire?" or "How can I improve my ability to align with the high-vibrational energies of the Universe?" Questions that begin with "Why" are big no-nos. For instance, "Why is my friend jealous of me?" won't work, because your conscious, thinking mind can jump right in and take over based on what you consciously want the answer to be. This means the answer is coming through your thinking mind and not through the higher consciousness of your Manifesting Avatar.

The same is true for time-related questions. "When will I make my first million?" isn't good because you're likely to receive an answer from your conscious mind, which is drawn to questions related to time. It's also not a good idea to ask a question for someone else. Your Manifesting Avatar is the best version of you and is wholly connected to your energy and your soul purpose. As such, guidance and answers you receive from it are for you and not for someone else, so resist asking questions like "Will my daughter get married by the end of the year?"

I've put together a quick list of helpful questions that I love and that you can use as a reference to kick-start your question-and-answer sessions with your Manifesting Avatar. Feel free to add your own questions to this list, but make sure your questions are aligned with the guidelines I just shared.

## Helpful Questions to Ask Your Manifesting Avatar

+ *What are the manifesting habits I need to have that I don't currently have?*
+ *Who are some of the people I need to speak to in order to elevate my manifesting experience?*
+ *What is the next best step in my manifesting journey?*
+ *What can I do to make manifesting my True Desires easier and more graceful?*
+ *What is my greatest block in receiving my True Desires?*
+ *How can I improve my chances of receiving my True Desires?*
+ *What is the Magical Manifesting Ingredient I need to focus on right now?*
+ *What is one thing I can do to improve my overall wellbeing and vibrational frequency?*

*Eight*

# Magical Manifesting Ingredient #6: Utilize the Power of Joyful Play

You've arrived at the most delightful and playful chapter in this book. I'm so glad we're here because I know I've asked a lot from you so far. You learned why mainstream manifesting methods might have let you down in the past. You connected with your Authentic Self through your intuition and uncovered your True Desires. You learned why toxic positivity is harmful, how to recognize it, and what to do about it. You fully embraced your shadow and learned to use easy-to-apply tools to activate genuine self-love and high-vibrational emotions. You discovered how to alchemize fear and generate embodied safety so you can effortlessly manifest the big, beautiful, bold changes you desire in your life. You also practiced the empowering art of Conscious Liberation and designed your Manifesting Avatar to supercharge your skills and become a masterful manifestor. Phew, that's a lot!

It takes a lot of courage to go deep within yourself and get up close and personal with who you truly are, so bravo to you on a job well done! And while there's no doubt that everything you learned will certainly support you in connecting with the limitless, loving, creative energy of the Universe so you can joyfully manifest a life you genuinely love, I must admit that some of the practices, activities, and processes in the previous chapters are not exactly what most people would consider fun. It's why I'm sure you'll be happy to know that we're about to take a break from deep self-exploration and shift into fun and games territory.

In this chapter, you'll learn to raise your vibration and accelerate the manifesting process with the energy of pleasurable, joyful play. You'll discover how sometimes just being in the energy of play can heighten your ability to manifest so your desires flow easily to you, and we'll practice inviting this energy into our life with processes such as creating the Sacred Container of Joyful Play and the ALIGN method. You'll also learn to lift your mood and overall sense of wellbeing by turning boring or mundane daily tasks into a game, so you never have to feel grumpy about doing another load of laundry or getting through that massive pile of dirty dishes you've been trying to ignore for the last two days.

But before we get started, I have a quick personal confession: this chapter was the most difficult for me to write. Creating space for joyful play and pleasure is a relatively new experience for me, and it felt disconcerting and even a little unsafe to simply relax and have fun. Looking back at my life, I can see why. My nervous system—and my entire energy system for that matter— were shaped by old-school self-help ideologies steeped in hustle culture.

## Letting Tony Robbins Down

I cut my personal development teeth on getting things done no matter what and doing it all with a smile (even if I had to smile through gritted teeth!). It was all about working all day every day to get to your goals, and if you failed, it just meant that you were not trying hard enough.

I love collecting motivational quotes, and I've been adding to my collection since I was about eight years old. I realized recently that some of my favorite quotes from my early days of diving into the world of personal development are actually generic hyperbole in disguise. I remember pushing myself past the breaking point at school in my attempts to follow seemingly helpful advice along the lines of "Success comes to those who take massive, fearless action," "Never give up, never surrender," and "Struggle is the price you pay to get to the top." For years, twentieth-century self-help philosophy felt like some kind of holy truth that would free me from a life of profound failure and shame. Books like *Awaken the Giant Within* by Anthony Robbins, *Feel the Fear and Do It Anyway* by Susan Jeffers, and *The Power of Positive Thinking* by Norman Vincent Peale were my constant companions. Tony, Susan, Norman, and many other personal development gurus felt like best friends and confidants.

Don't get me wrong: these are leaders in their fields and their books were hugely helpful to me. But when I didn't manage to hit a goal or if I failed to work hard, it felt like I was somehow letting them down. It got to the point where I set aside everything I loved that didn't seem to be immediately beneficial, productive, or profitable. I missed out on countless spontaneous opportunities to relax and just be. I said no when friends invited me to hang out on weekends just so I could finish my homework and prepare ahead for next week's lessons. For weeks I skipped doing origami (the Japanese art of folding paper into fun shapes) because I was trying to make sense of a bunch of technical manuals to get ahead at my first job. I bypassed reading a good novel on lazy Sunday afternoons—something I love to do—so I could check and edit some of the writing I'd done for clients (for the tenth time!).

For a long time, I couldn't shake the feeling that indulging in a hobby or an activity that felt like pure play and pleasure was a total waste of time. The only game I was playing at that time was an endless game of pushing and striving harder and harder to achieve bigger goals and reach for greater heights, except it didn't feel like a game to me. As I developed a holistic understanding of the art of manifesting and how all that we feel, think, and do has a corresponding effect on how we experience life and what we attract into our lived experience, it began to dawn on me that play was not a nice-to-have but a must-have.

## Remembering What It Means to Play

Can you remember when you were a kid and you raced across your playground or school field with your heart pumping and a big goofy grin plastered on your face? You didn't hold back and it felt like you had wings on your feet. Maybe you recall happily building castles in the sand by the beach. The hours slipped by and all you felt was the sun on your skin, the warm golden sand in your hands, and overflowing happiness in your heart. Stop for a moment right now and take yourself back to the times in your life when everything seemed to fall away and all that was left was the energy of pure, undiluted joy and pleasure. Can you remember? That's the energy of joyful play. When you feel this way, you are inside a powerful manifesting window where everything—and I mean *everything*—becomes possible. Playing makes time stand still, and it can help you achieve what feels like an impossible goal without even trying. It's magical, it's uplifting, it's transformative. As we discover more about this beautiful, joyful energy in the rest of this chapter, you'll come to see, like I did, that all work and no play makes Jack, Jill, and everyone else a dull (and ineffective) manifestor.

Just in case you're reading this and thinking, "Huh? I'm supposed to play more? Ridiculous! How's playing gonna help me manifest what I want?" the first thing I want to say to you is, "Hello, fellow Type-A!" The next thing I want to say is that play probably feels like a waste of time to you, as it did to me for so many years, because you believe in persistence, discipline, focus, and all of the other traits and habits we need to achieve our goals. I'm with you on that, but I'm also here to tell you that's just part of the story of success. You see, playing more in the context of manifesting is much more than a fun break. For one thing, it's certainly not an excuse to ignore your responsibilities or goof off, and for another, play is a powerful manifesting tool. It's possibly the most powerful Magical Manifesting Ingredient in this book.

Here's why I know play is a legitimate path to attracting your desires and successfully receiving what you want from the Universe: because the energy of joyful play and the energy of resistance cannot exist in the same space. When we play, we open our heart, mind, and spirit to align with powerful energies, like the energies of love, enchantment, pleasure, creativity, and so much more.

So if you're having trouble wrapping your head around the idea of having to play more, here's a mindset shift that can help: think of play as the advanced manifesting tool you need to be a world-class manifesting maven, because it is. Just as an award-winning chef works with advanced tools to elevate the cooking process and create artistic, beautiful, delightful food, you can tap into the energy of play to create an artistic, beautiful, delightful life.

Playing allows you to manifest without trying because the energy of joyful play easily and naturally takes you into perfect alignment with the remarkably high-vibrational energies of the Universe. Joyful play is the secret code that unlocks an endless flow of magic, such as miraculous synchronicities, incredible out-of-the-blue opportunities, and unbelievable coincidences that ultimately bring your desires right to your door. Play is an astonishingly empowering tool that lets you step into a space of manifesting what you want on autopilot, and it's crucial that we do all we can to release any resistance we may have when it comes to letting ourselves play. I've found that one of the most effective methods we can use to dissolve this resistance is to cultivate a deep and profound understanding of why we may resist play in the first place, and that's exactly what we'll do in the next section.

## Running through a Field of Sunflowers

For most of us, the resistance to play is seeded early on. As kids, we're told that play is something we get to indulge in only after we get the important stuff done, like our homework or chores around the house. Over the years, this tiny seed of resistance takes root deep in our psyche as we come to realize that we are consistently punished for playing too much at school, home, and work, but we are rewarded with praise and promotions for working hard or earning perfect scores. When you were growing up, how often were you encouraged to play more versus work harder? It's certainly no big surprise that most of us wind up feeling guilty about playing, unless we happen to take up a sport for fun, we're enjoying some downtime on vacation, or we take a few minutes away from our back-to-back weekend chores to play in the backyard with the dog and the kids.

We've been trained to believe that play gets in the way of getting something useful done or it holds us back from doing something useful with our time, and that's one of the biggest mistakes I made in my manifesting journey. For the longest time, it felt like if I just kept pushing and never stopped, if I tried harder, I'd finally manifest the life of my dreams. Yes, it's true that when you do the work, when you keep taking action, you will be rewarded with the results you're looking for as you attract your desires with the Universe as your loving friend and biggest cheerleader. But a big part of the process of manifesting *is* the process. When you manifest from a place of "I'm enjoying every second of this" instead of "I need to get to the end," you'll be amazed at how the exact thing you want, the thing you long for, the thing that feels out of reach, suddenly shows up out of nowhere. It's exactly how this book came to be—I owe it all to the energy of play.

Imagine running through a field of sunflowers. You're going nowhere, but you're feeling joyful, delighted, and excited the whole time. That's how I felt throughout the process of manifesting this book. I was in a state of play all the way, and I experienced each moment without an agenda, timeline, or outcome in mind. I was delighted when I connected with an amazing writer and coach who expertly guided me to craft a great book proposal. We got a lot of work done, but we also had so much fun together. I let myself feel joyful, excited, and enthusiastic about finding the perfect book agent for my book, and I ended up with one of the kindest, most respected agents in the business. I loved every second of the process of sending the proposal out to publishers, even though I knew my chances of landing a book deal on the first try were pretty much zero. I even extended the energy of play to reading my rejection emails, and as a result, I delighted in every single one (no kidding!). One acquisitions editor at a major publishing house said, "Love this idea, but we just signed with an author who is writing a book about manifesting," while another said, "This is a very interesting and new approach to manifesting. Unfortunately, it's not a good fit for our publishing list at this time."

Yes, I did feel that pinch of disappointment, but at the same time, being in the energy of play helped me see that every single rejection email I received was also encouraging and supportive. It was magical! (I learned later that my experience was unusual, because many authors, especially first-time authors, receive painful criticism in their rejection emails.) This book would not exist if I hadn't worked every Magical Manifesting Ingredient in this book—especially the power of joyful play.

By now, I hope you're at least a little bit curious about integrating play into your manifesting process to create eyebrow-raising results. But before we dive deeper, there's something I want you to keep in mind: the energy of joyful play is an accessible and effective Magical Manifesting Ingredient for sure, but only if we can keep ourselves safe and meet our basic needs, such as having enough food to eat and a safe place to live. It's hard to have fun when you're worried about paying the rent, if you're fearful of losing your job, or you're wondering where your next meal is coming from. It's why I've included play as the final ingredient in this book. We're ready to embrace the energy of play after we've learned how to generate safety from within.

*An important note:* If you get to the end of this chapter and you're still seeing a lot of resistance come up around play, it might be your intuition trying to tell you there's a hidden block, pain, or trauma that needs to be addressed around play. You might be feeling overwhelmed and tired, with a huge number of responsibilities on your shoulders. You might feel that the only thing standing between your family and life on the street is you, so who the heck has time for play?

If you're feeling intense resistance, frustration, or anger come up when you think about spending even a few minutes playing every day, I invite you to work with the Fear into Gold tool in chapter 5 (page 112). Follow the steps and ask yourself, "What is this resistance trying to tell me?" This will allow your intuition to guide you and will help you enter a state of calm. Try this practice at least two or three times. If you're still feeling agitated, frustrated, and stressed, consider working with an energy practitioner or somatic therapist to address what's creating strong resistance to taking some time off to kick back, relax, and enjoy yourself. Return to the activities in the rest of this chapter when you're feeling safe or when you're in a phase of life where you can fully feel the joy and freedom of play without also feeling like you have to look over your shoulder every second.

## Recognizing True Play

Dissolving our resistance to play through a deeper understanding of why we resist is the first step in connecting with the energy of play. In this section, we'll discover why not all play is created equal, and how to recognize pure play so we can gently start to invite and reintegrate this Magical Manifesting Ingredient into our lives.

The first thing to know is that when we are in the energy of joyful play, we have instant and unlimited access to the energy of creation, the energy of the Universe. The second thing to know is that this is great news because playing is the most natural activity in the world. The urge to play is a primal instinct and we are born knowing how to do it. Think about it: kids play all the time without ever taking a class on how to play. They engage in joyful play easily, intuitively, without reason, and often with nothing more than their imagination as a tool.

Since we've been playing almost from the day we were born, you'd think that we would instinctively know what play is, but if I asked you to define play, would you be able to do it? I challenged myself to define play, and when I did some research and also checked in with clients, friends, and family, much to my surprise I found that play means different things to different people. For some, play is basically anti-work, which means it's anything that's not a job, a task, a to-do, or a must-do. So play could be talking to a friend on the phone, reading a book, singing the latest Taylor Swift chart-topper in the shower, or enjoying freshly brewed coffee on the balcony at sunrise. Meanwhile, there are those who believe play doesn't count as play unless it's organized or coordinated in some way. These people are big fans of structured board games or outdoor sports that come with a bunch of rules and regulations. For them, play is a competitive game of soccer at the local community center or a challenging round of Scrabble on game night.

When it comes to defining play, an activity that's fun for some is the total opposite for others. For instance, one of my friends loves to cook and finds it deeply relaxing. It's her favorite way to play, especially at the end of a long, hard day. But another friend absolutely abhors cooking and feels like she's being punished when she has to juggle pots and pans in the kitchen. This brings us to a crucial point: play in the context of manifesting is all about how you feel and less about what you do. True play fills your heart with happiness, makes you feel more like yourself, and offers pleasure and respite from the everyday grind and routine. (I'd like to add that I'm defining rest as play because it's the most healing and pleasurable experience we can ever hope to have.)

I've put together the following five defining characteristics of play that you can use as a guideline to recognize the energy of pure, joyful play so you can integrate it into your manifesting journey.

## Play Is Timeless

Have you ever read a thriller all through the night even though you knew you had to get to work the next morning? How about becoming so engrossed in watching your favorite band perform live that it felt like the concert ended ten minutes after it began? When you're in the energy of joyful play, time ceases to exist. Play puts you in the space of timeless wonder where you're in flow, feeling excited and happy, and too absorbed in what you're doing to think about the clock.

## Play Is Pure Desire

Play invites that feeling of wanting more without needing anything to be different. Let's say you're on a swing at the playground and you find yourself wanting to swing higher simply because you want to. It's not to prove to yourself or anyone else that you can. You just love the idea of swinging high in the air, and that's all there is to it. That feeling of wanting without needing that gets you to swing higher is the feeling of pure desire, and it works like a powerful accelerant in your manifesting journey. Pure desire can speed things up like nothing else can, because wanting without needing is desire without attachment and you're essentially giving the Universe permission to bring you what you want with zero resistance.

## Play Effortlessly Draws You In

When you're about to do something you absolutely love, you don't procrastinate or put it off to a later date. You don't have to wait to feel inspired or motivated to get to it. If gardening feels like play, you'll read up on the art of planting tomatoes for days or weeks—no motivation necessary! You'll dedicate an entire weekend to watching YouTube videos to improve your composting skills without waiting for inspiration to strike. You'll think nothing of sacrificing your weekly trip to the mall for months so you can save up to get the best gardening tools you can afford. You'll be naturally and easily inspired to dive into anything and everything that has to do with gardening, and you won't have to be cajoled, influenced, convinced, or persuaded. You certainly won't have to force yourself to learn about gardening to improve your skills, and that's what it means to be in the energy of joyful play. You'll be drawn in by the activity you love, and you'll invest your time, energy, and money without hesitation.

### Play Requires No Reward

Play, in the context of manifesting, requires no reward and there are no winners and losers. Think of it this way: you're happy to play with your cat even if he never thanks you for it, and you'd play at the beach with your kids even if no one ever paid you to do it. It's the reason why games and organized sports don't make the cut in my definition of joyful play.

### Play Has No Goal

Play isn't about achieving an outcome. Yes, you may want to complete that origami dragon you started working on and you can't wait to serve that lasagna you made from scratch because you know it's so good, but those are not goals as much as the natural flow of desired results that arise from your playful creations. Play is inherently without a goal, without an aim or objective. True play is for play's sake, and you immerse yourself in it for the feeling you get when you allow yourself to let go and experience it fully.

Now that you have some guidelines to help you recognize true play, let's look at why inviting the energy of joyful play into your life is the most effective way to amplify your manifesting skills and speed up the manifesting process.

## Why Joyful Play Leads to Masterful Manifesting

Creating a vision board, visualizing your novel at the top of the bestseller list, or chanting positive, uplifting affirmations can be fun to do, but these activities can easily fall short of the powerful, focused energy of joyful play that you need to fuel the manifesting process and send a clear, unmistakable signal to the Universe that says, "I'm happy, I'm at peace, I trust you, and I'm ready to receive all that I desire!" It's because effective, masterful manifesting is not just about putting together a vision board with perfectly curated images that look great tacked up on your bedroom wall; it's the deeper emotional energies you experience while creating that board and every time you catch sight of it that make all the difference. If you're secretly fearful, anxious, or worried that some or all of the things on that board will never come to pass, then the life that you're dreaming of will continue to elude you.

But when you imbue the energy of joyful play into all aspects of your life, all that you do in your quest to manifest—and this includes the Magical Manifesting Ingredients and every single practice, activity, and tool you've learned so far in this book—will be supercharged with high-vibrational, magnetic frequencies that can bring you your True Desires and everything else you want in a heartbeat. In other words, with the energy of joyful play, everything you ask for, from the tiniest whisper of a wish for sunshine on a cloudy day to a lofty declaration to the Universe that you'll be the first self-made multimillionaire in your family, can happen just like that. It can all come together with ease, flow, and grace, in a seamless tapestry of magical synchronicities, astonishing opportunities, and inspired ideas popping into your mind when you least expect it. Tapping into the energy of joyful play can make you feel like you've suddenly acquired manifesting superpowers that you didn't even know you had. You'll find yourself walking through the world magically manifesting as you go, with everything working in your favor, and you won't even have to think about it. I know it sounds too good to be true, but it's not. Here's why.

## Joyful Play Instantly Raises Your Vibration

There's a reason that there's no such thing as fearful play. Play naturally and easily dissolves unwanted emotions like fear. The nature of play is such that it is free of all forms of low-vibrational energies such as disappointment or resentment. If you don't believe that's true, try engaging in your favorite form of play while holding onto feelings of sadness or shame, and you'll see it's really hard to do. The energy of joyful play cannot exist in the same space as lower-vibrational emotions. Entering into the energetic space of joyful play can instantly raise your vibrational frequency, and it's a wonderfully authentic way to keep genuinely happy emotions flowing through your system.

## Joyful Play Bypasses the Thinking Mind

Joyful play gives your thinking mind a break, so you can let down your guard and enter into a deep level of trust and faith in the Universe minus doubt, fear, worry, or anxiety. This allows aligned intuitive nudges, ideas, and insights to come through so you can make the choices and decisions that lead directly to your dreams.

## Joyful Play Offers Effortless Presence

While popular mindfulness practices such as meditation or observing your thoughts are great techniques in cultivating present moment awareness, most people don't realize that playing can also offer the same outcomes in ways that are often a lot more fun. Joyful play allows us to embrace the present moment without any effort at all. Whether you are making love, dancing in the rain, or rock climbing, joyful play brings you back to exactly where you are, which is in the here and now. We are consistently manifesting our next moment while allowing ourselves to occupy each moment in complete presence. It's why the energy of joyful play is like having access to the master key that unlocks the creative magic of the Universe.

## Joyful Play Protects You from Your Inner Critic

The energy of joyful play quickly brings you back to your core energetic essence, which is the soul and spirit that is your Authentic Self before self-criticism, self-judgment, and the concept of self-worth became a part of your inner world. When you're having fun in play, the voice of your inner critic recedes and disappears as you give yourself over to the flow of the activity you're engaging in. In this way, joyful play takes you home to who you truly are. It lets you experience everything and everyone around you with that beautifully innocent beginner's mind of a child, where unexpected, synchronous messages, ideas, insights, and answers can flow from the Universe so every experience and situation starts to work in your favor.

### Joyful Play Flips the Happiness Switch

Play is one of the few activities in our adult lives that has the power to activate true happiness in just a few minutes or even a few seconds. Joyful, intentional play works like a happiness switch, and as we know, happy people are much more likely to be forgiving, to be generous, to experience gratitude. These are wonderful emotions that will enhance the manifesting process.

### Joyful Play Unleashes Beautiful Creative Energy

The energy of manifesting, the energy of the Universe, is essentially the energy of creation. When we are manifesting, we are bringing the formless into form. The relaxing, calming energy of joyful play unlocks this wildly beautiful creative energy that belongs to us all, because it is the energy we are made of and made from. Play can allow you to tap into infinitely creative energy, which can come through as a sudden urge to pursue creative projects, like starting a business or writing a poem. The best part? You can complete creative projects that you thought were difficult or even impossible in a way that feels effortless and in flow. Consistently tuning into joyful play also allows you to receive creative ideas and insightful solutions to problems that you previously believed to be unsolvable.

## How to Invite the Energy of Joyful Play into Your Heart

I pretty much stopped playing by the time I was fifteen, believing that if I was super studious and ultra-serious and I applied myself so I could consistently achieve massive goals, then I'd somehow escape the heartache of losing my dad and the fears and anxiety that can come from growing up in a financially unstable home. So when it came time to tap into the energy of joyful play, I had no idea where to begin. It took a while, but I've assembled a collection of practices that work like a lighthouse when it comes to safely leading my spirit to its ultimate joyful destination of wondrous, childlike play. These practices can help you too, and you'll find that each of these no-muss, no-fuss practices is easy to do and inexpensive and can help you find your way back to playing again.

## Get Curious

Curiosity and joyful play go hand in hand, and it's because they have something important in common: they trigger dopamine, which is also known as the "happy hormone." Research shows that curiosity has the power to decrease anxiety and encourage positive emotions such as happiness and fulfillment. So you might be thinking, "That sounds great, but can I get curious on purpose?" I'm so glad you asked! The first thing you can do to intentionally awaken your innate curiosity is to introduce novelty into your life.

Start with little things, like rearranging the furniture in your bedroom or den so you can spice up your living space, and experience it in a whole new way, evoking your natural sense of "Ooh, this feels different and new!" You can also inspire curiosity by learning a new skill, and it doesn't have to be useful or necessary. Remember, this is about giving yourself permission to follow your curiosity wherever it takes you. You might be surprised and delighted to find yourself lost in the energy of joyful play as you learn how to dance the polka or master the art of making Korean fried chicken. I love spending hours at my favorite bookstore, and when I want to awaken my curiosity, I head to the shelves that I'd ordinarily ignore, like Young Adult Fiction or Graphic Novels. I usually wind up leaving with amazing books that allow me to dive into hours of joyful play and pleasure.

## Turning Boring Tasks into a Game

You can add the fresh, happy energy of joyful play to even the most boring, mundane task by turning it into a game, and this is easier to do than you might think. Imagine you have a massive pile of laundry that needs to be done on the weekend and it's the last thing in the world you want to do. You can easily turn it into a playful activity by giving yourself a little bonus boost, such as "I'll watch three episodes of my favorite series on Netflix the second I'm done." You can also make doing the laundry more exciting by introducing a fun challenge, like "How fast can I get this done? Can I do it in under an hour?" Try it and you'll be surprised at how quickly you get through those boring or hard-to-do tasks with the energy of joyful play in the mix.

### Create an Altar of Joyful Play or a Sacred Container of Joyful Play

A creative, inspiring, and super fun way to connect with the energy of play is to build an Altar of Joyful Play or a Sacred Container of Joyful Play. This sends a message to the Universe that you are ready to receive your True Desires in the effortless ease of joyful play. It also serves as a lovely personal reminder, because every time you happen to glance at your Altar or Container, you'll be reminded to connect with the energy of joyful play.

You don't need much space to create an effective Altar of Joyful Play. A little table in the corner of your bedroom or a shelf in your study will work. Even a raised platform made from a pile of books will do nicely. The idea is to make this space inviting, personal, and fun. Choose objects and items for your Altar with care. Anything that lifts your energy and your mood is good. My Altar of Joyful Play holds items I love such as my favorite crystals and oracle decks. My Sacred Container of Joyful Play is also home to things that made me happy as a kid and still do, like a bottle of bubble solution (I love blowing bubbles and watching them float through the air), a colorful pinwheel, a trio of baby dolls, and a box of marbles.

You can work with your Altar of Joyful Play or Sacred Container of Joyful Play to activate and invite play into your manifesting process in a few different ways. You could spend a few minutes each day gazing at the items on your Altar. This might not seem like much, but offering your attention to the energy of play is a quick and effective way to activate it in your life. You can also offer a heartfelt invocation as you stand or sit in front of your Altar. Do this daily or whenever you want. You can use the following invocation word for word or come up with your own:

*I call in a flow of delightful, easy, fun energy of joyful play into my day.*

Working with your Altar of Joyful Play or Sacred Container of Joyful Play releases stuck energy and loosens the grip of low-vibrational energies such as fear, disappointment, worry, and anxiety. Over time, you'll train your body, mind, and spirit to receive and accept the energy of joyful play as a natural state of being, and you'll be able to easily call up the energy of play in your manifesting activities.

### Take 1 Healing Breath of Play

Another great way to invite joyful play into your day is by taking 1 Healing Breath of Play whenever you can, either the In-the-Moment Edition or the Extended Edition. Doing this can help shift your energy so you're open to calling fun, delight, and pleasure into your day-to-day life. For an added boost, take your 1 Healing Breath of Play in front of your Altar of Joyful Play to help you evoke this energy. (As always, if you can't quite come up with a feeling, memory, or situation that symbolizes joyful play for you, feel free to refer to the image of 1 Healing Breath of Play that is available to you for free. It is part of a special collection of images that you can sign up to download at www.shantinirajah.com/manifest.)

### Use the ALIGN Method

Calling in a sense of joyful play to a creative project can be tricky, especially when there's a deadline looming like a dark cloud over your inner creative landscape. I developed the ALIGN method to help myself tune into a specific emotion that I want to imbue into my writing so I can connect deeply with my readers and write in the energy of joyful play and creative flow. ALIGN is an acronym for Activate, Listen, Invite, Get Connected, and Note.

The ALIGN method is also perfect for when you simply want to tune into the energy of joyful play as you work on a creative project. I've found that this easy-to-do technique can quickly shift your energy as it clears blocks that stand in the way of the infinite creative energy of the Universe, which can bring you wonderful downloads and ideas that you might never have thought of on your own.

The ALIGN method takes just a couple of minutes to do and it's perfect for when you need to write, design, create a work of art, or even put a vision board together. You can also turn to this method when you want to tune into the energy of joyful play to come up with creative ideas for new products and programs for your business or work project.

## *The ALIGN Method*

### STEP #1: ACTIVATE

Begin by taking 1 Healing Breath of Play, the In-the-Moment Edition, to expand into joyful play, creative flow, and the creative energies of the Universe. Don't forget to refer to the image of 1 Healing Breath of Play (which is part of a special collection of images that you can sign up to download at www.shantinirajah.com/manifest) if you need help in evoking the energy of joyful play or if you can't quite come up with a memory or vision that draws in this energy for you.

### STEP #2: LISTEN

Next, listen to your intuition as you choose the emotion you desire to tap into. When I write, I use my intuition to choose one of the emotions on the Emotions Wheel (see illustration), but you can choose an emotion that's not represented there. Ask yourself, "What is the emotion that will give me a sense of ease and joyful, playful flow?" Then listen to the answer that arises from your intuition. This is usually the first answer that comes to you.

## Emotions Wheel

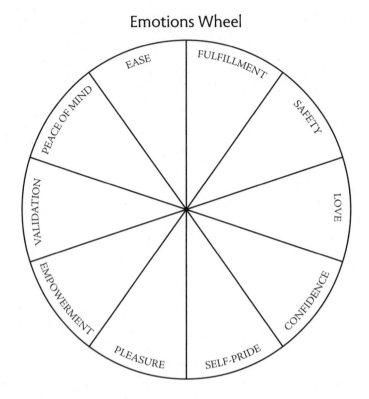

**STEP #3: INVITE**

Now you're ready to invite the emotion you chose in step 2 into your body, mind, and spirit. This step is simple. Take 1 Healing Breath of the emotion you chose, and let yourself feel the energy of that emotion rise up from within. For instance, if you chose ease from the Emotions Wheel, take 1 Healing Breath of Ease, either the In-the-Moment Edition or the Extended Edition. You can refer to a 1 Healing Breath image for additional assistance in connecting with the energy of your choice. (Again, feel free to refer to or find inspiration in one of the images in the special collection that you can sign up to download for free at www.shantinirajah.com/manifest.)

**STEP # 4: USE THE SPOTLIGHT RITUAL TO GET CONNECTED**

Most creative blocks arise because we focus on ourselves when we write or create art. "Will my work be criticized or judged? Is this piece of art or writing good enough? Am I making a fool of myself?" (That last question used to be my constant companion every time I sat down to write.) I've devised a quick tool called the Spotlight Ritual, which is about taking the focus off yourself and getting connected with the audience from a place of love and service so you can allow joyful play to flow through.

Start the Spotlight Ritual by closing your eyes. See yourself standing on a stage in front of an audience. There's a white spotlight (or any kind of bright light) shining down on you, from the crown of your head down to your feet. Now consciously and gently see this spotlight turn away from you and start to shine on your readers, clients, or audience. With your eyes still closed, set a powerful intention and make a commitment. You can use a version of the following intention or create your own:

*I'm [writing/painting/creating] to serve with love,*
*to connect deeply with my [audience/readers/clients],*
*and to offer [clarity/healing/comfort/inspiration/solutions].*

## STEP #5: NOTE

Steps 1 through 4 are about prepping your heart, mind, and energy to enter a state of flow. Now you're ready to dive into the task at hand. If you're using the ALIGN method to write, then put pen to paper or fingers to keyboard and begin. The same goes for painting, designing, or creating digital artwork. If you're looking to invite innovative ideas for your business or some other project, note the words, visions, and images that pop into your consciousness through your intuition. Let yourself follow through with these sparks of inspiration or insight. Every time you get stuck, return to step 1 and work through the steps to release energies that block the creative flow.

Joyful play is a wonderful way to practice presence and invite inspiration, creativity, and happy moments into our lives, even on the hard days. When we're absorbed in joyful play, the manifesting elements we often struggle with, such as mindfulness, trust, and letting go of attachment, can stream into our energy field without any effort at all.

# Manifest Now! Using the Magical Question to Enter into Joyful Play

I used to live by the belief that "anything worth doing is *hard* to do" and a mirror belief that said, "If it's easy, it doesn't count!" As a result, just about every goal I set my sights on, including manifesting my True Desires, felt like a challenge or struggle. Even worse, I'd quickly abandon goals that seemed too easy to accomplish (I know, right? Yikes!). Something in me consistently rejected and resisted ease until a few years ago, when a fabulous business coach asked me a powerful six-word question. I like to call it the Magical Question because it works like magic. Here it is:

## The Magical Question
*How can I make this easy?*

I practice using this question as often as possible every day, and that's what I'd like for you to do starting today. You see, play is joy. Play is delight. Play is wonder. And maybe most of all, play is ease. Asking yourself "How can I make this easy?" has the power to shift your energy so you are open to experiencing ease, and it helps to normalize ease in your life. I also recommend that you regularly ask yourself the Magical Question as you run through your True Desires list from chapter 3 (page 64). You'll be surprised at some of the creative ideas and insights that can come through for you as you do this.

Here's how that would work. Imagine that one of your True Desires is to find your soulmate. When you ask "How can I make this easy?" you might receive an intuitive nudge to accept an invitation to attend a friend's house-warming party this Saturday, which you were originally planning to turn down. Follow through with an open heart and mind and you'll be amazed at all that will unfold in full alignment with your True Desire of finding your soulmate.

Don't be alarmed if you find yourself feeling some kind of resistance in working with the Magical Question, at least in the beginning. When I first learned about this question, the idea that anything that is worth doing is difficult, complicated, and troublesome was so deeply embedded in my energy and in how I approached the world that it felt strange and wrong to ask, so I resisted the question altogether. This meant that I'd forget to ask it, and there were times when I totally forgot what the question even was (thankfully, I'd written it down in my journal).

I see this happen to lots of my clients, too. One client—a talented and gifted energy healer—couldn't bring herself to charge for her services even though she longed to create an expansive, aligned income with her healing practice. When I asked why she kept giving her sessions away for free, she said that her gifts came easily to her and it felt wrong to charge for something that was so easy! Working with the Magical Question helped release her resistance, and she went on to become one of the most successful energy practitioners in her niche.

If you're unfamiliar with the experience of joyful play and ease, you might notice that a similar resistance comes up for you. As we did with the Fear Check at the end of chapter 5 (page 117), I recommend that you write the Magical Question on sticky notes and place them where you can see them, like on your bathroom mirror, above the kitchen sink, and on your work desk. You can also set a timer that goes off every hour so you can get in the habit of regularly asking the Magical Question. This can help to bring ease to the deepest levels of your being. You'll find that allowing things to work in your favor without struggle is absolutely life-changing, and it can bring an immense, endless flow of joyful play and delight into your manifesting journey.

## Phase V

# Call In Your Destiny

In this final phase of our adventure together, we're focusing on action and implementation, so you can take everything you've learned and confidently create your very own manifesting system that's customized to fit beautifully into your life. In chapter 9, you'll discover exciting new ways to mix and match the six Magical Manifesting Ingredients in this book, using Essential, Expanded, and Elevated Manifesting Recipes designed to fit into your schedule (even if you're crazy busy), so you can keep taking action long after you've finished reading. In chapter 10, you'll take the Manifesting Archetype Quiz to discover your personal creative cycle and rhythm, so you can help yourself stick to your manifesting ritual or routine until you see the results you're looking for. Finally, in chapter 11, you'll learn to seamlessly weave the 1 Healing Breath practice into your daily life in fun, creative ways so you can raise your vibrational frequency and improve your manifesting skills all day every day and with effortless ease.

# Your Magical Manifesting Recipes

I'm the not-so-proud owner of a huge pile of unread self-help books plus a bunch of incomplete digital courses on personal growth and metaphysical topics that range from creating abundance and becoming superconscious to healing core wounds. It always begins the same way: I flip to the first page of a new personal growth book, filled with excited anticipation, or I start a course, fully prepared to complete every activity and exercise. But sooner or later, my sizzling enthusiasm fizzles out, and I'm left disappointed that I didn't get to the last page in the book or the last activity in the course yet again. As it turns out, I'm a self-starter, but I'm also a self-stopper, and I'm guessing I'm not the only one.

Like me, you might have started a personal growth program or book and promised yourself that this time you would apply everything you learned every single day until you got what you wanted, no matter what. But thirty pages into the book or a few days into the course, you found yourself faltering. Your heart was still in it, but that promise that you made to yourself at the start became a distant memory as you found yourself returning to old emotional, behavioral, and thought patterns that gave you the same results as before.

If this is you (or if you think this could be you in a week or so after you finish reading this book), I've got some great news: you've successfully reached the final phase of our exciting manifesting adventure together, which means you're *this close* to making the transformational manifesting practices in this book a part of your daily life and seeing your True Desires come to life. So let's not stop now.

In honor of your persistence, patience, and passion in getting this far, I've decided to devote this final phase of our journey to helping you design a fun, inspirational support system you can use to take action on everything you've learned so far. In this chapter, you'll discover a collection of Manifesting Recipes you can use to consistently practice all six Magical Manifesting Ingredients—the concepts, activities, and tools—you've learned so far. Just so we're on the same page, let's begin with a clear definition of what I mean when I say "Manifesting Recipe."

## The Power of Ritual

A Manifesting Recipe is essentially an easy-to-follow daily or weekly practice that you perform consistently so you can create the momentum and magic you need to see your True Desires come to life.

Rituals have been around for centuries, and if you're anything like me, you love them. When we think of rituals, we tend to picture extravagant, magical, mystical experiences and activities. But rituals can be much simpler than that, and many are inextricably woven into our everyday lives. Marriages, funerals, religious gatherings, rites of passage, and even oaths of allegiance (like to a national flag) are considered rituals.

Rituals bring us together and offer a sense of belonging and continuity in ways that few other things can. From the outlandish to the ordinary, rituals date back to our collective ancestral past and are an important part of our instinctive tribal nature. Whether we realize it or not, each of us has a deep need for ritual embedded in our unconscious. A ritual creates a sense of ceremony and celebration, which is what I love about it, and unlike a habit or a routine, a ritual can make an otherwise mundane, repeated task feel incredibly special. Our thinking mind relaxes as we gently coax our intuitive nature to come forward.

This is why I'd love for you to approach the Manifesting Recipes in this chapter as powerful rituals that offer new, exciting, and innovative ways to blend and integrate one or more of the six Magical Manifesting Ingredients. When you embrace a ritual mindset, you'll find that practicing what you've learned so far starts to become a natural part of your life, and you'll be able to easily tune into the unlimited power of the Universe for amplified, accelerated manifesting results and have fun at the same time.

## Essential, Expanded, and Elevated Manifesting Recipes

I've created three categories of Manifesting Recipes for you: Essential Manifesting Recipes for when you're super short on time, Expanded Manifesting Recipes for when you have *some* time to spare but not a whole lot (ten minutes or less), and Elevated Manifesting Recipes for when you have time for a luxurious experience that takes a couple of hours or more.

## Essential Manifesting Recipes

Essential Manifesting Recipes take less than five minutes to complete (some can be completed in seconds), which makes them incredibly convenient and easy to do. Perform the recipe of your choosing at least once a day, but feel free to repeat it as many times as you wish throughout the day. If all else fails and it happens to be one of those days where you can barely make time to brush your teeth, just take 1 Healing Breath of your choice, using the In-the-Moment Edition (refer to the steps in chapter 2, page 39), and you're done for the day. A 1 Healing Breath is more than enough to begin helping you rise to a higher-vibrational frequency, especially on days when the world feels like it's not the friendliest place to be.

### *Magical Manifesting Ingredient #1 (from Chapter 3)*

1. Set an intention.

   Do the Stop segment (step 1) of the Stop and Drop Technique (page 54). Say the declaration on page 55 or your own version first thing in the morning.

2. Delightful desires.

Simply read through the True Desires list you created (based on the exercise on page 64). This is a wonderful way to consistently offer the powerful energy of your awareness to activate your True Desires. It also doubles as a great high-vibrational practice to raise your spirits as you turn your attention to a brighter, more beautiful future.

## Magical Manifesting Ingredient #2 (from Chapter 4)

1. Love your Secret Shadow.

Set a timer to ring once an hour throughout the day. When you hear it, say the Secret Shadow Mantra (page 81) to yourself or out loud: "I love you, [insert your name here]. I love you wholly and completely. I love you, my Secret Shadow. I love that which is my Light and I love that which is my Secret Shadow."

2. Catch the Coulda-Woulda-Shouldas.

Set an intention to practice self-kindness by releasing self-judgment. As discussed on page 88, phrases that include "could," "would," or "should" are symptoms of self-judgment. Observe your thoughts and speech throughout the day when you say "I could have," "I wish I would have," or "I should have" out loud or in your mind. Bringing your attention to this habit is a wonderfully simple way to begin to let it go.

## Magical Manifesting Ingredient #3 (from Chapter 5)

1. Learn to accurately identify your fears.

Every time you experience fear or its close cousins, worry and anxiety, use the guide on page 105 to determine if it's Helpful Fear or Harmful Fear. Knowing that most of your fears are Harmful Fears that exist only in your mind will serve as a powerful reminder that you are safe and ready to experience positive changes in your manifesting journey.

2. Practice releasing Harmful Fear in the moment.

Choose one of the activities from the Easy-to-Do Techniques to Alchemize Fear section on page 115 to safely release Harmful Fear and rapidly raise your vibration.

## Magical Manifesting Ingredient #4 (from Chapter 6)

1. Commit your heart and mind to Radical Receiving.

Chant the Radical Receiving Mantra (page 129) as often as possible throughout your day.

2. Ask for a sign.

Have some fun connecting with the Universe. Ask for a sign that your desires are close at hand using the ideas in the Let the Universe Talk to You section on page 144.

## Magical Manifesting Ingredient #5 (from Chapter 7)

1. Connect with your Manifesting Avatar.

Tune into the energy of your Manifesting Avatar using the Symbolic Gesture you received from the Asking for Your Symbolic Gesture Visualization (page 168).

2. Feel into the energy of your favorite words.

Look at your collection of words that are virtues, character attributes, traits, and skills for your Manifesting Avatar that you created in Step #1: Assemble (page 161). Read through your list of favorite words or phrases, and take a moment to tune into the energy of each word.

## Magical Manifesting Ingredient #6 (from Chapter 8)

1. Instantly enter into the energy of joyful play.

Ask the Magical Question on page 192 at least once every day. Repeat it throughout your day, especially if you're feeling blue, stuck, or uncertain.

2. Keep a living list of joyful, playful activities.

Refer to the How to Invite the Energy of Joyful Play into Your Heart section (page 186) to teach yourself to recognize the energy of joyful play. Reflect on an activity you can do that brings in the energy of joyful play for you, and note it down in your journal or digital device. Keep this list alive by adding to it at least once every day. Doing this will inspire and motivate you to invite joyful play into your day-to-day life.

# Expanded Manifesting Recipes

Expanded Manifesting Recipes take a few minutes to complete (typically less than ten minutes), and while this is longer than for the Essential Manifesting Recipes, you'll find they're pretty doable even if you're juggling a tight schedule. Do one of these activities at least once a day, but feel free to repeat as many times as you wish throughout your day.

## Magical Manifesting Ingredient #1 (from Chapter 3)

1. Invite your intuition to the party.
   Do the entire Stop and Drop Technique (page 54).
2. Recognize True Desire versus False Desire.
   Hone your skill in telling the difference between True Desire and False Desire. Use the exercise on page 63 to make simple choices during your day, like what to have for lunch or what show to watch.

## Magical Manifesting Ingredient #2 (from Chapter 4)

1. Practice self-kindness.
   Feel refreshed, rejuvenated, and much more inclined to be kinder to yourself by taking a Self-Kindness Nap (page 91).
2. Cultivate self-compassion.
   Encourage self-compassion with the Practicing Common Humanity for Self-Compassion exercise (page 87). Take five minutes to

bring your attention to the unassailable truth that no matter who you are or what you're going through, you are not alone.

## Magical Manifesting Ingredient #3 (from Chapter 5)

1. Dissolve fear in the mind.
   Apply the Fear into Gold tool (page 112) to dissolve fears that enter your mind.

2. Release fear in the body.
   Apply the Relaxed Protection tool (page 114) to teach your body to release fear.

## Magical Manifesting Ingredient #4 (from Chapter 6)

1. Call in Conscious Liberation.
   Say the Mantra of Light (page 134) to invite the energy of Conscious Liberation.

2. Embody the spirit of Conscious Liberation.
   Hold the Mudra of Light (the Garuda Mudra) on page 135 for 60 to 120 seconds. Do this as many times as you wish.

## Magical Manifesting Ingredient #5 (from Chapter 7)

1. Uncover your Symbolic Gesture.
   Do the Asking for Your Symbolic Gesture Visualization (page 168). If you've completed this exercise and you already have one, you can do it again whenever you feel called to update or change your Symbolic Gesture.

2. Receive wisdom from your Manifesting Avatar.
   Identify a problem or challenge you're facing. Use your Symbolic Gesture to bring your Manifesting Avatar forward, then spend five to ten minutes journaling or recording a voice message about this issue *as* your Manifesting Avatar. You'll be amazed at the wisdom that flows through!

## Magical Manifesting Ingredient #6 (from Chapter 8)

1. Create your list of joyful, playful activities.

   Think back to when you were a child. What were some of the activities you loved to do? Draw, run, swim, dance your heart out? Make a list of three to five activities and commit to doing at least one today. If you have a living list of joyful, playful activities (refer to the Essential Recipe for Magical Manifesting Ingredient #6 on page 201), you can choose an activity from that list.

2. Turn a boring task into a game.

   Pick a task that bores you to tears and turn it into something you enjoy. Refer to the instructions in the How to Invite the Energy of Joyful Play into Your Heart section (page 186).

# Elevated Manifesting Recipes

Here's where things get delightfully, deliciously juicy and deep! The following are go-to practices for times when you have a couple of hours, half a day, or maybe even an entire weekend on your hands. Elevated Manifesting Recipes are designed for you to fully immerse yourself in the magic of the Universe to speed up your manifesting journey.

## Magical Manifesting Ingredient #1 (from Chapter 3)

1. Create your True Desires list.

   If you haven't yet, create your True Desires list using the instructions on page 64. If you've already listed your True Desires and chosen your top three to five, use the exercise in the True Desire versus False Desire section (page 63) to check if you are feeling fully aligned with each one. If you want to go even deeper with this, use the following journal prompts to clarify, energize, and activate your True Desires by tuning into the wisdom of your Manifesting Avatar. Use the instructions in the Manifest Now! Stay on Track with Your Manifesting Avatar section in chapter 7 (page 170) to do this.

Prompt 1: *I'll know my True Desires have come to pass when...*

Prompt 2: *When I need support or help in manifesting my True Desires, I will...*

Prompt 3: *When my True Desires are a part of my reality, I will feel...*

Prompt 4: *It's easy to manifest my True Desires because I am...*

Prompt 5: *I deserve to have my True Desires enter my reality because...*

Prompt 6: *These True Desires will let me contribute to the world because...*

2. Take your intuition out on the town.

   Take a trip to your favorite restaurant or shopping mall or out into nature. Use your intuition to guide your choices every step of the way. For instance, if you're walking in the woods, let your intuition guide you on which path to take, when it's time to stop and go home, or at any point when you have to make a choice or decision.

## *Magical Manifesting Ingredient #2 (from Chapter 4)*

1. Raise your vibration.

   Complete the entire How to Authentically Elevate Your Vibe with 1 Healing Breath exercise (page 73). When you're done and you feel attuned to a higher-vibrational energy, allow yourself to sit still for a moment so you can take in the feeling of genuine positivity.

2. Shine a light on your Secret Shadow.

   Complete the entire Loving Your Secret Shadow exercise (page 80).

## *Magical Manifesting Ingredient #3 (from Chapter 5)*

1. Become masterful at recognizing Harmful Fear.

   Bring awareness on how Harmful Fear shows up in your day-to-day life for ten straight days (refer to the lists in the section called

Helpful Fear versus Harmful Fear: How to Tell the Difference on page 105 to help yourself accurately identify and recognize Harmful Fear). Journal about your experience every single day. When you're done with day 10, read through every entry. See if you can detect patterns and commonalities to identify how Harmful Fear shows up for you. Does it come up every time you speak to your supervisor at work? Does it show up when you're in social situations? Detecting these patterns and knowing that Harmful Fear is a perceived threat that lives only in your mind will help you loosen its grip on your life.

2. Embody deep safety.

Do the Building a Bridge of Safety exercise, parts 1 and 2 (pages 112 and 114). You can go ahead with this activity even if you're not feeling afraid. It's always a good idea to teach your body and mind what it feels like to be truly safe. Regularly building a Bridge of Safety can help to rewire your brain so you can trade low-grade fear that often shows up as anxiety and worry for deep safety that you can generate at will.

## Magical Manifesting Ingredient #4 (from Chapter 6)

1. Invoke the Light.

Do the Invoking the Light Candle Ritual (this happens to be a favorite of mine!) on page 142 twice a day for three months.

2. Activate Conscious Liberation.

Perform the entire Light of Empowered Serenity: Deep and Delightful version (page 135) to fully experience and activate Conscious Liberation.

## Magical Manifesting Ingredient #5 (from Chapter 7)

1. Design your Manifesting Avatar.

If you haven't done so yet, design your Manifesting Avatar, referring to the guidelines that begin on page 160.

2. Connect with your Manifesting Avatar.

Look for opportunities to tune into and connect with your Manifesting Avatar using the exercises in the Consistently Working with Your Manifesting Avatar section (page 168).

### *Magical Manifesting Ingredient #6 (from Chapter 8)*

1. Create your Sacred Altar of Joyful Play or Sacred Container of Joyful Play.

Set aside a day (or more) to create your Altar of Joyful Play or Sacred Container of Joyful Play (page 187).

2. Play big!

Choose a skill or hobby that you want to do just for fun, and take the first steps to make it happen. For instance, if you want to learn to play the guitar, look online for guitar lessons or self-taught classes, search for music stores in your area, and consider purchasing a guitar.

I've created these Essential, Expanded, and Elevated Manifesting Recipes based on my personal experiences and my work with clients and friends. These recipes are extraordinarily powerful and effective, especially when practiced regularly. Having said that, I'm all about taking what you learn and making it your own, so please feel free to play with these ideas and adapt them according to your personal needs and preferences.

## Manifest Now! Creating Accelerated Results with Your Magical Manifesting Recipes

You've just discovered a whole bunch of Manifesting Recipes—in the Essential, Expanded, and Elevated categories—and now it's time to put what you've learned into practice. But don't worry—you don't have to implement every single recipe every day to see results (that would totally defeat the purpose of doing these easy-to-do Manifesting Recipes!). You can simply start by choosing just one Manifesting Recipe that you'd like to work with once a day over the next week or a few times throughout the week.

I encourage you to adopt an experimental approach where you test a new Manifesting Recipe each week so you can decide on the ones that you want to work with regularly. You can certainly test every single one of the 18 recipes in this chapter if you wish, but if that feels overwhelming, choose just one recipe from each of the three categories and allow your Authentic Self to guide you.

You can easily adapt the exercise in the Connect with Your Authentic Self section (page 65) to do this. Just replace your True Desires list with the Manifesting Recipes in this chapter and you'll arrive at the three recipes that will work best for you at this time. Gentle persistence and consistency are the keys to success, and this means the more you work with the Manifesting Recipes of your choice, the faster you'll see your True Desires manifest. When you're done choosing your Manifesting Recipes, start practicing right away so your efforts will quickly become a beautiful manifesting ritual that you love.

# The Quiz: Find Your Manifesting Archetype

Whether we realize it or not, each of us has a personal creative cycle and rhythm that helps us design, write, make art, come up with ideas for a business, and, yes, manifest our dreams in flow and with ease. For some, this creative cycle can show up as short, powerful, and often unexpected bursts of energy that allow them to work with unrelenting focus and flow. For others, it can feel like gentle waves on a sandy beach—their creative energy comes and goes with fairly regular predictability.

I help my clients identify their personal creative style by having them complete a unique quiz that I designed based on hours and hours of experience working closely with spiritual entrepreneurs from diverse cultures and backgrounds, so they can express themselves authentically, bravely, and effectively in their writing. It's a fun, eye-opening quiz that consists of custom-designed questions that can help anyone gain an understanding of the natural ebbs and flows of their creative energy. My clients have used their quiz results to honor and respect their individual cycles and rhythms so they can effortlessly channel their creative energy to write for their business and achieve great results in increased income flow and significant growth in their audience and client base.

Writing isn't so different from manifesting. Both are profound acts of creation that can powerfully transport ideas, visions, and dreams from the intangible world of energy into the tangible world of our physical reality. Using this quiz, you can accurately identify your creative cycle and rhythm to manifest anything you want.

## The Manifesting Archetype Quiz

The Manifesting Archetype Quiz will reveal your personal manifesting and creative style, and your results will help you to faithfully and consistently stick to just about any manifesting ritual under the sun, including every single one of the 18 Manifesting Recipes from the previous chapter.

Your quiz results will tell you if you're a Divine Nurturer, an Incarnated Goddess, an Earth Angel, a Cosmic Spirit, a Sacred Seeker, or a Spiritual Warrior. You'll also discover a Magic Mantra based on your Manifesting Archetype. Your mantra can help to create a sense of safety for both the conscious and the unconscious mind so you can allow creative energy to flow freely and easily. Use your Magic Mantra any time during the day or whenever you need a little creative boost.

1. It makes me feel so special and so loved when others …
   a. Offer genuine praise and compliments
   b. Recognize my accomplishments and appreciate my input and advice
   c. Tell me I'm special and that my opinion is important to them
   d. Let me be who I am
   e. Reassure me that they are always there for me
   f. Are honest and direct with me and stand up for me
2. I would NEVER …
   a. Get into an angry, aggressive confrontation with someone, even if I feel I'm right
   b. Go on a holiday without a clear daily agenda

    c. Enjoy being the center of attention in a large gathering

    d. Feel motivated to complete a project that I'm not deeply passionate about

    e. Make a major decision without doing some deep research

    f. Hide my true opinion just so I can agree with everyone and be part of the group

3. People who know me might say I'm...

    a. A peaceful dreamer

    b. Ambitious and a bit of a perfectionist

    c. Sensitive and gentle

    d. Fun-loving and charming

    e. Smart and likable

    f. Independent and reliable

4. Which of the following is your biggest challenge when it comes to being productive at home or at work?

    a. Following a routine and creating systems and processes so things run smoothly

    b. Getting caught up in what you're doing and then having difficulty being on time or sticking to a timeline because you want everything to be absolutely flawless

    c. Not second-guessing yourself. You have a hard time moving forward with confidence.

    d. Sticking to one project until it's done. You're always juggling a million tasks at the same time.

    e. Feeling relaxed and in control. You constantly worry something's going to go wrong.

    f. Asking for help even if you desperately need it

5. If you could wave a magic wand and change one unwanted trait in yourself, what would it be?

    a. Being too sensitive about other people's opinions and criticism of your actions and decisions

    b. Your need to control and get everything right. It's exhausting.

    c. Being a people pleaser. You end up feeling angry and resentful of everyone, including the people you love.

    d. Lack of commitment to and focus on your own future success. It stops you from achieving your highest potential.

    e. Your inability to fully trust yourself

    f. Your tendency to be too direct. You hurt people without meaning to.

6. Which word are you deeply drawn to?

    a. Peace

    b. Immaculate

    c. Love

    d. Freedom

    e. Wisdom

    f. Truth

7. Which of the following closely describes your personal preference when it comes to working on creative projects, such as writing, arts and crafts, learning or playing a musical instrument, cooking, etc.?

    a. You work on it when you're inspired. You tend to be spontaneous and unpredictable, but when you start, you can get a lot done.

    b. You are focused and methodical, and you like to take your time so you don't make mistakes.

    c. You create in cycles. You do things consistently for a while and then stop for long periods of time.

    d. You tend to work on many different creative projects at the same time. You know you'll get bored and give up if you don't.

    e. You're slow and steady. You like to go deep so you know you're doing quality work.

    f. You work on your projects only when you feel strongly inspired or intensely motivated.

8.  Your ideal vacation is...

    a. Restorative, revitalizing, and healing. To you, vacations are about experiencing simple, leisurely pleasures, like going for long walks by the beach or in the woods or losing yourself in the beauty of a sunrise or sunset.

    b. Indulgent, luxurious, and pleasurable. When it comes to taking time off, it's all about extravagant spa retreats, five-star hotels, and first-class travel all the way.

    c. Peaceful, cozy, and quiet. It's not your dream holiday if you're not meditating, reflecting, and writing in your journal.

    d. Thrilling, exciting, and adventurous. Skydiving, bungee jumping, or any activity that gets your adrenaline pumping is perfect.

    e. Exotic, expansive, and eye-opening. You can't think of anything more exciting and rewarding than experiencing new cultures and ways of living.

    f. Helpful and useful. You'd love to spend at least some of your vacation time supporting your favorite cause, whether that's planting trees or volunteering at a soup kitchen or an animal sanctuary.

9.  Your aunt's book club members (you don't know them well) have asked for your help in throwing her a surprise birthday party. What do you do first?

    a. Get to know everyone so you feel comfortable working with them

    b. Think about how you can come up with the best possible ideas, insights, and input before you contribute

    c. Start by letting everyone know that you're there to help them as much as humanly possible

    d. Immediately dive in and start getting things done

    e. Research themes and ideas around "how to throw awesome surprise birthday parties"

    f. Take the lead and organize a group meeting so everyone can collaborate and work together easily

10. Which animal captures the essence of who you are?
    a. The whimsical and colorful butterfly
    b. The elegant and flamboyant peacock
    c. The sweet and friendly puppy
    d. The energetic and playful dolphin
    e. The wise and observant owl
    f. The powerful and protective lioness

11. Which crystal energy calls to you right now?
    a. The magical, healing energy of a clear quartz crystal
    b. The abundant, potent energy of citrine
    c. The comforting, loving energy of rose quartz
    d. The bright, revitalizing energy of carnelian
    e. The positive, confident energy of aventurine
    f. The stabilizing, clarifying energy of amazonite

## If Your Answers Were Mostly "A"

Your Manifesting Archetype is the Divine Nurturer and your Magic Mantra is:

*Trusting myself intuitively allows me to help others
and to create positive transformations in the world.*

You are a highly evolved soul, full of deep compassion and generosity for Mother Earth and her children. You have a natural ability to feel aligned and one with the Universe, and you are devoted to the vision of all sentient beings living and working together in harmony. You dislike confrontations, raised voices, and angry outbursts, but you will find the courage to take a stand and speak up when you feel strongly about a cause or an issue.

You love coming up with creative ideas to support your manifesting journey, and you can easily receive these ideas through Divine Downloads from the Universe, Source, or Divine Perfection or higher beings such as angels or your spirit guides. You are gifted at seeing the big picture when it comes to manifesting your True Desires, but you quickly lose interest if you have to spend a lot of time drilling down the specifics and details.

*Your Personal Manifesting Style*

Working with step-by-step manifesting rituals, such as the Manifesting Recipes from the previous chapter, will give you the structure and consistency you need to attract what you want. Give yourself permission to adapt or redesign mainstream manifesting methods (such as building a vision board) based on intuitive insights or Divine Downloads you may receive.

You can accentuate your ability to manifest when you show up as who you truly are. This will allow you to naturally align with the Universe. You can create magical momentum in your manifesting journey when you implement any of the self-love practices in chapter 4.

# If Your Answers Were Mostly "B"

Your Manifesting Archetype is the Incarnated Goddess and your Magic Mantra is:

*Enjoying the journey and the flow of life allows me to*
*create my highest vision with grace and ease.*

You are inspired by high ideals and a clear sense of right and wrong. You are not afraid to work hard, and you will go to great lengths to align with the Universe so you can bring your goals and dreams to life. Your incredible drive and self-motivation are legendary. You dislike chaos and losing control more than most people, and you can be a bit of a perfectionist.

Your natural optimism and magnetic personality effortlessly inspire faith and trust in people. You may or may not know it, but you easily inspire those around you, and this is a big reason why it's good to share your manifesting efforts and wins with others.

*Your Personal Manifesting Style*

You'll probably enjoy working with the Manifesting Recipes from the previous chapter more than any of the other Manifesting Archetypes will because it will give you that sense of control and focus that you love. Your natural optimism and high energy are major plus points when it comes to attracting your True Desires, so make sure you choose a Manifesting Recipe that feels inspiring, exciting, and energizing to you.

You like to get to the point and get things done quickly, so think about starting with an Essential Manifesting Recipe. Consider doing the Garuda Mudra from chapter 6 (page 135) multiple times during the day to invite the energy of Conscious Liberation and release the tendency for perfectionism that can block your manifesting process.

## If Your Answers Were Mostly "C"

Your Manifesting Archetype is the Earth Angel and your Magic Mantra is:

*Knowing on the deepest level of my being that I am important
lets me shine bright and light up the world.*

You have a heart of gold. Your kind, loving, and generous nature makes everyone around you feel loved and cared for. You are happy to have others take center stage while you remain behind the scenes doing what you do best: creating an environment of love, kindness, and caring. Offering support and helping others comes naturally to you, and there's a good chance that some of your True Desires include attracting wonderful things for others. You take longer than most people to collect your thoughts before you communicate, and you think carefully before you decide on what you want to manifest. You're not afraid of hard work, but your generous, giving nature can sometimes leave you feeling drained and unmotivated.

### Your Personal Manifesting Style

Take as much time as you need to reflect on the six Magical Manifesting Ingredients in this book and how they could work for you. When it's time to choose a Manifesting Recipe, go with the one that feels intuitively expansive right now—something that makes you feel relaxed and lighthearted when you think about adding it to your daily or weekly schedule. Work closely with your Manifesting Avatar using the practices in the Consistently Working with Your Manifesting Avatar section in chapter 7 (page 168) to uncover what you need to stay motivated and supported throughout your manifesting journey.

It's also good to invite a trusted, loving friend or partner to cheer you on in your manifesting journey. Support from people you love will create a big boost in your energy and your overall ability to successfully manifest your True Desires.

# If Your Answers Were Mostly "D"

Your Manifesting Archetype is the Cosmic Spirit and your Magic Mantra is:

*Giving myself permission to be who I truly am
is the most powerful and aligned path to abundance, joy, and success.*

Within you lives the soul of a joyful wanderer who enjoys spontaneity and fun. You love being a part of activities and experiences that allow you to express your adventurous soul. You like to travel and meet new people, and you believe in living in the moment. You possess magical, irresistible charm, and others are easily drawn to you.

Your imaginative, impulsive nature inspires creativity, enthusiasm, and excitement in all those whose lives you touch. You love discovering and learning about various manifesting activities in quick succession, and you can quickly feel bored if you are confined to just one method for too long.

## *Your Personal Manifesting Style*

You'll love having the flexibility and the option to choose your own adventure in creating or adapting a manifesting ritual. When it comes to choosing from the Essential, Expanded, or Elevated Manifesting Recipes in the previous chapter, consider going with the flow based on how you feel and what resonates for you on any given day. Feel free to switch between Manifesting Recipes any time you want to.

Sticking to a manifesting ritual in the long term might prove to be a challenge, so go ahead and talk to a friend or partner who can help you stay accountable, or work with the Altar of Joyful Play or the Sacred Container of Joyful Play from chapter 8 (page 187) so you don't end up disinterested and bored. To maximize your overall manifesting efforts and to speed up results, think about joining or starting a manifesting group, online or in person, where everyone can inspire and motivate one another by sharing their experiences, hopes, dreams, and wins.

## If Your Answers Were Mostly "E"

Your Manifesting Archetype is the Sacred Seeker and your Magic Mantra is:

*It is good to relax and open myself up to beautiful new experiences.*
*Everything is happening for my highest good.*

You can bring love, harmony, and clarity to any situation with your profound ability to uncover and share the truth. You are a wonderful judge of character and you hold yourself—and others—to a high level of integrity. You value knowledge, and you need to know and understand as much as you can before you make a decision.

You enjoy reading and research and can go on doing these things for hours at a time. You like going deep into any subject that interests you, and this includes the art of manifesting. You will not stop until you have discovered the facts and truth about various aspects of manifesting and attracting what you want, but your love for additional knowledge can sometimes turn into indefinite procrastination.

### Your Personal Manifesting Style

You'll enjoy the predictability of working with a repeatable manifesting ritual or the Manifesting Recipes from the previous chapter. To avoid delays and unwanted procrastination, make a commitment to yourself to dive in and put your ritual or Manifesting Recipe into practice even before you feel you're ready. If you find yourself procrastinating, use the Fear into Gold tool in chapter 5 (page 112) to help you release the need to put things off.

It's also good to give yourself permission to research and read other books and sources on manifesting so you'll have a vast reservoir of knowledge and wisdom to work with during your manifesting journey. The only caveat? Make sure you start taking action sooner rather than later.

# If Your Answers Were Mostly "F"

Your Manifesting Archetype is the Spiritual Warrior and your Magic Mantra is:

*Life is easy when I relax, let go, and allow myself
to reignite my creativity and replenish my soul.*

You are the soul of authenticity and honesty, and you wouldn't dream of shying away from standing up for what's right. You are a devoted supporter of causes that protect and provide for those who can't fight for themselves. You are independent and have the drive and focus to motivate others, but you can sometimes push yourself too hard and be incredibly self-judgmental.

You love using your manifesting skills and working with the Universe to help support your community, the environment, animals, the world, or all of the above. You don't have a lot of patience for manifesting tools and techniques that feel vague and "up in the air," and you prefer working with methods that are effective and down-to-earth.

## *Your Personal Manifesting Style*

Reliability is the name of the game for you when it comes to partnering with the Universe. You'll find yourself drawn to working with the Manifesting Recipes that feel practical and actionable to you.

Allow yourself to experiment with, customize, and expand on any of the Manifesting Recipes from the previous chapter or create something totally unique that supports you in your quest to live a life of meaning, purpose, and contribution. Doing this will appeal to your independent, self-reliant nature and will inspire you to consistently implement your custom Manifesting Recipe so you can quickly see your True Desires manifest. You can effectively elevate your manifesting skills by implementing the antidotes to self-judgment in chapter 4 (page 89).

Now that you know your Manifesting Archetype and manifesting style, you have everything you need to align with your personal creative cycle and rhythm so that manifesting what you want becomes inevitable.

Keep in mind that because we are complex, creative beings, you might find that you resonate with the description of one or more of the Manifesting Archetypes other than your own. This is to be expected and is perfectly normal. Your results reflect the energy you are in at this time, and you were led to the Manifesting Archetype that is most prominent within you right now. I invite you to trust your answers and your results, and I highly recommend that you work with your current manifesting style plus your Magic Mantra for three months. After that time, feel free to adopt some of the ideas from the other Manifesting Archetypes or combine various ideas and insights to create your own manifesting style.

# Manifest Now!
# Release Resistance with Self-Forgiveness

Performing a daily or weekly manifesting ritual in alignment with your Manifesting Archetype and your personal manifesting style is likely to feel strange or even stressful, especially in the beginning. This is absolutely normal, and it certainly doesn't mean you're doing anything wrong. Know that integrating new actions and behaviors, even when we know it's for our highest good, can bring up unexpected internal resistance in the form of procrastination, frustration, and other unwanted emotions. This can lead to unconscious self-sabotage, where you can become more and more inconsistent in performing your manifesting ritual and eventually stop altogether. I've found that the most effective way to heal self-sabotage for good is to practice self-forgiveness. An unforgiving heart is shut tight against all that is divine and resists all that is expansive, including our right to manifest and create what we desire. Whether we realize it or not, self-sabotage and inner resistance arise from deep-seated feelings of inadequacy, feeling like we're not good enough just as we are, or believing we are flawed, wrong, or imperfect in some way. But nothing could be further from the truth.

We are born from the unlimited creative energy of the Universe, which is the energy of Divine Perfection. We are all children of Divine Perfection and we are meant to learn, grow, and evolve throughout our lives so we can remember our innate divinity. It is our birthright to live with pleasurable ease, love, passion, and harmony and to attract anything we want, which includes everything that lifts us up and raises the collective energy of our world. But we are taught to believe that we must earn the right to get what we want, and so we hold back from allowing ourselves to be completely happy and fulfilled, even though we are worthy simply because we are born. It's why practicing self-forgiveness can be supremely challenging for so many people.

I developed the following self-forgiveness exercise while working with a client, and I promise that no matter how much you may resist self-forgiveness, this practice is gentle on the spirit, soothing to the heart, and deeply comforting to the mind and body. Like the 1 Healing Breath practice, this beautiful, uncomplicated exercise dropped into my mind and heart from Source as an instantaneous Divine Download. Here's how to do it.

### Self-Forgiveness Practice

Begin by connecting with the Divine Perfection within and the boundless divinity of the Universe with the In-the-Moment Edition of 1 Healing Breath of Divinity. (You can find the activated image of this 1 Healing Breath in the free gift bundle that you can sign up to download at www.shantinirajah.com /manifest.) When you've taken your 1 Healing Breath of Divinity, continue to keep your hands over your heart for this next part of the activity. Bring your awareness to the warmth of your hands over your heart, and as you experience this warmth, repeat this word to yourself: *forgiving*. Keep repeating this word until you feel a shift in your energy as you begin to relax and feel the soothing comfort of forgiveness flow through you. Do this for just a moment or two or as long as you wish.

Practice this self-forgiveness ritual as many times as you wish. You'll find that this simple process is deeply healing and transformative—maybe even a little addictive, but in a good way—as it draws you closer and closer to your innate divinity each time you do it. In time, you'll fully reconnect with the truth of who you are, and you'll find that you no longer feel undeserving or unworthy of going for bigger, bolder goals and dreams. You'll be able to commit to your own happiness, stick to your manifesting rituals, and attract anything you want with ease, grace, joy, and freedom, knowing in your soul that you deserve all that you desire just because you are alive.

Eleven

# Breathe Your Way
# to Anything You Want

As you made your way through this book, you probably noticed that the thread that connects just about every practice, activity, and Magical Manifesting Ingredient is—yep—the 1 Healing Breath. I like to say the 1 Healing Breath practice is an invitation and a reminder to come home to yourself. It's a Microaction Manifesting practice that allows you to create what you want with every intentional breath you take throughout the day, and it's also Microaction Meditation that inspires presence in seconds.

The beauty and power of the 1 Healing Breath practice lies in its incredible versatility. It's one of the simplest spiritual practices around, and it can be applied to just about every manifesting tool, practice, technique, or modality you can think of. You can use it to connect with the Divine during a chaotic day or create a moment of rest, play, and self-love when you need it most. It's for anyone who feels they don't have the bandwidth to do a bunch of complex, complicated methodologies or time-consuming self-care routines. You don't need to spend a week meditating in the middle of a forest and you don't need to draw a bath, visit a spa, or book an expensive luxury vacation. You just need to breathe with intention, and the results are extraordinarily deep and expansive.

## A Wonderful New Way of Being

When you consistently practice 1 Healing Breath, you'll find that you'll be able to achieve and sustain high-vibrational states with ease as you continuously rise to greater levels of freedom, abundance, and creativity. You'll also find that you can successfully release painful emotions and difficult thoughts whenever they arise. In a very short period of time—a week or two and sometimes even in a couple of days—you'll realize that you are starting to let go of habitual cycles of stressful rumination and anxiety that you may have been struggling with for years or even decades. In time, you'll embrace a wonderful new way of being in this world as you train your energy system to shift from needless stress and worry to fully experiencing genuine, positive emotions like joy and tranquility in just a few seconds or sometimes even in an instant.

That's why it's crucial that you find ways to make 1 Healing Breath a natural, ongoing part of your life so you're intentionally shaping your experience, moment to moment, many times a day, as you manifest the life that you've always dreamed of.

## Creative Ways to Use 1 Healing Breath

Here's a quick list of ideas and suggestions you can use to seamlessly integrate the 1 Healing Breath practice into your life.

Use your 1 Healing Breath practice to:

+ Begin and end your meditation practice or yoga routine
+ Get unstuck from rumination
+ Unlock creativity before you write, paint, or work on a creative project
+ Open your energy to receive ideas, Divine Downloads, and messages from the Universe
+ Improve your mood and overall sense of wellbeing

+ Instantly attune your energy system to high-vibrational energies or emotions such as gratitude and love

+ Invite calm before or during a difficult experience, such as a challenging conversation with your partner

+ Center yourself before a spiritual practice such as an oracle card reading. Create a powerful "I AM" affirmation. Just say the words "I AM" followed by your chosen energy as you take your breath. For instance, if you're taking 1 Healing Breath of Calm, as you take your healing breath, say to yourself or out loud, "I am calm."

+ Rapidly refresh, revitalize, and reinvigorate your body

That's just a handful of ways to include 1 Healing Breath in your daily experience. The list could go on and on. Give yourself permission to test, experiment, and get creative with how you want to work with this deceptively simple yet powerfully transformative practice, and you'll find, like I have, that there is no limit to how you can use 1 Healing Breath to heighten your vibrational frequency and elevate your manifesting skills by enhancing focus and inviting inner calm, no matter what else is going on around you.

## Pairing 1 Healing Breath with Popular Manifesting Practices

I love every manifesting activity I've ever tried—even the ones that don't work well! Most of these techniques are fun to do, and in this way, they're great for stepping into the energy of joyful play. Plus, just about every manifesting practice in existence aligns beautifully with 1 Healing Breath, which is a lovely little healing experience to add to your day. In other words, you can't lose!

I've compiled a collection of popular manifesting activities that pair well with 1 Healing Breath. I recommend that you take a 1 Healing Breath of your choice, either the In-the-Moment Edition or the Extended Edition, at the start and end of your manifesting practice, and continuously work with the In-the-Moment Edition throughout the activity. (Remember that you have access to a free collection of powerful, positive images to choose from if you need ideas. Just go to www.shantinirajah.com/manifest to sign up to download them.)

You'll find that opening and closing with 1 Healing Breath and also taking 1 Healing Breaths during the activity is a beautiful way to create a sacred ceremonial container, invite positive energy into your experience, and continuously rise into higher consciousness so you can easily tap into your Authentic Self and your intuition and align with the Universe.

## Creating Your Vision Board

Ah, the always popular vision board! It's a must-have tool in any manifestor's tool kit. It helps to focus your energy and attention on your desires and effectively communicate with the Universe in a language that gets the message across loud and clear: the language of images and emotions.

## Scripting

Scripting is one of the oldest manifesting practices around. For hundreds of years, magical, mystical folks used a quill and ink, then pen and paper, and now fingers on a keyboard to write their intentions and desires like they have already happened. For instance, if you're looking to manifest a peaceful world, you could write, "All beings are living in peace and harmony all around the world with effortless ease." There are a bunch of interesting guidelines when it comes to scripting, and my favorite is the 369 *method*, which is about writing down your intention three times in the morning, six times in the afternoon, and nine times in the evening. A friend did this for a month and manifested a total of $7,000, which she received through multiple channels: two payments from clients, an unexpected gift that was transferred directly into her account, and prize money that she won at the mall!

## Performing a Burning Ritual

A burning ritual or ceremony is a transformative practice that's used to release that which no longer serves you or that which you no longer need or desire. It's perfect for letting go of low-vibrational energies that show up as thoughts, emotions, beliefs, and experiences that can hold you back from receiving your desires from the Universe. The ritual is simple. Write what you no longer want on a piece of paper, place it in a nonflammable container or space, then burn it safely and watch the fire burn out. You can state an intention as you watch the paper burn. Something easy and to the point works best, such as this:

*I release this from all levels of my being. I am healed and I am free.*

If you've never performed a burning ritual, I encourage you to give it a try. The feeling of release and relief can be palpable, and you'll notice a positive shift in your thoughts, your emotions, and possibly even your entire outlook by the time the fire burns out.

## Using a Cosmic Chest

Also referred to as a God Box, the Cosmic Chest is any kind of physical container (such as a shoebox, crate, or drawer) that holds your doubts and fears related to manifesting or anything else. Here's how it works. Every time you feel stressed, worried, or anxious, write a short note about how you feel and why. Then place it in the box and say to yourself or out loud:

*I release this to you, Universe/God/Source/Divine Perfection/Higher Intelligence, to remove, clear, and resolve in the highest and best good.*

Releasing your worries and fears in this way offers healing and comfort, as it brings your attention to the truth that you have a Higher Power on your side and you are never alone. This is an incredibly powerful and effective way to heal, release, and step into higher-vibrational energy, which can sometimes happen in seconds.

## Designing a Sigil

A sigil is a creative, symbolic representation of your desire. Sigils have been used in metaphysical ceremonies for centuries to great effect. To create your own sigil, start by writing your desire on a piece of paper. Next, list just the consonants in your written desire (write each consonant only once, even if it appears more than once). For instance, if your desire is to "Build one hundred animal sanctuaries around the world," first write the consonants, listing each one only once: B L D N H R M S C T H W. Now it's time to have some fun. Design a single symbol with the letters. You could overlay some of the letters or maybe arrange them in a concentric circle. Your design can be as simple or as intricate as you wish. If you're stuck, feel free to Google "sigil designs" for inspiration. Have fun with this! When you're done, it's time to activate your sigil. The easiest way to do this is to give it your attention and energy, so devote a minute or two to gazing at your sigil at least once a day.

## Concocting a Magical Elixir

A magical elixir allows you to physically absorb and fully embody your intention, and I happen to think it's a super cool manifesting tool. Concocting your elixir is easy. All you need is a drinking glass, a cover for the glass, water, and a clean clear quartz (optional), which is known to amplify focused energy. First, decide on your manifesting intention. Then fill the glass with water and place your crystal quartz inside if you're using one. Next, whisper your intention over the glass of water. This could be anything you want, such as "I desire to feel the energy of gratitude all day," or "I'm ready to experience Radical Receiving," or "My intention is to enjoy deep sleep tonight." Cover the glass and let your intention "sit" in the water for an hour or two. Drink the water, knowing your intention is being absorbed into all levels of your being.

## Tapping

The Emotional Freedom Technique (EFT), or *tapping*, is wildly popular with thousands of people around the world, and for good reason. It's super simple to do and creates noticeable results. Based on concepts from Traditional Chinese Medicine, EFT works by gently stimulating specific meridian points on the body to encourage the smooth flow of energy to restore balance while saying a script to address and improve your emotional, mental, and physical state. In manifesting, tapping can be used to release unwanted beliefs, thoughts, or emotions and to activate positive energies. Google "tapping scripts for manifesting" for a step-by-step process, plus countless scripts you can use to release inner blocks to make way for a successful, healing manifesting experience.

## 1 Healing Breath Is All You Need

The 1 Healing Breath isn't so much a manifesting technique as it is a way of life. We're breathing all the time, every moment of every day, even when we're asleep, so let's breathe in a way that serves and supports our manifesting journey.

When you take conscious healing breaths every day, what you're really doing is gently and intentionally rewiring your thinking, safely experiencing your emotions, and living your life in a way that's fully aligned with your Authentic Self. With every healing breath you take, you're giving yourself permission to take care of yourself and love yourself unconditionally, and at the same time you're sending clear messages to the Universe that you're ready to receive your True Desires. The way I see it, when we teach ourselves to become conscious and intentional with our breath, we are in effect learning to manifest what we want with every breath we take. It's why I like to think of 1 Healing Breath as the next level of manifesting. The best part is that you already have everything you need with you at all times: oxygen and your body.

I've seen this unbelievably simple practice lead to changes, transformations, and astonishing manifesting results. You can rise up to living your greatest purpose and experiencing your wildest dreams with just 1 Healing Breath at a time, because as it turns out, 1 Healing Breath at a time is all you need.

## Manifest Now! Higher Consciousness Journaling for Next-Level Manifesting

Unlike most books, courses, and programs about the art of manifesting, you might have noticed that this book did not feature one of the most well-known manifesting activities around: the ubiquitous daily gratitude list or gratitude journal. This is an incredibly popular manifesting tool, and the idea is to essentially answer one question: "What are you grateful for today?" Depending on whose teachings you follow, you'll be asked to list 10, 20, 30, or even 50 answers to this question in a gratitude journal.

Gratitude is, undoubtedly, one of the most powerful and high-vibrational energies you could ever experience, and it can work like rocket fuel for manifesting what you want. But I've found that simply listing what you're grateful for without fully immersing yourself in the experience and energy of gratitude greatly diminishes the value of this tool. At best, this powerful practice will start to feel like an empty, meaningless activity that brings little or no benefit to your manifesting experience. At worst, forcing yourself to think about what you're grateful for when you've just had an argument with your partner or you're nursing a headache can become something stressful that you must do—yet another thing to add to your never-ending to-do list. It's why I've devised an alternative journaling technique that lets you experience gratitude without having to stress over it, strive for it, or even think about it.

The Higher Consciousness journaling method lets you fully accept, on all levels of your being, that you are a masterful manifestor and you have the power to bring through beautiful, inspiring, life-enhancing manifestations, both big and small, without trying and even in the middle of an otherwise difficult day, week, month, or even year. This unique journaling method involves intentionally practicing the sensory art of noticing all that you have successfully manifested that day and then journaling about it that night, so you can progressively rise up to higher levels of consciousness while experiencing a spontaneous flow of gratitude at the same time.

Noticing, in this context, simply means resting your attention, lightly and gently, on all that is going well in your life and owning that you have attracted these beautiful experiences and things even if you feel like you had nothing to do with it. Remember that you were born from the unlimited creative energies of the Universe, and as a creative being, you are continuously manifesting your experience even if you are not aware that you are doing so.

Here's how to do this deeply empowering practice. Begin by noticing all that is good and true for you throughout the day. You certainly don't have to wait until you manifest something big or significant from your True Desires list to enter it into your journal. It could be noticing something simple, like the way sunlight bounces off the glistening dew of the early morning or the pretty yellow bird singing outside your window, and then giving yourself over to this experience in the moment, knowing that you have successfully attracted these positive experiences. Don't feel like you have to do anything special here. Just bringing awareness to the truth that you have manifested these good things in your day is extraordinarily powerful.

Next, do the In-the-Moment Edition of 1 Healing Breath of Awareness, or any other 1 Healing Breath energy that feels aligned for you, so you can transform your noticing practice into a multisensory experience. (Feel free to refer to or find inspiration from one of the collection of images and energies you have access to for free as part of the gift bundle that you can sign up to download at www.shantinirajah.com/manifest.)

Bringing your breath into your moment of noticing will allow you to fully absorb the experience while it is happening and anchor it in your mind, heart, memory, and energy for easy recall. Then, at the end of your day, take five or ten minutes, or even just a minute or two, to write about the delightful, uplifting things you manifested and noticed in your journal. Feel free to jot down points or write short phrases. There is no need to craft full sentences or fill page after page in your journal if that's not what you want to do.

The Higher Consciousness journaling method allows gratitude and appreciation to arise spontaneously while you are journaling, without you having to think about it. The act of writing in your journal will let you bring forward all the good things that happened to you and for you in your day from the energetic realm of your mind to your physical reality on the page. This transition is important, as it helps you to see yourself as the creator of your life that you are, and you'll find that as you keep doing this practice, unexpected good things will begin to appear in your life and you'll be manifesting wonderful new experiences without having to actually do anything to manifest them. That's how you'll know that you've finally made the transition from manifesting as an act of doing to becoming a masterful manifestor where you are intuitively and effortlessly attracting all that you desire and more simply by being who you are.

# Conclusion

Believe it or not, we've arrived at the end of our journey together. I deeply hope you enjoyed the ride! You have successfully assembled a phenomenally powerful manifesting tool kit that includes six Magical Manifesting Ingredients along with 18 Magical Manifesting Recipes, plus techniques, processes, and exercises, including simple, effective spiritual practices that you can supercharge with the uplifting energies of the 1 Healing Breath practice. Regardless of your beliefs, background, or perceived limitations, you've learned how to activate your innate manifesting power so you can live each day as a purposeful creator of your own life experience as you attract your True Desires, whether that's starting your dream business, finding true love, helping to create a more peaceful, inclusive, and loving world, or simply and courageously speaking your truth. You now have everything you need to manifest anything you want and to transition from approaching the art of manifesting as something you do to wholly embracing manifesting as a way of being, knowing that you are becoming a masterful manifestor moment by moment as you design your reality with every intentional 1 Healing Breath you take.

Intentionally manifesting a life that you truly love is about embodying and accepting this truth: You are here to live at the highest levels of consciousness in alignment with your values as you experience life to the fullest. Accepting this truth is not a denial of what is; it's about embracing the promise and purpose of the infinitely miraculous life that is yours to live without apology or regret. You are not meant to put up with your lot in life such as it is if it's not what you want.

You see, the promise of your life is held within you as a part of your essence, just as the promise of a rose is held within its seed. Embodying this promise is vital as you embark on this journey into yourself and into realizing that you were born a masterful manifestor, even if the circumstances of your birth and your current life don't seem to support this promise at this time. This is not to say that you'll float through it all without a care in the world. Make no mistake, the journey of manifesting with focused intention, inner safety, and deep alignment is a path for the brave and those who are willing to dig deep and get real about who they are, who they are meant to be, and how they want to show up in the world. Yes, it takes some effort, but the rewards are so worth it. As you tread upon this path using the tools you've discovered in this book, you'll find that manifesting what you want starts to happen on its own, almost as a side effect of living a life that's true to yourself—a beautiful, abundant life that feels like yours and not someone else's expectations for you.

If you read between the lines, you'll see that this book is not just about manifesting what you want; it's about being who you are—and there's nothing more important, more healing, and more loving that you can do for yourself and for the world. Why? Well there is only one of you in the entire cosmos. There has never been anyone else like you and there will never be anyone like you ever again. This makes you special, magical, and rare. You are a star unlike any other star that ever was or ever will be. *When you manifest all that you desire by being yourself, you are serving, contributing to, and expanding the Universe and all of existence in a way that only YOU can.* And if you turn away from who you are, then all that you are meant to be, to create, and to bring forward, and that beautiful, precious, unlike-any-other energy that is you, will be lost to all of us.

So know this: No matter who you are or where you're from, you are worth it, you are deserving, and you are here to embrace all that the Universe has to offer. You are here to be you. The adventure we've experienced together through the pages of this book is ultimately about fully receiving and embodying an undeniable truth now and forever: when you love, accept, and become who you truly are, you will be unstoppable, and manifesting anything you want will become inevitable.

I hope this experience of unearthing the truth about what you want and giving yourself what you need and desire so you can rise up to the highest and best version of yourself has been as enlightening and empowering for you as it has been for me. Thank you from the bottom of my heart for trusting me to be your guide.

With love and deepest gratitude,
Shantini Rajah

# Recommended Reading

My personal development and spiritual journey began when I was a young teenager, and I'm deeply grateful that I've had an to opportunity to read countless books by some of the world's greatest teachers and healers as well as innovators, trailblazers, and rebels in the personal and business development space over the past few decades. The books, courses, and trainings by these incredible people have influenced, inspired, and shaped my life and the writing of this book.

The following is a recommended reading list that will help to elevate your manifesting journey like it did for me, but please know that this is by no means a static list! If you'd like up-to-date recommendations and suggestions, you'll find me sharing my ever-expanding list of transformational books, courses, and trainings @shantinirajah on Instagram, Facebook, and Threads and on my website, www.shantinirajah.com.

Brach, Tara. *Radical Compassion: Learning to Love Yourself and Your World with the Practice of RAIN.* London: Penguin Life, 2020.

Brewer, Judson. *Unwinding Anxiety: Train Your Brain to Heal Your Mind.* London: Penguin Random House UK, 2021.

Bush, Ashley Davis. *The Art and Power of Acceptance: Your Guide to Inner Peace.* London: Gaia, 2019.

Conner, Janet. *Writing Down Your Soul: How to Activate and Listen to the Extraordinary Voice Within.* Newburyport, MA: Conari Press, 2008.

Dondi, Dahlin. *The Five Elements: Understand Yourself and Enhance Your Relationships with the Wisdom of the World's Oldest Personality Type System.* New York: TarcherPerigee, 2016.

Dyer, Wayne W. *The Power of Intention: Learning to Co-create Your World Your Way.* Carlsbad, CA: Hay House, 2010.

Eden, Donna, with David Feinstein. *Energy Medicine for Women: Aligning Your Body's Energies to Boost Your Health and Vitality.* New York: Jeremy P. Tarcher/Penguin, 2008.

Fay, Deirdre. *Becoming Safely Embodied: A Guide to Organize Your Mind, Body and Heart to Feel Secure in the World.* New York: Morgan James Publishing, 2021.

Goodman, Whitney. *Toxic Positivity: Keeping It Real in a World Obsessed with Positivity.* New York: TarcherPerigree, 2022.

Hanson, Rick. *Hardwiring Happiness: The New Brain Science of Contentment, Calm, and Confidence.* New York: Harmony Books, 2016.

Hanson, Rick, with Forrest Hanson. *Resilient: How to Grow an Unshakable Core of Calm, Strength, and Happiness.* New York: Harmony Books, 2018.

Hicks, Esther, and Jerry Hicks. *Ask and It Is Given.* Carlsbad, CA: Hay House, 2004.

Jenett, Marilyn. *Feel Free to Prosper with the Simplest Prosperity Laws Available.* New York: TarcherPerigee, 2015.

Kennedy, Russell. *Anxiety Rx: A New Prescription for Anxiety Relief from the Doctor Who Created It.* Sioux Falls, SD: Awaken Village Press, 2020.

Neff, Kristin. *Self-Compassion: The Proven Power of Being Kind to Yourself.* New York: William Morrow, 2011.

Nemeth, Maria. *The Energy of Money: A Spiritual Guide to Financial and Personal Fulfillment.* New York: Wellspring/Ballantine, 2000.

Schafler, Katherine Morgan. *The Perfectionist's Guide to Losing Control: A Path to Peace and Power.* New York: Portfolio/Penguin, 2023.

Scher, Amy B. *How to Heal Yourself When No One Else Can: A Total Self-Healing Approach for Mind, Body, and Spirit.* Woodbury, MN: Llewellyn, 2016.

Scher, Andrea. *Wonder Seeker: 52 Ways to Wake Up Your Creativity and Find Your Joy.* New York: Harper Design, 2021.

Silver, Tosha. *It's Not Your Money: How to Live Fully from Divine Abundance.* Carlsbad, CA: Hay House, 2020.

Stanley, Elizabeth A. *Widen the Window: Training Your Brain and Body to Thrive During Stress and Recover from Trauma.* New York: Avery, 2019.

Van der Kolk, Bessel. *The Body Keeps the Score: Brain, Mind, and Body in the Healing of Trauma.* London: Penguin Books, 2015.

# Bibliography

Bolte, A., T. Goschke, and J. Kuhl. "Emotion and Intuition: Effects of Positive and Negative Mood on Implicit Judgments of Semantic Coherence." *Psychological Science* 14, no. 5 (2003): 416–21. https://doi.org/10.1111/1467-9280.01456.

Goodman, Whitney. *Toxic Positivity: Keeping It Real in a World Obsessed with Positivity.* New York: TarcherPerigree, 2022.

Hanson, Rick, with Forrest Hanson. *Resilient: How to Grow an Unshakable Core of Calm, Strength, and Happiness.* New York: Harmony Books, 2018.

Hicks, Esther, and Jerry Hicks. *Ask and It Is Given.* Carlsbad, CA: Hay House, 2004.

Lienhard, John H., founder and host. *The Engines of Our Ingenuity.* No. 265, "Inventing Benzene." University of Houston. March 20, 2023. https://www.uh.edu/engines/epi265.htm.

Masters, Robert Augustus. *Spiritual Bypassing: When Spirituality Disconnects Us from What Really Matters.* Berkeley, CA: North Atlantic Books, 2010.

Neff, Kristin. *Self-Compassion: The Proven Power of Being Kind to Yourself.* New York: William Morrow, 2011.

Perry, Christopher. "The Jungian Shadow." The Society of Analytical Psychology. August 12, 2015. https://www.thesap.org.uk/articles-on-jungian-psychology-2/about-analysis-and-therapy/the-shadow.

Rosenberg, Stanley. *Accessing the Healing Power of the Vagus Nerve: Self-Help Exercises for Anxiety, Depression, Trauma, and Autism.* Berkeley, CA: North Atlantic Books, 2017.

## To Write to the Author

If you wish to contact the author or would like more information about this book, please write to the author in care of Llewellyn Worldwide Ltd. and we will forward your request. Both the author and the publisher appreciate hearing from you and learning of your enjoyment of this book and how it has helped you. Llewellyn Worldwide Ltd. cannot guarantee that every letter written to the author can be answered, but all will be forwarded. Please write to:

Shantini Rajah
℅ Llewellyn Worldwide
2143 Wooddale Drive
Woodbury, MN 55125-2989

Please enclose a self-addressed stamped envelope for reply,
or $1.00 to cover costs. If outside the U.S.A., enclose
an international postal reply coupon.

Many of Llewellyn's authors have websites with additional
information and resources. For more information,
please visit our website at http://www.llewellyn.com.